REMAKING
MEMORY

REMAKING MEMORY

Autoethnography, Memoir
and the Ethics of Self

John Freeman

First published in 2015 by Libri Publishing

ISBN 978 1 909818 59 0

A CIP catalogue record for this book is available from The British Library

Cover and book design by Carnegie Publishing

Front cover image by Sancintya Simpson

Back cover photograph of John Freeman by Koufar Belarus

Printed in the UK by Short Run Press

Libri Publishing
Brunel House
Volunteer Way
Faringdon
Oxfordshire
SN7 7YR

Tel: +44 (0)845 873 3837

www.libripublishing.co.uk

Nothing will unfold for us unless we move
toward that which looks to us like nothing.
Alice Fulton

Contents

We've only just begun…
Roger Nichols and Paul Williams

Are You Talking to Me?

First and foremost, this book is intended to function as something of a critical friend to autoethnographers and memoirists. It asks questions about what it might mean to write oneself into research findings and narrative reports, and what happens when one's self goes further and *becomes* the research. It will draw on extant writing in the field from around the world and offer fresh perspectives and provocations that are informed but not bound by this body of thought. Suggestions will jostle with warnings and readers at whatever level of experience are invited on a journey (not remotely chronological and not always logical) through self-writing as it relates to the vagaries of memory, the illusion of truth and the possibilities for presentation. This journey will cover ethical territory and, in turn, the ethics of university research will be challenged and critiqued.

The journey also moves through understandings of research. The most widely agreed upon characteristics of research are that it uses systematic and controlled procedures; that it strives for validity, rigour and logicality; and that it is driven by critical thought, objectivity, accuracy and repeatability. This agreement amounts to a convention; and this convention dictates that without due adherence to the stuff of this list a researcher cannot make much progress in any investigation. Furthermore, research is innately incremental inasmuch as one researcher's findings are transferred to others to prevent duplication. In other words, findings are accumulated from one generation to another and each researcher's work either stands on the shoulders of the past or looks to sweep previous thought to the ground. Most importantly, research is about repeatability: what works today under a particular set of conditions must work in the same way tomorrow. This is the basis of all trials and it is this that gives us the confidence we have in results.

It will come as no surprise then that autoethnography, with its emphasis on unrepeatability, emotion, mood, subjectivity and (at one extreme) a solipsistic focus on self, has ruffled the old school feathers that it has. Autoethnography, memoir and creative nonfiction inevitably negotiate the relationship between the stories we want to tell and the histories we have lived through; between the necessary fictions of publication/presentation and the real-world experiences we draw upon. As such, the forms make their own virtue of the telling of stories that are so laden with emotive detail that they will elicit a similar emotional reaction in the reader. This at least is self-writing's hope. This has not quite been the hope that has driven the more dispassionate aspects of this book; nevertheless, despite its occasional claims to the contrary, and despite some of its best early intentions, *Remaking Memory* is itself a work of at least partial autoethnography.

A partial autoethnography might be neither fish nor fowl, and might yet be so curious a hybrid that it satisfies neither one camp nor the other. Be that as it may: in a very real sense, this book's subject of autoethnography allowed, if not quite demanded, a particular form. In selecting and shaping the chapters to come, as well as through the inclusion of case studies from research students more or less in my own fields of practice and endeavour, some of the concerns of autoethnography and memoir have been woven here into a new narrative. This narrative reveals the marks of personal engagement and original experience no less than academic construction and referencing.

All research is experiential, whether this is the experience of reading in the library or observing in the field. Autoethnographers write their experience into narratives and are themselves key participants in the research, and often also its subject. For autoethnographers, and to a lesser extent for memoirists, the idea of research as a neutral process is abandoned in favour of a self-reflective form that explores the researcher's perspective on the subject in question. If this is a reasonable description of autoethnography then this book can be said to be reasonably autoethenographic in its tone and approach. Certainly the book lays a trail of some of my personal thoughts and observations, and at times these are laid fairly bare. They function as a way of providing readers with insight into the thought processes at play during the book's construction and they exist alongside a through line of text that is the result of more conventional research methods. In other ways, *Remaking Memory* can be read as an objective trawl through its subject that only occasionally deviates into personal territory. One reader's autoethnography is another's study of authoethnography. What can be said is that I have not deliberately censored out the ad hoc impulse to comment directly. Hopefully, the result does not come across like an intrusive B-movie voice over.

We make arguments to the contrary, yet the tensions that exist within conventional academic writing and autoethnography are not dissimilar to those encountered elsewhere. Autoethnography suggests that in certain cases writing about and through oneself can be illuminating in ways that add to rather than diminish traditional scholarship; and in other investigative processes, it is accepted that one's gender, race or sexuality can be grist to the mill of enquiry. In books and articles, research reports and essays, theses and dissertations, writers' personal, lived experiences are increasingly used to offer insights that more traditional academic approaches might deny. Again, that, at least, is the idea. And so this book is neither quite one thing nor the other. There are relatively few forays into the deeply personal, but there are more than some readers might expect.

As a self-reflexive miner of my own professional life the impact of being regularly delighted and occasionally disappointed by the autoethnographies I have encountered has left traces of feelings in amongst the debris of findings. These traces augur against any claims for objectivity, and the chapters that follow this introduction mark (as I now come to read them) a journey that has been on one level hugely immersive and on another strangely peripheral: immersive because this book's subject matter could not be closer to my professional heart and peripheral because there were times in the writing when my heart was not fully in my profession. Indeed, the writing of this book covers periods when there was no calling I felt more removed from than university teaching and research, leadership, management and administration. Rather than edit those moments of disconnection out, they now remain as a form of palimpsest, registering a journey of doubt and embracing, engagement and denial, admiration and admonishment.

Reflection is a part of all writing and late stage reflection generally leads to a strict process of self-editing. Within the chapters of *Remaking Memory* this has certainly taken place, but not to the extent that each chapter has been revised to form a falsely cohesive whole. The chapters are presented in the order in which they were written and where changes of perspective occur these have been left to bear testimony to the realities of writing as an active form of process. As a counterpoint to the book's title, my own memories have not been fundamentally re-made in a final draft.

Through everything from its title to its format, a book promises to take us on a particular journey; and we trust that it will do so. In this way, an introduction forms a contract of sorts with its readers, albeit a contract that promises only as much as its conceit will allow. Leaving chapters to evidence or even betray my shifting concerns is an attempt at sticking to the facts of what took place during this book's process, in the knowledge that this attempt has been prey to my own inevitable acts of misunderstanding and misrepresentation. Memories are malleable rather than infallible, partly because the world around us contains too much information for us to deal with and partly, when it comes to our own writing, because none of us can occupy anything like a neutral starting position. Our systems of perception are not capable of paying attention to everything going on around us and when we remember events, our memory fills in the gaps with what we think could or *should* have taken place.

To say that someone's memory is bad or inaccurate is an easier thing than to suggest that someone is deliberately reinventing or remaking events to fit their own agendas; but we know well that all people lie, and not least to themselves. If we told no lies, we would need few if any courts of law. People lie, and for many reasons. Despite their contract of truth based on accuracy of recall and ethical intent, autoethnographers, memoirists and the writers of books such as the one you are reading are no less susceptible to misremembering than anybody else; and neither are they (or we) any less likely to lie.

When I was a child, my first cousin once removed, who was a fiery young adult at the time, plucked the cowboy book I was reading from my hand and, cursing the bias that depicted Native American Indians as bloodthirsty savages, referred to the publishers (although interestingly not the author) as 'swine'. It was a useful early lesson for me that the printed word holds no monopoly on truth and all these years later it is that memory (which I believe to be entirely accurate even in my knowledge that it is very probably not) which runs beneath this book in a seam of purposive doubt. For better or worse, my mother's cousin Cliff Jones shaped my perspective on writerly truth in ways I have never been able to shake and in ways I have never wanted to.

The notion that all memories are in some way false is not quite the same thing as the phenomenon of false memories, or false memory syndrome. Due to the reconstructive nature of memory, some recollections will always be distorted through the incorporation of new information. The mind is also subject to believed-in imaginings that are not based on lived experience but which are nonetheless firmly believed to be true. These pseudo memories are often the hardest to break down because the subject's belief in this false version of events, which might range from memories of alien abduction to seeing a ghost or suffering an act of abuse, is so strong. Because s/he 'remembers' the event, no amount of contradictory evidence will ever change his/her mind. It is axiomatic that somebody with an internal or professional desire to please or to conform can easily be affected by such influences.

There is ongoing controversy about the accuracy of repressed memories that adults claim to have of incidents from their childhood. These claims are generally problematic because they are often made many years after the alleged events. When there is no external corroboration, things are problematised further still. Where this book will consider issues of false and repressed memories, the matter is not about whether somebody was or was not abused in any particular case. At all but the most minor end of the spectrum, abuse is a serious social and legal problem that requires precisely the attention it currently receives; and it requires a type of attentive expertise that neither I nor the field of study I work within are capable of providing. For the purposes of this book, the issue is the extent to which people may or may not accurately remember incidents from their past, whether these are incidents of childhood abuse or the circumstances surrounding an autoethnographer's taking of field notes. The book is concerned with the accuracy of all memories; and recovered and repressed memories of abuse form one small part of this address.

The form of any autoethnographic text impacts on its content. In this way, an ethics of writing is always present, and if the medium is not quite the message, then writing is part of the ethical relation rather than a report on it. An engagement with ethics is central to communication, but ethics can be used to cut two ways. In the mid-1980s, the actor Leslie Grantham was welcomed onto the UK television soap series *EastEnders* despite his prior conviction for the attempted robbery and subsequent murder of a German taxi driver, Felix Reese. In 2004, Grantham was banished from the screen for a webcam sex scandal which, whilst unsavoury in its details, resulted in no criminal proceedings. Ethics equate to a social system in which morals are applied. In other words, ethics point to standards or codes of behaviour expected by the group to which an individual belongs. Within this definition (and whilst believing that once a sentence has been served, that, generally speaking, should be that), it is hard to fathom the reasons why shooting a taxi driver in the head might be easier to forgive than sending explicit and private images of oneself to a fully consenting adult.

In similar cases of ethical cleansing, the reasons are clearer but the results are no less confused. In 2013, and to predictably low-level sales, a CD box set of UK Glam Rock from the 1970s was released (*The Best Glam Rock Album in the World... Ever!*). The usual suspects of Suzi Quatro, T Rex, Wizzard and The Sweet were present, but not the disgraced sex offender Gary Glitter, despite his status as one of the key glam rockers of his time. Glitter's music was no better or worse than that of his contemporaries and his exclusion (like the BBC's refusal to re-run old *Top of the Pops* programmes that were hosted by the disgraced Jimmy Savile) is based on his sex offences rather than his lack of talent. In effect, an entirely understandable ethical and/or moral decision results in an inaccurate impression of the music of that period.

Glitter's musical output was insignificant on a global stage, certainly compared to the film directing of Roman Polanski. In 1977, Polanski was arrested and charged with offences against Samantha Gailey. The charges were lewd and lascivious acts upon a 13-year-old girl, furnishing a controlled substance to a minor, and sodomy. Not to put too fine a point on it, this refers to Polanski drugging a 13-year-old girl with Quaaludes and champagne, luring her into posing for naked photographs, ignoring her protests and then anally raping her. In response to imminent imprisonment, Polanski bought a one-way ticket to England and fled the United States; yet mainstream Hollywood actors queue up to work with Polanski and the director won an Oscar (and a prolonged standing ovation) for his 2002 film *The Pianist*. There is an act of obvious cultural relativism at work here, writing Glitter out of one world and applauding Polanski in another. I am offering no argument as to the rights and wrongs of deleting a person's creative output based on their criminal activities, nor am I seeking to mitigate the severity of one criminal's actions through comparison with another's. The hypocrisy and moral incoherence of the entertainment industry is legendary: all that I am pointing to is the fact that basing adoration or contempt on an offender's creative standing rather than on the nature of his or her crime is clearly antithetical to any form of accuracy. I am also pointing to the fact that our own moral hypocrisies can massively colour our attempts at accurate writing.

The temptation to imbue events with our own ethical perspective can be overpowering. If we do not often go to extremes of censorship, we do it in semi-hidden ways when we support our views with one set of references rather than another. We do it in the ways we deal with gender on the page, opting, as I have already done in this introduction, for 's/he', choosing 'she' over 'he' when gender is unknown or using 'humanity' rather than 'mankind' – all fairly clunky techniques which can be clunkier still when faced with the reality of English, in which many words equally apply to men and women. Only a woman can be an actress, for example, whereas both women and men can be actors. The word 'actor' refers only to one who acts and is not gender specific. Citing examples from popular culture might have more to do with a writer's desire to be seen as in touch with the modern world than anything else; referring by name to the universities writers have graduated from might set them apart from and above we readers from lesser institutions, if ever we graduated at all; citing examples from ancient works might demonstrate a writer's classical education and so on. Our writerly choices do more than denote a certain style: they seek to persuade particular readers to take particular points of view.

Writing effectively means knowing and respecting one's readers, but it also means appealing to some at the expense of others. It is obviously important to be sensitive to issues of race, ethnicity, age, socio-economic standing and gender, but the ways in which we demonstrate this sensitivity also demonstrate the ways we choose to be read. With autoethnography and memoir we look to report what was said, but does that extend to sentences that contain racial, ethnic, gender and sexual slurs and/or offensive stereotypes? Does it extend to the inclusion of vulgar content, generally regarded as material that is crude, graphic or coarse? This is a genuine concern. In 2012, Susan Candiotti, a reporter for CNN, apologised on-air for repeating the word 'nigger' during a live broadcast. Candiotti said she regretted using the term while reporting on the story of two men accused of shooting five black people. Candiotti's apology took the form of explaining that, in reading a *Facebook* post from one of the suspects and quoting from it directly, she had repeated its offence. After the report aired, a news anchor in the studio apologised again to viewers for using the word on air.

Doug McGray, editor of the 2011 reprint of *The Adventures of Huckleberry Finn*, announced that the same word would be replaced throughout the book with 'slave'. As a teacher, I can empathise with those who have had difficulty speaking the word out loud in a classroom; but substitution feels like the weak end-product of a flawed line of reasoning – and a dangerous one. Whatever we might think of his book and whatever the passing of time might have done to it, the book is Twain's and it seems to me that the discretion to like or dislike the book based on its author's word choice is the right of the reader rather than an editor. Changing an author's words a century and a quarter later is more than part of an awkward precedent: it is censorship based on the attitudes of our time rather than Twain's. On its original publication, several US libraries decided not to stock the book and banned it from their shelves. In subsequent years, controversy has shadowed and foreshadowed the work. We can read it or ignore it, stock it or not, but changing Twain's words is no different in kind to Cosimo III de Medici's order, three centuries after the event, that fig leaves be painted over the naked genitals of Masaccio's Renaissance fresco *The Expulsion from the Garden of Eden.*

Within the context of this book rather than Twain's, should I, like Candiotti, also apologise for using the N-word? Is it ever appropriate or proper to use the term? Does my use read as somehow racist, inflammatory or demeaning? Naturally, I hope not. I am quoting a news report. Nothing more. But of course *it is more.* It's a nasty word in any context and my use of it exposes that, without (again, I hope) furthering it. George Orwell's *Nineteen Eighty-Four* showed how society is susceptible to manipulation by having his Ministry of Truth destroy words that might lead to thoughtcrimes. Words are potent and explosive. They also change what they describe. We choose our words carefully and this applies even to the ways we deal with ostensibly verbatim reports.

A section of this book will focus on the ethics of appropriation as these relate to Australian Indigenous and Torres Strait Islander stories. That section changes if I use different words. Aboriginal people are a diverse group of individuals and if I were to use the term 'Aborigine' might this have accidentally negative connotations? Might this term then perpetuate prejudice and discrimination, and might Australian readers regard this differently to those elsewhere? Might my status as a European cut me some slack based on my relative lack of familiarity with Indigenous Australian matters, or might my Englishness stir still-bitter feelings of colonialism? Should I follow the recommendation of the Aboriginal Advisory Group of Community Legal Centres in New South Wales and use 'Aboriginal people' or 'Aboriginal person' on the assumption that these are more positive and empowering terms? The words we use matter, even when one's intention is to be respectful, because being respectful can sail close to being patronising, even if the words we choose do their best to match the mood of the moment. And the moment of this book's writing is no indication of the various times at which its words might be read.

Our writing points a camera at what we want to be seen, and can dictate how and in what measure this will occur; and this extends even to the notes we take that are intended for our own eyes only. Memoirists and autoethnographers rely massively on the taking of field notes, and debates rage as to the superiority of one form over another. The internet has allowed for blog posting as a means of providing an in-situ and synchronous coverage of given events from an autoethnographer's work. Blogs can be time and date stamped and made publicly accessible on the internet and they demonstrate the researcher's participation in a given social world alongside a written and participatory account. Live field notes posted as blogs benefit from immediacy and openness, but in essence they are no more true or false than notes scribbled with a pencil in the pages of a dog-eared book. We distort our own experiences with the innate faults of memory and this is a theme that runs through each of the following chapters; self-writers' impossible searching for truth, or what passes for it on the page, is another.

In seeking truth, we find there are three main types: contextualised, evidential and interpreted. These deal, respectively, with truth as the liberal arts research tradition this book springs from states it to be; truth as scientific and statistical evidence demands; and truth as a matter of deriving possible non-statistical meaning from our findings. When we write about what we have lived through, we make reference to the extent to which we are committed to the propositions expressed; and we do so in statements that are always in one form or another about truth. In general terms, an autoethnographer or memoirist who tells a lie shatters his or her contract with the reader. But there is perhaps something more insidious than telling a lie: to dissemble with a half-lie (or half-truth), a slippery mistruth that hides a lie beneath its vocabulary of honesty. These seeming truths are so seductive that we want to believe them, even when evidence reveals the lie lurking beneath.

This book will argue that the conditions and techniques of autoethnography and memoir are such that they render the goal of providing an objective portrayal of a cultural reality impossible. Every element that contributes to an ethnographer's account or memoirist's narrative is filtered through impressions that are inherent in one's research strategies, theoretical positionings, socio-economic status, gender, geography, nationality, integrity, aspirations, age, influences and personality. There is then no possibility of neutral observation, just as there is no observation that is pure and unsullied. Can I write in a way that resists my first-world and gendered status? Can I write a line that is not male and white and European? Can I write a chapter that references the best sources without giving in to the temptation to cite the writers I prefer, or those I choose to affiliate myself with? And what does referring to myself as European, rather than British or English, say about how I might hope to be seen?

Most of us are reasonably familiar with memoirs and have been brought up reading them, but what is there to autoethnographic research? What is it that autoethnography is doing that is just so valuable? In essence, an autoethnographer is a detective in search of clues as to motivations, desires, beliefs, ways of thinking and words for description. An autoethnographer will look for absence as well as presence: what and where are the gaps, and the differences as well as similarities; what explains why we say one thing and do another? The aim is to draw out the clues that explain behaviour and researchers have to be acutely aware of their role in any discussion. An autoethnographer, like a memoirist, needs to be sharp enough to probe beneath the surface of a subject and to tease out the contradictions. Autoethnography argues that even the most liberal qualitative research techniques are themselves artificial standardisations of process, which may result in findings that are no more than manufactured predictions.

We live our lives in the present and yet all forms of research, like all detective narratives, are backwards looking, fuelled by interrogations into what happened, when and why? We can ask about the future, but the future is unplanned, indeterminate and impossible to know. Hence the reasons we like to think of researchers as academic detectives, engaged, as we conjure them, in a search for the truth that in its complexity eludes the rest of us. When researchers mistake their inquiry to find out what happened and why for a more lawyer-like approach, piling evidence in favour of either guilt or innocence, things seem unfair – because fairness is linked to neutrality. Partiality is in the domain of lawyers who work this way so that a jury can decide which argument is stronger; not in order for truth to win out so much as for the lawyer to win her or his case. That may do nicely for practitioners in the legal system, but that is not how most of us feel that research is supposed to work. Researchers are not supposed to begin with the goal of convincing others that a particular idea is true by assembling as much evidence as possible in support of that idea. Researchers are supposed to be detectives looking for clues to get to the bottom of what is actually going on, and they do this by repeatedly asking 'why?' Researchers are thus committed to following the trail of clues, wherever that may lead. We are charged with an interest in searching for the information that will help decide what is true, not just for data that supports a preconceived idea.

And yet, researchers are rarely (if ever) like dispassionate, unbiased detectives (if such a person could ever exist). Rather, researchers *are* akin to lawyers and we try relentlessly to convince an audience that our particular narrative of events is correct. Recent autoethnographies have begun to emphasise the inevitability of researchers selectively and/or subconsciously gathering information that is consistent with their existing preconceptions (and the more unsavoury-sounding *prejudices*). When this happens, researchers can reveal in their interpretation of other cultures rather more of the student than the studied. This is an echo of postmodernism's embrace of reflexivity and when it is foregrounded, a lie can morph into the truth by dint of nothing much more than its self-declaration. The problem comes when we confuse our memories of what occurred with what really took place. As Cousin Cliff well knew, black ink on a white page can read with a power that is hard to erase. It may well be the case, to paraphrase Ray Bradbury, that we have our creative arts so we won't overdose on truth, but the line between creative writing and reportage is often too fine for even the writer to see.

A memoir is a literary device. So too is an autoethnography. And literary devices differ in form and function from transcripts. They are versions of events, part fact, part fiction, part exaggeration and part composite, part other and part self. Where this amounts to deliberate lying in one's writing, rather than telling truth with a forgivable spin, will be considered in the pages to come; and not all lies are as identifiable and deliberate as those told by mock-memoirists such as James Frey. Beyond the slippery nature of description and deceit we need to remember that memoirs are rarely dispassionate accounts of what happened. When we write we take on a particular endeavour, and this relies on creativity. But being creative is a more subtle and complex activity than simply inventing events to suit a story's arc. Writerly flourish is easily transformed into embellishment and, whilst no-one would wish for a world of bland prose, there are ethical implications that come with the worlds of research and self-writing.

Remaking Memory stakes its place as an addition to the literature in the burgeoning fields of autoethnography and memoir, carving out fresh territory in at least the following four ways.

1. Although this is not featured in the title, it should be said that this book flirts heavily with autoethnographic performance. The final chapter of this book is offered as a stand-alone and lengthy contribution to this field, and the case studies each address various aspects of autoethnography as they apply to their particular, and particularly performative, research projects.

It should also be said that there are good reasons for this, beyond, I hope, my own background in contemporary performance and its study. The key principles regarding the experiential nature of autoethnography and memoir are closely aligned with the performative nature of identity, and the desire for narrative authenticity is dynamically connected to wider ideas of self-presentation as an often unknowing fiction about origin. By bringing together both literary and performed work pertaining to self-generating narratives, *Remaking Memory* looks to document and critique the mosaic of stories that constitute autoethnographical and memoir-driven identity in the making. In this way, readers whose interests are innately performative are invited to read Chapter 5 and the book's case studies as useful, and I would argue *necessary*, forms of address to the concerns all other readers are likely to share.

2. The book has a focus that is not limited by geography or to the usual suspects of academia. The writing was carried out on three continents and self-writing is accordingly regarded as a broad and international church. We live in a world of increasingly unfixed borders between high and pop culture; in this spirit, the book's index sees David Beckham nestling next to Samuel Beckett, *EastEnders* next to Umberto Eco, Bob Dylan next to Marcel Duchamp and Bruce Springsteen next to the post-porn modernist Annie Sprinkle. Beginning each chapter with song lyrics provides a further nod toward this collapse.

3. *Remaking Memory* takes a somewhat revisionist approach to its subject. Many effective autoethnographers (and perhaps even all) will argue that their form is always already revisionist in its rethinking of what makes research tick and stick, and this much is clearly so. But autoethnography has spent enough time in the light for its own occasional myths and misdirections to have assumed the status of fact, and many of these are challenged in the pages to come. Any book that looks to expose these misdirections at the same time as it offers broad and hopefully useful support for researchers needs to tread a fine line between views; and where the writing falls too heavily on one side or the other the reader's patience is necessarily sought.

Readers should be alerted at the outset to a strong dose of devil's advocacy in *Remaking Memory*. Whilst all of the questions I ask in this book are the product of genuine rather than manufactured concern, the ways in which they are asked will sometimes collapse healthy challenge into an aggressive-seeming provocation.

In a book about truth and belief it would be perverse to ask readers not to believe all that they will read between this book's covers, but readers *are* being asked to consider the fact that antagonism drives writing faster than agreement. All of which is to say that, at those times when buttons might be pressed a little too hard for the comfort of readers, they are many times pressed in pursuit of dialogue rather than diatribe. On other occasions they are pressed because they simply need pressing, which is not the same thing as being disrespectful or intending any professional slight.

Academic argument always depends on ideas being made subject to some form or other of scrutiny, and this will often involve attacking opinions that other academics hold dear and have themselves argued strongly for. Because of this the possibility of causing offence is ever present and the gap between fair comment and perceived rudeness is as subjective as it is slippery. It is axiomatic that the status of any argument depends in part on the cultural or disciplinary context within which it is made, and within the world of university research autoethnography and creative nonfiction are each liberal, provocative and somewhat outlaw forms; indeed, they are forms that have assumed the status they have through their own attack on the traditional rules of academic writing. Very few parts of my own published work in recent years have not been autoethnographical and the practices this book will scrutinise are very often the self-same ones I draw upon (and not least in this book's pages). In this way, *Remaking Memory* forms a challenge to my own practice as much as to any other. I offer these words not as a form of self-flagellation so much as a reminder that my perspective here is inside rather than out.

4. The book's chapters are laced through with a series of case studies from PhD and DCA students working with and through autoethnography. The case studies lend invaluable first-hand engagement with the realities of creating and submitting work that breaks many of the hitherto accepted rules of research in the arts, humanities and social sciences.

Inasmuch as this book looks to practise a little of what it preaches, I have little choice but to acknowledge that autoethnography can suffer when it privileges the monologic voice of one person. While the case studies are individually too brief to be classed as a form of co-generative dialogue, collectively they run to several thousand words and in so doing they provide more than five spaces for other people to speak their mind: they serve to remind the reader (and me) that a sole authorial voice is usually suspect. Contributors were approached because they had interesting things to say for themselves and interesting ways to say them. There was never any intention that the case studies would somehow conflate into one homogenising voice; rather, they exist to hint at the multiple approaches to autoethnography through the inclusion of diverse experiences and agendas.

In terms of familiarity and disclosure, I first met Kate Rice and Jamie Coull in 2011 and Nazar Jabour the following year. As the principal supervisor of their research degrees, I met regularly with each of them over the ensuing months and years. I met Steph Brocken once only, at the introduction of Professor Allan Owens; and to date the closest I have come to meeting Rebekka Kill has been a fractured conversation on Skype. The generosity of the case studies' authors has allowed *Remaking Memory* to speak with half a dozen voices rather than one. On an invaluable level the studies punctuate and puncture five very long chapters, as well as speaking to fellow researchers with the type of clarity, purpose and application that my own protracted and more discursive ramblings will be less likely to achieve. My appreciation of the wisdom they bring to this book is no less than the appreciation readers will feel when they encounter their sections.

Autoethnography and memoir are examples of the writer rendering his or her self visible and inviting readers into a dialogue with ideas and practices. *Remaking Memory* is simpatico in its intention to function as a conversation (no easy thing in the bombast of print): one that invites reader response rather than acquiescence or dismissal. If the pages that follow might miss their mark of giving readers the sound of talk on the page then they will I hope give a sense of thinking and writing in action, where issues are returned to as much because they force themselves back into the fray as because they are knowingly recalled as exemplars. The writing process has thus been a journey in which ideas were experienced that both confirmed and conflicted with the book's drive. Indeed, my own temperamental subjectivities, moods, memories, emotions, intentions and arguments created the book rather than being controlled in order to adhere to some pre-planned scheme.

Perhaps the circularity of this type of self-referencing will cause more problems than it can ever solve. Perhaps Jerome Bruner is correct in his belief that one's self is a perpetually rewritten story and that we are all constantly engaged in acts of self-making until 'in the end we become the autobiographical narratives by which we tell about our lives'. (Bruner, 2004, p.694) Perhaps we should all embrace the well-documented fact that telling and retelling events from one's past creates the very changes in detail that our memories hope to resist. Perhaps, if our every act of recollection leads to alteration, so that the more often we narrate our histories the further we move away from the truth of who we are, we should acknowledge autoethnography and memoir as fiction offered under an always false flag of truth. Perhaps we struggle with our doubt in the possibility of truth precisely because the need for self-writing to be true is steeped both in history and logic: if the things we describe are not real, then what is there to reward or to redeem? Perhaps the harshest reality of all is that the most authentic voices are the ones that resist the contemporary urge to speak, speak, speak.

Be that as it may, it is not enough to fail, Beckett taught us. We must try our best to fail better.

Research is an extension of academics' lives rather than an adjunct to them and although many of us struggle hard to guard against subjectivity and to separate the self from research activities, autoethnography and memoir make the case that research in the arts and social sciences is so closely connected to personal interest, experience and familiarity that objectivity is an increasingly moveable feast. What choice then but to speak what we believe to be our best approximation of the truth and shame whatever demons we substitute for the devil? Wherever and whenever one's research interests combine features of life history alongside the area under study, the result is likely to require researchers to make their own experience a topic in its own right rather than attempt to create a document that seems as if it could have been written by anybody coming into contact with the same source material.

Damned if we do and damned if we don't. In a relativist and post-postmodern world in which we are as free as birds, we are also always doomed to fail.

Fail and fail better, and still try to succeed. Taken as a whole, *Remaking Memory* forms a unique perspective on the creation of work in the areas of autoethnography and memoir. The inclusion of a dedicated chapter on ethics and an end-of-book appendix is significant not least because it will provide new university researchers with the opportunity to work through an ethics application form of the type that all students and members of academic staff now encounter. An additional appendix will offer guidelines for prospective higher-degree-by-research students. Inclusions like these provide readers with a blend of practical purpose, theoretical engagement and personal journey; and as ever, a book without reader response is no more than a collection of words. Each of the chapters will conclude with a running out of time and space rather than a sense of having done anything approaching complete service to their themes. Many books do.

In much the same way, introductions serve in some ways to delay the moment of their own surrender; to hover between ownership and release. This book is now released and ownership is passed from the writer to the reader.

Hear what I say, 'cause every word is true.
You know I wouldn't tell you no lies.

Eric Clapton

CHAPTER ONE

Obscene Truths

Objectivity, subjectivity, methodologies and mantras; free will and William
Zinsser's checklist; weasel words and love-me writing; skepsis, blogging,
truth and fact; reality television; Picasso; Rebekka Kill's case study

This book will cast a wide net and will range across many fields of practice. In doing so, the book's coverage will very probably be a little uneven and some sections are likely to speak more eloquently – although hopefully not more usefully – than others. Chapters will turn from the general to the particular and back again in ways that intend to cut through a surface treatment to the heart and blood of autoethnography. In taking writing as a theme, the chapters that follow will weave form and content in ways that are not always quite deliberate and perhaps not always fully under control. For these moments to come, I can only ask the reader's patience and hope that the book's searching for answers rather than documenting that which has already been found will read less like structural collapse than a genuine and purposive attempt at practising a little of the things that we self-writers are often wont to preach.

If the macro of this book is writing, its micro is research, brought face-to-face in the idea of communication that legislates against its own concealment of construction. The etymology of *obscene* is 'off scene', hidden, out of sight. In most traditional forms of research, the investigator's self has likewise been historically hidden, camouflaged in borrowed cloaks and behind the representation of the studied other. In a similar way and with some notable exceptions, the researching writer's self has traditionally been excised from all but autobiographical publication, limited to the idea of observation from a distance; as though this act of disentanglement would somehow result in rigour; as though 'good research' could only take place if and when the researcher stays firmly outside the frame.

Essentially researchers' positions to their subject have been regarded as not at all interesting; indeed, convention has preferred the neutrality of the term 'disinterested'. Nor have we generally regarded the researchers' perspective as important, with the main schools of thought being that one's research should echo that of a dispassionate and essentially objective observer, of an articulate and intelligent *uber*-everyman grounding findings within a coolly coherent body of sustained theoretical prose.

As an alternative to this, the autoethnography focused on in this book functions as a pedagogic and creative tool for focusing attention on the inevitability and indeed the *usefulness* of overt subject positioning. Its concern is also with acknowledging the inevitable overlaps between the maker and the made, and with a hopefully cautious relationship with truth.

This caution is not something we need take as suspect. On the contrary, it stems from recognition that ideas of truth are sometimes no more than the opinions that have been spoken by the loudest and most powerful voices and that in most cases truth is a construction at best. In this context, any and all claims for objective truths that might creep into this book's pages should be treated with healthy disdain: they may well be not as deliberate or deliberately placed as they seem.

Alphonse Bertillon wrote that one can only see what one observes, and one observes only things which are already in the mind; whilst in his essay *On the Decay of the Art of Lying* Mark Twain famously told us that everybody lies – every day, every hour, awake, asleep, in his dreams, in his joy, in his mourning. If he keeps his tongue still his hands, his feet, his eyes, his attitude will convey deception. And truth is indeed an impossible prey to catch, not just because it is elusive but because it is different in kind to fact. If the following chapters are likely to seem antagonistic toward a more rigorously held relationship between truth and fact, they are also intended to be read as a plea for a more rigorously held relationship between methodology and quality.

The methodologies of memoir, autoethnography and creative nonfiction have become so commonplace in the arts, humanities, health, education and social sciences that they are in danger of appearing as little more than research spin doctoring. Certainly in some authors' and postgraduate students' hands, self-writing has come to honour no audience greater than itself. And when self-writing slides into self-justification, self-indulgence is never far behind.

If the personal can hold sway as evidence (and this book is all about that very thing) then I can say that in my professional life I have read a few too many weak autoethnographies to be left with much of the *a priori* faith in the term that many of my genuinely valued colleagues seem to possess. If this results in a book *about* autoethnography that is in part a book *for* autoethnographers that is also in places a book *against* autoethnography, then that confluence should be seen not as cynicism so much as a form of sceptical embrace that is desperately seeking conviction. The book's abiding battle then is with the quality of writing in the field rather than with the battleground itself. More than this and because quality is almost as hard to define as truth, the battle is with autoethnography and memoir as these have become deployed in the hands of the idle, the self-deluded and the faux. Truth be told, these thoughts, part-claim and part-disclaimer, part-provocation and part self-protection, will be returned to throughout the next few thousand words. Truth be told. If truth can ever be told.

The idea of truth in art and literature is a hoary one, done to near death as far back as Plato and beyond. Nevertheless, both autoethnography and memoir trade on truth so relentlessly that it is simply not a theme that is possible to sidestep; indeed, research that is not concerned with truthful pursuit of verifiable facts is notoriously hard to justify as research at all. As readers of this book will well know, feelings segue into findings and emotions can muddy the waters of information to the extent that facts become the first casualty of creative research. As we also well know, our own part-truths are easier to believe than those of other people. Everyone is a liar but us.

Picasso told us that art is a lie that tells the truth and we know that art in its various forms has its own covenant with veracity. The words *truth* and *fact* are often used interchangeably but one can generally say that a fact is easier to define than a truth inasmuch as a fact is something that possesses objective reality. To say that the sun rises in the east is regarded as a fact. To say that gravity exists is a fact. To say that a certain person loves coffee is at best a risk, because the factual evidence of that individual's consumption of many cups each day is not at all proof of love. A man who, as a matter of fact, buys flowers for his wife every Wednesday cannot argue convincingly that his bouquets are evidence of the truth of his love, any more than a cynical outsider might claim that his gifts are evidence of his having something to hide. What stands for truth in everyday life is generally no more than opinion offered as fact. Scientific facts may well change from one generation to the next as new methods of observation come into use but for the most part it is safe to regard facts as assertions that can be made subject to proof.

Truth on the other hand is not so easy to pin down: a work of creative fiction or a painting can, in the sense Picasso meant, be said to be true to life or true to human nature. For a philosopher or a theologian the opposite may be true: facts may be fleeting in their temporary specificity whereas truth (the truth of faith and conviction) is something eternal and unchanged. But for most purposes a fact is a concrete reality that no amount of reasoning will change, something that cannot be logically disputed or rejected. A truth is almost the opposite. The idea that a particular god exists will for many people be held an absolute truth without ever having come close to being a verifiable fact. Swathes of atheists aside, a greater number of people will always disbelieve in the existence of any one god figure because they are locked into faith in their own particular deity and because their monotheism asserts (and often demands) the existence of a unique and solitary god. The common noun *god* is capitalised into the proper noun *God* and the ubiquitous assumes the status of the particular. Unlike members of the Flat Earth Society, who sit outside accepted normative worldviews, followers of mainstream religions are generally able, within their own cultural groups, to position their beliefs as uncomplicated truths.

Writing in the magazine *America*, Terrance W. Klein likens Mary of Nazareth to a great work of art and God as the ultimate artist. (Klein, 2012) This is hardly a factual statement, despite the author's obvious sense of his and his own subject's truth. Just as I could write truly that I believe neither in God nor the widely accepted bible story of Mary of Nazareth and yet I would not be able to propose my version as being based on any facts, not even by calling upon the scientific implausibility of a child being conceived as a result of a mother's union with a god who inseminated her by methods unknown. I could not regard my beliefs as being factual despite *knowing* with the same level of certainty that a Christian might have for the opposite view. Many people continue to regard creationism as a truth in spite of more hard scientific evidence than one could shake a Darwinian stick at. Even for those of us who do not share the peculiar beliefs of the particularly religious, truths matter to us in life at least as much as facts, yet they are essentially fluid, malleable and open to endless challenge.

Facts are often used to substantiate our assertions on particular truths; just as truths may be used to help us better understand particular facts. But to offer a truth as a fact is always problematic. It is also one of the great pitfalls of autoethnography. Describing our beliefs as truths makes them sound rather grand at the same time as it discourages challenge; and when we confuse the truth of our memories with the fact of what really occurred, we are generally heading for trouble. All writing balances on the razor edge of deception and description but few forms have the inbuilt capacity to self-delude better (or worse) than autoethnography.

The English language has many words to express the concept of truth – such as integrity, sincerity, authenticity, honesty – and wanting them to be a part of our work is almost always a good thing; but the words themselves do nothing to make our content *true*. In autoethnographical research terms they can become no more or less than weasel words, used to create an impression that something specific, accurate and meaningful has been written about in words that are equally accurate. When Stewart Chaplin wrote of 'words that suck the life out of the words next to them, just as a weasel sucks the egg and leaves the shell', (Chaplin, 1900) he might have been thinking of the ways that autoethnography and memoir would evolve.

Added to all of this is the fact (or is it a truth?) that we are living through a time of rapidly increasing technical sophistication, to the extent that digital techniques, not least on the internet, are generating a huge interest in manipulative deception and deceptive manipulation. The art world is already well able to create remarkably convincing images, conjuring the false into seeming reality and Baudrillard's notion of *simulacrum* has come to haunt representation in more ways than we (if not perhaps he) could have ever imagined. Just as the term *art* has grown ever broader in meaning, so *truth* has lost even more sense of fixity or permanence. In standard research practice there is no longer the illusion of absolute methodological certainty and, as Art Bochner describes it, there is no 'single, unchallenged paradigm... for deciding what does and what does not comprise valid, useful and significant knowledge.' (Bochner, 2000, p.268)

Reality television in all its guises generally deploys very little sophistication with which to conceal its editorial bias and yet we have become so seduced by the image that we still look to buy truth where only lies are up for sale, just as we lap up *X Factor* contestants when they dedicate trite songs to dead relatives and *Masterchef* cooks who prepare meals so evocative of their tormented childhoods that they shed crocodile tears into their skillets. The international talent show *The Voice*, which is ostensibly about singing, focuses heavily on the narrative behind each contestant's choice of song and/or reasons for entering the show. Vanity, careerism and the pursuit of celebrity are never given as reasons, but promises made to dead relatives whose spirits watch over and inspire the singers like guardian angels are relentlessly invoked. From chat shows to marketing and from the well-intentioned myth-making of memoir to the world of confessional performance (where the larger clue might be in the word *performance* rather than in the claim of confession), it would appear that we are hungrier than ever for a slice of the real. What is clear too is that this paragraph has used terms like *truth*, *reality*, *authenticity* and *genuine* without any noticeable sense of discernment. This may be no more or less than evidence of my own hazy thinking and lazy writing but it may also be a way of collapsing these words into something that is at once manageable and clean, and readers are asked to go with the flow of an authorial conceit that, in terms of memory re-made, sees no easy distinction between a YouTube clip, an autoethnographically written thesis, a memoir and a tightly scripted revelation to a chat show host. The issue is the extent to which truth might matter in art and the personal might have currency in research. These ideas come together in autoethnography; and if this does not quite expel my own weasel words, it does at least expose them to the light.

Where photographs were once held to be records of a moment in time and considered factual enough to be presented regularly as evidence in legal matters, photographers can now manipulate their images to the extent that little that we see can be taken as true. Words are the same. Anything that is typed, the manuscript for this book for instance, can be edited by someone else to be something that it was not before. In the past, the next edition of a book could always be changed but the original was retained for posterity. Any changes to original records were generally crude and usually obvious. In the digital world the new edition is *the edition* and distinctions between what was and what is are eroded. It was possible in previous times to compare different originals to get to some idea of the truth but it is not easy any more to know what to regard as an accurate recording of an instant in time. It is too simple a task to manipulate an image digitally to make it seem real, or even *more real*, after the event. The questions asked of truth have been with us forever but they are rendered considerably more problematic in the digital age. For sure, if there is one universal truth of today it is that there is too much content and not enough time to consume it; and if there is one more, it is that we can no longer have any trust in the images we see and the words that we read.

The Vatican no less is well aware of this and, in line with that ancient institution's desire to keep up with the times, Pope Benedict's pre-retirement 2013 message for the World Communications Day was entitled *Truth, Proclamation and Authenticity of Life in the Digital Age*. In his address, Benedict called for a 'creative and responsible use of the latest technologies in order to communicate the lasting truth of God's love for the world.' (Vatican, 2011) Young people in particular, the then Pope told his followers, are increasingly involved in social networks, posing important questions about the authenticity of one's own being. In the search for sharing and finding new friends, the message stresses, there is the challenge to be authentic and faithful and not to give in to the illusion of constructing an artificial public profile for oneself. With every new medium comes a new disruption to the ways we communicate and the ways we receive; and it may well be that autoethnography is enjoying the honeymoon period that it is precisely because of the intensity with which we crave a truth that, as we know in our heart of hearts, we cannot really find.

Matters of fact and even truth have been replaced with matters of signification and in almost everything we see, truth has become no more than a copy of truth. Little wonder then that autoethnography and memoir are in danger of becoming the two last turkeys in the shop of the faux real. What has changed for all of us has been the huge rise of digital socialisation and the endless array of electronic outlets to express anyone and everyone's versions of the truth. This zeitgeist of the digital world has dramatically influenced the negotiability of truth in all arenas because it has democratised global communications. So-called citizen journalists, bloggers who see themselves as playing (and indeed, who *do* play) active and vital roles in the process of collecting and disseminating news and information, now participate actively in content formation in ways that shape the public narrative on issues ranging from celebrity deaths and a country's reasons for going to war to local authority lawsuits and innuendo dressed up as *reportage*. Regardless of the subject matter, the underlying facts (a weasel word in this context) are negotiated and debated by a newly empowered social media: one that is unbound by the rules governing lawyers and traditional journalists. The currency of individual blogs is premised on independence, on the writer's freedom from the dictates of media moguls and politically prejudicial editors. But who monitors the individual's bias? And what makes an independent perspective tapped out on a hand-held device innately better than that of a newspaper-employed news reporter? We are none of us independent and free will has been shown on countless occasions to be something of a myth.

The medical anthropologist Daniel Moerman has shown how the recovery rate of patients is linked to the colours of the pills they are prescribed. People with depression get better more quickly when their tablets are yellow; blue sleeping pills work better than the same compound with different colouring; green pills cure anxiety quicker than pills of any other colour; and the health of patients improves when they believe that their prescribed drugs are expensive. (Leslie, 2012, p.292) Every pharmaceutical producer knows this to be absolutely the case, yet precious few of us believe that we are so easily duped.

In 1966 the psychiatrist Charles Hofling arranged for 22 unsuspecting nurses working in a large hospital to receive separate telephone calls from an actor who identified himself as Dr Smith. The assumed doctor told each of the nurses that they were to give a 20mg dose of a highly toxic drug called *Astroten* to a specific patient. The actor posing as Dr Smith (and there was no Dr Smith at the hospital) told the nurses that he was *en route* to the hospital and that he would sign the necessary paperwork as soon as he arrived. The drug was an invention of the experimenters. It had been placed in the drug cabinet several days before the bogus telephone calls, marked with a prominent warning which reminded staff that 10mg was the maximum safe dose and that any more than this was potentially lethal. Hospital protocol was emphatic in its ruling that no drug should ever be administered based solely on a phone call, yet 21 out of the 22 nurses were about to deliver the 20mg dose when they were stopped. (Hofling, 1966) The nurses had bowed to the imagined authority of the doctor and were in the process of killing patients. Not much evidence of free will there, and what would make us think that our minds are more our own than those of the duped nurses? The last half century's research into human behaviour suggests that we are no more than puppets dancing on society's strings. In a very real sense, we can never be sure of ourselves and those of us who think we are free are perhaps doubly deluded.

Within these notions of autoethnographic free will and truth, creative nonfiction has come to play as the seeming saviour of agenda-driven personal research. Creative nonfiction looks to foreground issues of truth in personal writing; but the term has always been something of a slight misnomer, for isn't all writing creative? And for many of us – and despite its new university embrace – the term 'nonfiction' can read at times as just a little naïve and more than a little desperate. Writers of creative nonfiction would have it that their code denies fabrication or the tawdry manipulation of facts, that we are getting true stories well told; that creative nonfiction is about telling stories, using dialogue, description and character to give information from a particular point of view while at the same time avoiding straying away from the facts. But who can say how far they stray from truth when we no longer trust the idea of authenticity itself? Under these circumstances creative nonfiction can seem as much an act of evasion as a literary adventure. Like the term 'artist scholar', which can be spun in research-framing documents to dress bad art and weak scholarship into something much greater than the sum of its parts, creative nonfiction is fuelled by artistic freedom with respect to its construction and fidelity in terms of the information it conveys. In skilled hands, this is something to behold. In unskilled hands, it is yet another entrée into publication for the writer *manqué*.

The term 'nonfiction novel' was coined by Truman Capote when he wrote *In Cold Blood*; Ernest Hemingway did similar things with his short stories and his reporting to the extent that one became inseparable from the other. Capote and Hemingway set a very high bar, beyond the reach of many but touched by the likes of Tobias Wolff, Maya Angelou, Susan Sontag, Gore Vidal, Norman Mailer and Alex Haley. The great skill of these writers notwithstanding, truth was once a less slippery ideal. Readers were more trusting of the teller and so more trusting of the tale. Time now is at its messiest moment and whilst exposing the writer-at-play breaks through the surface sheen of objectivity, it does little these days to expose the real.

Creative nonfiction will be addressed more thoroughly in the chapter on autoethnography, for this is where the marriage of convenience between the hidden-false and the fake-real is invited to take its honeymoon. I should confess here that my hard-to-shift distrust of the term is based more on experience of truth tellers who feel free to invent in pursuit of that which they describe as a *larger truth* than with any stuffy adherence I might retain to literal fact. Creative nonfiction can be an incredibly powerful form of expression (and not least in the hands of some of my current and recent colleagues) but this power is considerably weakened, I would argue, by its ubiquity: ubiquity that speaks too often to ease of access rather than expert expression. And this reaches both zenith and nadir in the blog. 'Blog' is an abbreviation of weblog, an online journal that is frequently updated and intended for public consumption. We know that blogs can be dynamically intercultural and interdisciplinary, that they can connect people from around the world in newly direct and intimate ways; we know too that they can also be published by anyone who thinks she or he has something to say.

The writers' blog is sympathetically aligned to the idea, beautiful in its appeal, that each of us is a story waiting to be written and that, once written, these stories will result in a person explained. Perhaps we are all stories waiting to be written and perhaps we each have our stories to tell. The problem is that few of our stories are interesting enough to make the journey worth taking and, harsh though this sounds, most people do not have much of public interest to say at all and do not want to work hard enough to say it particularly well. Too much of a good thing drifts from good to bad very quickly. If immediacy is not antithetical to quality then neither is it a guarantee of it, and the publication of creative nonfiction online *can* be little more than litter on the wind.

Proponents might well (and doubtless will) argue that creative nonfiction and autoethnographical research outcomes are prime cultural agents in the interrogation and dissolution of assumed binaries between the watcher and the watched and the maker and the made. And on some occasions these arguments will be sound. At other times, such as when Norman Denzin refers to (presumably all) autoethnographers as public intellectuals who produce and engage in meaningful cultural criticism and autoethnography itself as providing 'a framework against which all other forms of writing about the politics of the popular under the regimes of global capitalism are judged' (Denzin, 2005, p.259) or when Andrew Sparkes suggests that autoethnography is superior to the 'standard boring writing of the academy' (Sparkes, 2007, p.541), the hyperbole clearly exceeds the facts. Nevertheless, in its implicit acknowledgement that all observation is participant observation (because all observation is participatory and involving) autoethnography has emerged as one of the very few contemporary methodologies with something genuine to say about the ways in which art, society and research are moving forward into practices that are new and germane.

Research doublespeak aside, this is a book, ultimately, about ways of writing the self – and this is where the book begins, or rather begins again: with a discursive address to the activity of constructing one's self through words on the page. This first chapter will weave through various paths but its concern remains with forms of writing which are predominantly autotelic. In T.S. Eliot's terms, this refers to work which is about itself, which is a central concern of autoethnography and memoir. (Eliot, 1932, p.30) If the book intends a particular purpose, it is for self-writing better to be able to break free from allegations of self-indulgence. To this end, it is hoped that engagement with the constructed nature of writing might lead to greater control and the book is intended to support research students and their supervisors as much as it offers provocations to memoirists, autoethnographers and autobiographers whose work may well sit happily beyond academia. Equally importantly this book is not intended as some form of charter, and less still a cheat's charter: a 'How To' guide that sets out to defend the indefensible. If all researchers have the freedom and some have the wherewithal to write their positions and experience into the frame of a thesis or article, book or performance then so much the better, because research demands variety and because methodologies are innately unfixed. But this is not the same thing as arguing autoethnography's problems into merits and self-writing's potential failings into unqualified success.

As Robert Frost told us, if there is no surprise for the writer then there will be no surprise for the reader. If writing is always an act of discovery then it is certainly true that in the process of writing this book I did not always realise quite what I thought until I saw the words on the screen in front of me. Writing does that. Active writing at least, where we sometimes write through what we think we know in order to discover that we actually think something else entirely. The writing thus changes the writer as much perhaps or even more than the reader. This was certainly the case for Michel Foucault who stated 'I write in order to change myself and in order not to think the same things as before.' (Foucault, 2000, pp.239–40) Objectivity does not necessarily get lost in this mix but it does disguise itself sometimes in subjective language, just as subjectivity often hides behind the refusal to use the personal pronoun. All of this makes defining a book as an act of research (rather than as a book that is just *about* research) problematic.

Perhaps these late opening words are a type of self-acknowledgment, a statement of how awkwardly this book will present its own acts of autoethnography. It is clear at the outset that any easy distinction in these pages between writing *about* autoethnography and writing that *is* autoethnographic would be an impossible aim – even if this were the intention behind this book. It is a positive feature of our times that academic and creative writing are no longer seen as oppositional factions, just as autobiography and fiction are fruit from the same poisoned tree: poisoned because the act of writing is nothing if not the pursuit of persuasion.

Whilst mainstream research was at one time (and for many, still is) informed by critical perspectives born out of the literary canon, we know that contemporary research in the arts, humanities and social sciences is now largely informed by a huge body of post-structural theories. The autoethnography focused on in this book is informed by a loose application of these theoretical interventions, each of which posits self-reality as no more than a composite of historically situated language constructs within which our individual or subjective perspectives are programmed to play their part. We witness this on a regular basis with autoethnographic practitioners whose work conforms to post-structuralist ideals by presenting material that acknowledges and investigates the relationships between subjective perspectives and the social–historical manifestations of construction. At its best, this makes for powerful work; at its worst, it creates a cycle of what is often little more than the language of oppression, obscured by the babble of hypersubjectivity. As Noam Chomsky sees it, this hypersubjectivity can take a form that seeks to deprive the working classes of the tools of emancipation, playing working people and vulnerable, excluded communities against each other through claims that all projects of enlightenment are redundant, in so far as inequity is never anything more than one illusion in a world of simulacrum. (Chomsky, 1993) Foucault's observation that truth is an effect of power has created telling critiques on notions of objectivity; but where oppression is a fact of daily life, my own placing of inverted commas around the word 'truth' threatens to add casual intellectual insult to savage social injury.

Partly because of Foucault, we can say that we are at a point in history where much that might once have been edited out of academic writing is now as likely to be edited in as left intact, and autoethnography is evidence and application of this. For one of autoethnography's long-time champions, Carolyn Ellis, this inclusivity goes so far as advocating research which is likely to 'start with my personal life. I pay attention to my physical feelings, thoughts and emotions... to try and understand an experience I've lived through.' (Ellis & Bochner, 2000, p.737) We are told that his excavation and exploration of self takes its toll. Ellis elaborates:

> honest autoethnographic exploration generates a lot of fears and
> doubts – and emotional pain. Just when you can't stand the pain
> anymore, well that's when the real work has only begun. Then there's
> the vulnerability of revealing yourself, not being able to take back what
> you have written or having any control over how readers interpret it.
>
> (Ibid., p.738)

Ruth Behar adopts a similar line when she writes that autoethnographers need to learn to be comfortable with their own 'passionate vulnerability', knowing that their writings will be published in hostile and unforgiving environments. (Behar & Suárez, 2008, pp.13–14) Speaking perhaps to those same hostilities, Kathryn Church is emphatic in her belief that foregrounding one's own voice in research 'is not narcissism; it is not an egocentric indulgence'. (Sparkes, 2002, p.216) Church's argument is that her subjectivity is filled with the voices of other people and that writing about the self is a way of writing about those others and about the worlds which she both creates and inhabits. If these are reasonably standard claims for autoethnography then they also comprise its standard defence. The notion of autoethnography is regarded with some degree of suspicion by university colleagues – and not only those in the hard sciences

– and the risk of confusing self-indulgence with self-knowing is as potent as it is seductive. If we acknowledge Primo Levi's writing of 'the need to tell our story to the rest', of achieving 'an interior liberation', (Levi, 1997, p.15) we should also heed Charles Marowitz's dismissal of those who write about their own practice as masturbators; an idea echoed in Blake Morrison's belief that confessional writing without some sort of tempering judgement is little more than masturbation in print. (Marowitz, 1991) Autoethnograpers, memoirists and followers of Levi beware.

In the autoethnographical spirit of disclosure and of all things having potential significance, there is an assumed imperative (or is that an *opportunity?*) to make clear something of my intentions for this book and also something of my background. But that is no simple thing. No simple thing at all. Doing so involves both choice and judgement. And these two elements, so fundamental to traditional notions of research, are not always easily found in autoethnography where the specificity of data has given way to the inclusivity at all costs of personal material. Autoethnography's fusing of the self and the social, in Deborah Reed-Danahay's terms, famously locates the *self* as innately ethnographic rather than touristic. (Reed-Danahay, 1997) This is a shift from Karl Heider's view of self, which referred solely, in the autoethnographic terms he introduced, to the self of the informant. (Heider, 1975) Autoethnography is more commonly regarded now as a form of autobiographical ethnography in which researchers are able to insert all of the variants of their personal experiences into their investigation and documentation; which is to say that the feelings of the researcher, or the researcher's emotional journey, are generally accepted as being grist to the mill of research activity and that which was once thought of as spoiling the research is now seen as going no small way towards creating it. Carolyn Ellis, Tony Adams and Art Bochner see in this a recognition of 'the innumerable ways personal experience influences the research process.' (Ellis et al., 2010)

Ellis, Adams and Bochner suggest that 'autoethnographers vary in their emphasis on the research process (graphy), on culture (ethno), and on self (auto)'. (Ibid.) This is indeed the case and, when each of these elements is given due time, space and attention, autoethnography can achieve excellent results. The methodology is prone to suffer, however, when healthy emphasis leads to gross imbalance and research focuses too strongly on the auto. Locating oneself as part of an investigated community can understandably lead to insights that are likely to have external value in research terms. Locating one's self as the sole object of investigation, framed but not significantly *informed* by the society one belongs to is likely to lead to some quite reasonable allegations of navel-gazing; and this book would be doing its readers a disservice by sidestepping these problems rather than engaging with them. At times this engagement with criticisms of autoethnography and memoir will go so far as agreement. Despite believing that counter-narratives deserve to be heard no less than the grand narratives of modernism, despite knowing that injustice goes hand in glove with silence and despite being aware that autoethnography is at core anti-hierarchical and subversive, it is hard for me to find much immediate argument with Jill Taft-Kaufman's view that:

> Despite claims that autoethnography is a mode open to all, certain narratives are discouraged (discourse that echoes those dead white males, for example), and other stories are favored (especially from voices considered marginalized). Autoethnography is touted as a practice that does not participate in the perpetration of ideology (advocacy and responsibility are two of those thorny issues). However, many of the autoethnographies that appear in journals and at academic gatherings explicitly structure and relate the points in their stories to the doctrines that underlie the practice, imparting an almost formulaic sameness to these supposedly subjective expressions.
>
> (Taft-Kaufman, 2000)

It is probably fair to say that whilst not all research endeavours are autobiographic in flavour or intent, many are driven by a strong sense of self. In choosing to investigate certain things in certain ways, we make our interests, passions, compassions and fears overt to others, probably more cleanly than we will show them to ourselves. In acknowledging its emphasis on self, autoethnography functions as a way of controlling self-interests through their exposure; putting a positive spin on this, it follows that autoethnography is not so much the *ipso facto* method towards self-indulgence that its critics often claim as it is a methodology that places the researcher's self-motivations front and centre, bringing to the fore that which other approaches adopt and also conceal. Taking a more cautious tone we should note and remember that in the case of autoethnography, methodology is all too easily replaced by mantra.

Because we do not often engage in deliberate, conscientious and self-conscious reflection upon our own processes of experience we do not generally privilege the personal as a form of evidence. Nevertheless, Kristi Gerding Scholten suggests that our acts of communication will always already embody projections of the self, even if at a subconscious level, so that we are presenting and/or performing versions of our selves each time we speak or write. (Scholten,

2007) For autoethnographers this type of self-reflection and self-projection can be described as a harrowing process but one which leads to identification and learning from experience. Instead of concealing personal experience, because it is resistant to notions of rational argument and systematic results, ideas are articulated *through* one's experience, leading to a form of communication that is offered up as being at once heartfelt, honest and authentic. Rather than assuming a sense of borrowed objectivity, which is often no more than the *language* of objectivity, autoethnography asks whether we are doing ourselves an injustice by not examining the way we write ourselves and our readers into our research findings and outcomes.

Apropos of which, in a publication focused on another area of research it might be enough to simply state that my subject specialism is contemporary European and US theatre, that I have lectured in this field at many universities for many years, and that I am currently an associate professor and Head of Theatre at a university in the UK and hold an adjunct role at a university in Western Australia. I might go further at this point and write that I have considered and addressed issues of autoethnography, self-writing and subjectivity in a number of previous works. This would be enough, probably, to place a legitimate frame around at least some of my arguments and to justify the inclusion of staged or performed examples of autoethnography alongside the more expected written ones, not least through the existence of this book's stand-alone chapter on auto-performance. But is this enough for a book such as this, for a book about autoethnography?

Should I also disclose here, as part of a contract with the reader, my historical distrust of and even at times *distaste* for much professional and faux professional performance that I saw? Should I explain in these relatively early pages that there have been times when nothing filled me with a deeper sense of dread than a night at the theatre, unless perhaps it was conversing with those half-baked Stanislavskian actors who describe their well-told lies as acts of holy truth, or worse still those teachers of acting who cast themselves as guru figures to students too young and filled with dreams to see through them? Should I attempt to articulate the ways in which my respect for universities and love of theatre translates too often into disappointment at university theatre's self-satisfied embrace of the commonplace, the facile and the middlebrow, middle-of-the-road *ordinariness* of much that we produce? Should I mention the fact that I cringe when I read some of the self-satisfied claims for theatre that are made by the people who make the work rather than those it is ostensibly for; or when I come across articles that are coded applications for tenure, employment or promotion?

Should I cite the one performance seen on a cold evening in Sarajevo that rekindled my faith in theatre after a long time in the wilderness? Should I come clean about the fact that I am a reasonably committed advocate of autoethnography even though the bulk of my published writings in the field demonstrate more than a little concern for many of autoethnography's *results*, just as my commitment to practice-led research in performance is tempered by serious and seriously growing doubts as to the quality and efficacy of many of the resulting performances? Should I write about my own decades-old research for PhD – research from a more innocent and, if I am to be honest, somewhat less-rigorous time for research, where ethical approval from my study's participants involved no more than cheerful verbal consent given during a between-rehearsals coffee break and where my supervisor shrugged and told me simply to 'get on with it'?

And I am inordinately glad that he did. His name is Barry Edwards and he was an expert supervisor. In fact, the difference in the levels of ethical control determined by UK universities then (in the mid-to-late 1990s) compared to UK, US and Australian universities now is vast. My PhD explored the creative and reflective processes of making work with a group of undergraduates; each member of the group was working with me on a formally assessed final-year project. At the time, securing students' consent to include description and analysis of their time spent on the project was easily and painlessly obtained; the notion of changing their names was discussed with the students, my supervisor and my university colleagues but at the time this all felt a little unnecessary: an exaggerated caution, too much like belt and braces.

I am aware now, as I was then, of the power imbalance and of the difficulty my students might have felt had they not wanted to be included in the thesis, and we all worked as conscientiously as we could (or needed to) *at the time* to provide spaces for withdrawal. What was interesting, then and now, is that the students were adamant that their own names should be used. Partly this was about the pleasure that came from the students seeing their names in print, firstly in the thesis and then when that document was reworked into a book, published in 2003; but I think the students also appreciated the sense of mutual trust and informed respect we were engendering.

Ultimately, whilst I know that this way of working would be unlikely now to get through the fine print and tick boxes of a university's ethics committee (in the same way that a student acting in a play would be unlikely to light a cigarette), I have no regrets about the ethical approach we settled upon. Years after the research, thesis and publication I attended the weddings of two members of the group and have intermittent but good contact with all involved. And it appears that no student participants were harmed in the research process.

Like Carolyn Ellis, I believed I had a general notion of what it meant to engage in ethical research based on my personal understanding of the term: which amounted to little more than the ubiquitous intent to do no harm alongside a vague commitment to reciprocity. At that time and at that university, there were no compulsory discussions of ethics in my research programme and perhaps no optional ones. This was at Brunel University, west London. The absence of sessions on ethical research was a feature of the time and times have changed. Brunel University, and not least the School of Arts, remains an innovative and supportive environment for students pursuing higher degrees by research.

If my status at that time was clearly one of 'researcher' it was not uniquely so: I was also 'lecturer' and passably also 'theatre director', as well as being somebody who had a considerable say in my participants' university grades: a complex and problematic ethical soup if ever there was one. Should I include those experiences here, detailing where things went wrong and how value was often massaged out of failure? Should I try to explain how my professional concern for the teaching work I was doing *with* the group as students was sold quickly into a manipulative and strategic concern for the research work I was doing *on* them? Should I articulate something of my earlier and non-professional, non-academic life, a life just about as far removed from the one I currently enjoy as it is possible to imagine? Should I make public and dwell upon formative hardship: of beatings and poverty and evictions, of failings and loneliness, picking at the scars of experience until they open into wounds where blood serves as a type of ink?

Should I expose my own often-questionable relationship with truth (and sometimes fact) and my track record of occasional misdirection; the slipperiness of authorship as it relates to promotion, tenure and all of the murky unseens of university life? Should I be attempting at all a book about authorial perspective that is not quite transparent enough about my own only half-convinced approval of my subject? Should I refer directly to my age, my gender, my physical health, my marital status, the names and whereabouts of my children? Should I, in the spirit of Alexander, Moreira and kumar's tri-autoethnographic exploration, delve deeply (they would, I know, prefer the term 'courageously') into my relationship with my late father, or my very much alive and wits-about-her mother, or my powerfully no-nonsense brother? (Alexander et al., 2012)

My personal history, like everybody else's, grounds my understanding in lived experience but does this mean that everything I have experienced is of potential value here? Should I explain how I got from factory floors and building sites to university common rooms and from Hastings to Coventry to West Australia and on to California and back again, with undue haste, to a seaside town in Cornwall; and should I talk about what I lost and found along the way? Should I try to describe how I quickly came to regard the heat of the West Australian sun as a force that bleached away the melancholia necessary for art despite the fact that the term 'artist' was wilfully thrown around the state like the cheapest confetti? Should I note too that despite my commitment to a wide range of practices that might be seen to stand as art and despite my predilection toward inclusivity, *artist* is a term I still find difficult to assign to anybody who doesn't hold a brush and stand behind an easel?

Should I write of the feelings I developed for an absent Europe and my reluctance to put roots down in other countries, believing increasingly that roots matter and that mine remained steadfastly elsewhere despite how welcome I was made to feel in the new/old world of Australia? Should I describe the view from my various office windows and compare these with the view I have when I work at home, teasing out differences between writing styles and moods and locations? Should I write about friendships kept and enemies made and relatives lost? More pertinently perhaps, should I write about those conversations with students and colleagues that have inevitably impacted on my thinking for better and for worse? Should I acknowledge key writers, performers and colleagues in the field, those I enjoy and those whose work I find an increasing embarrassment? Should I mention those people here, rather than listing them purely alphabetically in the index at the end of the book? Should I refer directly to the PhD students I have supervised whose struggles, triumphs and occasional evasions have done much to shape this book's address? Should I be heroically up front in cautioning the reader every time I develop an idea from my own back catalogue of work or re-hash a favourite phrase? Is it the case, as Bernadette Barton suggests in regard to her own work, and like Scholten before her, that almost every element of one's life becomes data? (Barton, 2011) Should I introduce this book's case studies from PhD students in ways that impose my own readings over the students' own, or should I leave the work and their words to speak without interference?

This is probably a good time to say a few words about the case studies: about where they come from and what their intended value is to this book.

Firstly they are each real-world examples from PhD and DCA students. And they are real world in multiple ways. Other than as a natural process of proofreading, the written sections have not been re-edited by me for this book. The case studies as you will read them come more or less directly from the students' own thesis material, inasmuch as this was the invitational brief, and they deal with issues that were germane to those studies at those times and within the particular context of higher degrees by research. All of which is to say that the writing is not primarily designed to be book friendly (although a number of the people concerned are also published elsewhere); rather it was (and is) aimed at that most critical of academic readerships: an examining board. What mattered to these students, in the writing, was that they dealt with aspects of autoethnography that relate to justification, argument, persuasion, methodology, intent and account. This is the stuff of academic research and their sections, which are offered here as case studies that stand as chapters in their own right, will provide exactly the type of detailed specificity that the rest of the book skirts around.

The case studies describe particular moments and circumstances, intrinsically exploring and exposing the ways that those encounters shaped their writers' understanding. Taken together, their shared intent is to introduce, describe and debate some of the prime issues arising out of the overlap of performance and autoethnography, both in theatrical presentation and in print. The case studies make for diverse voices, assembled here as a means of exploring the frontiers of a large territory delineated by these paired fields, producing autethnography in a self-reflexive mode through the contributing autoethnographers themselves.

Whilst the value of these sections will be clear to students pursuing higher degrees by research, much that is valuable remains for those people whose writing falls outside this tight academic frame. In a similar way, the case studies' predominant focus on performance does not in any way limit their usefulness to writers in other areas of endeavour. When Kate Rice wrestles with the role of theatre based on fact, she is working within a form that has re-established itself in recent years as a distinct body of work which includes verbatim theatre, plays about real events, and fictionalised plays inspired by personal experiences. Rice explores the genre's ability to make particular claims about its relationship with real-world experience, taking the work's implicit promise apart through her own playwriting and raising timely and invaluable questions of ethical responsibility which are intertwined with the issue of on-the-page and on-the-stage authenticity.

Nazar Jabour's thesis on Iraqi memory in performance was an attempt above all else to analyse the experience of having lived in countries that treat makers of art as dangerous people and having been known to the United Nations High Commission as Refugee Number 424. Jabour's work asks how artistic inquiry might further the exchanges between historical events and life narratives as these were made in and through theatre. In discovering how the people most affected by war have managed to find the strategies of creative perspectives to deal with memory, hardship and hope, Jabour's thesis emerges as an exploration of theatre as a meeting place for stories to be told and heard. The remarkable nature of Jabour's work is added to by the fact that English is his fifth language of expression.

Jamie Coull's research interests include identity formation in performances of desire and fantasy, imaginative persona play in adulthood, and how notions of the private, the public and the act of performance might be challenged in the age of online media. At the core of this is research into faux queening, where Coull discusses a relatively new iteration of drag by biologically female performers who consciously and affectionately parody femininity in a similar manner to conventional male drag queens. With reference to Simone de Beauvoir's theorising of woman as construction and man as transcendental given, Coull finds the male body is prioritised as the authentic site of drag while women in female drag are considered to be, unfortunately, in the wrong bodies. Faux queens present as cisgendered females who perform female drag, biological women, of mixed sexual orientations, in a gay-male-dominated performance genre. Coull's immersion in her practice (one outcome of which is a website http://agorafauxbia.com) results in an autoethnography which critically explores these notions with reference to her personal interest in faux queen drag and adult play.

Steph Brocken's research focuses on the uses of interdisciplinary and contemporary arts practices in work with children and young people in non-formal educational settings and the impact that this can have on young people's social and political development. In so doing, Brocken analyses the experience of collecting data from her chosen participant group, using approaches which allow for their general working process to remain as uninterrupted as possible. For Brocken, this is about enabling the researcher to gain an accurate perception of the effects of the methods and work that are undertaken with the group. Her searching for a democracy in process leads into exploration of the ways that researchers strive to be as fair minded as possible in the ways in which they observe and analyse process. Brocken casts a perceptive eye on issues of ethical research with young people, questioning the tendency to assume that voice is something that can be distributed, from those with power to those without, in ways that see young people as 'somehow incomplete in their ability to articulate experience or opinion'.

Rebekka Kill's PhD thesis represented an original foray into the very stuff of being and *thinking like* an academic in contemporary performance, art and design. This process required Kill to examine the literature and her various and variously intertwined roles and practices as performer/teacher/researcher in a reflexive and relational way; the social turn and the reflexive process were both highly evident in Kill's work, which was both bold and successful in its endeavour. Kill's methodology and presentation was a hybrid that articulated and critiqued a body of academic knowledge at the same time as it provided an analysis of the author's pedagogic and creative practice; and this self-reflexivity, robustly focused and underpinned by theory throughout, combined to create a significant body of knowledge.

As has been previously noted, another aspect of the case studies is structural and no less valuable. They punctuate and puncture my own chapters at the same time as they provide the reader with different perspectives and different voices. No bad place then to include this book's first contribution. Rebekka Kill's writing below is the opening and closing parts of her PhD, completed in 2011. It was a PhD by practice and the middle part (not republished here) included drawing, performance and poetic writing alongside academic writing. The PhD was submitted as one artefact, a twelve-inch-square hardback book, which has the scale and feel (but not the weight) of a gatefold album.

Beginnings

Rebekka Kill

This research is an exploration of academic identity construction in creative practice academics in higher education. Yawn, that sounds terribly dull. Try again.

Over the last eight years I have tried to uncover something about academic identity. I wanted to find out how it is constructed, how it changes and develops, and how we can talk about it. I am particularly interested in the academic identities I am surrounded by every day. Those staff who sometimes call themselves artists and other times lecturers, teachers or academics. These staff may work in art, design or performance but this dual naming is the same. This

PhD work has taken a long time. The main reason for this is that along the way I have taken many wrong turns. On this journey there are so many other PhDs that were nearly written that this final draft becomes like a palimpsest, and if you look closely these other texts are hidden underneath; barely visible but not legible. This PhD is half practice and half text. Not exactly 50:50, split down the middle, but I hope something that is hybrid half and half: a chimera. This is, however, the only way to explore this hybrid identity of half artist and half academic: a submission that is also half art and half academic.

In the early stages of this PhD I really struggled with the notion of methodology. I couldn't understand the requirement to decide on a methodology for the research before I carried it out. In my studio practice, methodology was always developmental and discovering new methodologies was at the heart of this work. During the course of this PhD I have read a large quantity of material on practice-based research, and there are a couple of issues in relation to methodology that are worth mentioning here. Desmond Bell's 2008 article 'Is there a doctor in the house? A riposte to Victor Burgin on practice-based arts and audiovisual research' discusses the 'intellectualisation of art practice'. (Bell, 2008, p.173) He is rather critical of Burgin's assertions about what a PhD in practice should looks like, and he describes this as a tripartite system partly because this system is based on the number and type of words that the artist is required to produce and partly because Burgin asserts the need for a separate 'Doctorate in Fine Art' that doesn't necessarily need much writing. Burgin's 'tripartite' system can be summarised as follows:

> A humanities, or social science, type PhD in History and Theory with a full-length dissertation;

> A practice-based PhD with a body of work and a half-length dissertation;

> A 'Doctorate of Fine Art' with minimal written requirement and the emphasis on excellence in practice.

For Bell, this way of thinking enforces a hierarchical division between manual and intellectual labour; I might refer to this as logobias or logocentrism. He states:

> The issue I believe is not one of defending an outmoded notion
> of academic rigour by demanding that PhD candidates produce a
> dissertation of a stipulated word length, nor is it one of romantic

resistance that demands that practice candidates be free to present creative work without an obligation to contextualise this in a body of writing. Rather our aim as doctoral supervisors should be to encourage a circle of reading, making, documenting, reflecting, writing up, public communication and criticism.

(Bell, 2008, p.177)

So, in PhDs in practice there is a great deal of discussion around the location and status of any written research associated with the project. And central to this debate is the quantity, weighting and also the type of writing. There has also been an ongoing debate on the status of practice as research; this debate is also explored later in this PhD thesis.

However, in parallel to this, there have also been developments around research methodologies in the social sciences.

During the last forty years, social scientists have looked to the arts for qualitative and non-traditional research methods and methodologies. As far back as 1967, Guba identified a notion of an 'art' to enquiry as research moved away from explorations of technique towards generating theory. In the early 1970s, prompted by ethical issues around research relationships and the position of researchers as either community member or the figure with the capacity to 'other' the subject of research, new modes of qualitative research emerged including what Finley calls 'arts-based social science enquiry'. (Finley, 2005, p.682)

In creative arts education, there are several examples of the appropriation of our practices by social science and pedagogical researchers. For example, in Schön's (1983) *The Reflective Practitioner* he uses the example of the fine art 'crit' as best practice in critical reflection; another example would be the recent proliferation of literature around 'creativity'. However, Finley's positioning of this 'arts-based social science enquiry' is interesting in its alignment with activism and reform. In this context Finley cites Eisner's (1991/1998) work on the skill base required of researchers.

He proposed a graduate school curriculum that values students' developing skills of imagination, perception, and interpretation of the qualities of things.

(Finley, 2005, p.683)

Eisner, like Seale (1999), describes a studio apprenticeship model for social science researchers modelling a research training environment on the way that artists learn painting and drawing. Tierney (1998) discusses the use of experimental narrative and tone of voice in research writing, and Casey (1995) and others explore storytelling as a research tool. Finley characterises this paradigm shift as politically and ethically charged, she also cites Columbia University's Program in Narrative Medicine as an excellent example of this radical change, where medical students study literature and critical theory.

So, for Finley, appropriating arts-based inquiry is radical, ethical and revolutionary. She goes on (quoting Freire, 1970/2001 and Denzin, 1999) to discuss these types of methodologies as guerrilla warfare. Describing such tactics as 'mystory' performances and using visual arts with young adults she outlines the benefits for both self-reflection and expression and social change. Finley finishes with a series of questions including 'What is good arts-based research?', 'Who is an artist?' and 'Who is a researcher?' So, the situation is this. Social science researchers have begun to explore the use of arts-based methodologies and are often using 'off the shelf' pre-used versions of this and yet it is often the artist researcher who has the responsibility for innovation in methodology. Thinking about this in relation to my requirement to declare my PhD methodology in advance of beginning the work, the question I came to was: Am I an artist researcher in this project or am I a pedagogic researcher? Depending on my answer, different rules applied. As an artist researcher methodology could be developmental and as a pedagogic researcher I needed a clear understanding of methodology in advance, one that would help me structure and organise my research. However, it was also clear that social science and pedagogic research was (in some types of research) realigning its methodology. If I return to Finley's questions of 'Who is an artist?' and 'Who is a researcher?' then, in the context of this research, the answer to both is me. Luckily, at this point I had a breakthrough: I discovered autoethnography.

The purpose of this research is to explore a notional identity that is both artist and academic, and my struggles with methodology are related to the different approaches of practice-based research and social sciences research. There has also been, in some sense, a convergence between these two fields recently. Qualitative researchers in social sciences have begun to employ a range of approaches that they call 'arts based' and practice-based researchers have begun to explore the status of writing and its role in the methods and outcomes of practice-based PhDs. There are a number of definitions of autoethnography available. For Tami Spry, a performance studies professor, autoethnography is 'a self-narrative that critiques the situatedness of self and others in social context. (Spry, 2001, p.710) In many ways, this definition sits at one end of the spectrum. For Spry, autoethnographic performance and writing seems to be highly poetic, creative, political and confessional. At the other end of the spectrum is the highly analytical work of Leon Anderson.

Anderson describes an analytical autoethnography that has five key features. It is qualitative research in which the researcher has '(1) complete member researcher (CMR) status, (2) analytic reflexivity, (3) narrative visibility of the researcher's self, (4) dialogue with informants beyond the self, and (5) commitment to theoretical analysis'. (Anderson, 2006, p.375) This is highly complex so I will deal with each of these five criteria in turn. Firstly, complete member researcher status is not simply being able to speak in the first person, or witnessing; it must be much deeper than that. The autoethnographer needs to be a full and equal participant in the group, the situation or the conversation, but unlike other participants the autoethnographer is described as more self-conscious, introspective and analytical. (Anderson, 2006, p.382)

In order to discuss analytic reflexivity, Anderson quotes Atkinson, Coffey, and Delamont:

> (Auto) ethnographers-as-authors frame their accounts with personal reflexive views of the self. Their ethnographic data are situated within their personal experience and sense making. They themselves form part of the representational processes in which they are engaging and are part of the story they are telling.
>
> (Anderson, 2006, p.382)

Anderson states that:

> Not only do they form part of the representational processes, but they are in part formed by those processes as the cultural meanings they cocreate are constituted in conversation, action, and text.

So, analytic reflexivity is about researcher mutability in the context of research. It's about co-creation and being 'part of' it. This being 'part of' it is also important in terms of the narrative visibility of the researcher's self in the research. In autoethnographic research the researcher isn't invisible, or subordinated to the research, they are for Anderson 'a highly visible social actor within the written text'. (Anderson, 2006, p.384) He warns though that:

> Given this nomothetic commitment, analytic ethnographers must avoid self-absorbed digression. They are also constrained from self-absorption by the ethnographic imperative of dialogic engagement with others in the social worlds they seek to understand.

Dialogue with informants beyond the self also comes as a kind of warning against navel gazing. Anderson strongly states that 'No ethnographic work – not even autoethnography – is a warrant to generalise from an "N of one."' Finally, Anderson declares the importance of a commitment to an analytical agenda warning that autoethnography isn't just describing an insider perspective or facilitating a work of creative non-fiction. Autoethnography, for Anderson, must be analytical, must offer grounded opportunities to explore the relationships between the personal and the general and is a 'radically non-traditional, poststructuralist form of research'. (Anderson, 2006, p.391) In many ways, I like the rigour of Anderson's definition. It is a clear, intense and serious structure for a methodology that is often, in practice, very messy and hard to develop. I like the clarity of Anderson's description but I prefer Stacy Holman Jones' (2005) discussions of autoethnography. For her:

> Autoethnography is a blurred genre… a response to the call… it is setting a scene, telling a story, weaving intricate connections between life and art… making a text present… refusing categorization… believing that words matter and writing toward the moment when the point of creating autoethnographic texts is to change the world.

> (Holman, 2005, p.765)

Autoethnographic approaches appealed to me because they allowed me to site my own creative and pedagogic practices in and around the theoretical ideas that I am interested in. They also allow a loose and blurry framework for exploring both the personal and the general. But most importantly, autoethnographic approaches expose the many processes and varieties of thinking and *that* is at the heart of this research.

My central question in this research is:

How is academic identity constructed in contemporary creative arts higher education?

Furthermore I will ask:

Why is disciplinarity important?

What is the effect of language and logobias on academic identity construction in the arts?

How, and why, do collaborations with students effect a shift in the process and pace of academic identity construction?

These questions will be explored using both practice approaches and pedagogic writing. However, these two approaches are not separated in this research they are combined, or hybridised. If you imagine arts-based inquiry in social sciences as a point on a line and 'intellectualised' (Burgin) practice-based PhD research as another point on the same line, then this research, in terms of both methods and methodology, occupies the space in between these two points. Autoethnography, in this context, becomes a guiding principle, something that anchors the research and stops it from floating off into chaos. With this autoethnographic security, notions of the relationship between personal first-hand narrative and more general or transferable principles can be explored in multimodal ways driven either by practice or by radical (new) qualitative approaches.

So, this work is messy, and complicated, and ambitious, and necessary, and important, and relevant. It has taken a long time, two institutions and lots of supervisors. At points it has seemed too difficult and has been abandoned; at other times it has picked up speed. This is a story of more failures than successes, of paradigmatic battles won and lost, of risk and of chaos, of development and of framing.

My first chapter will explore the notion of academic identity. What exactly does that term mean? What is it made of? And how can we represent academic identity effectively so that we can talk about it?

Trust

Throughout this thesis I have alluded to this thing called trust and stated that it functions as a catalyst. This is a complex idea and is explored succinctly by Aidan Curzon-Hobson in 'A Pedagogy of Trust in Higher Learning' (2002). In this text, risk and trust are closely aligned. For Curzon-Hobson the perfect environment for higher learning, and change, is one that can generate what he calls a 'will to potentiality'; that is, an environment that promotes the desire, in the student, to change, to become their potential selves. In this environment, risk is essential and transformation is possible. In this framework, both lecturer and student are in a state of becoming: they are both learners and both incomplete. For Curzon-Hobson an essential component of this environment for trust and risk is teachers telling stories about their own learning, their own struggle to understand and describing how their ideas have changed.

Teachers could also share their research with students and encourage collaboration. In both cases their understanding is revealed as incomplete, needing the help of others, and that they welcome and trust the student to work with them. In all these cases, a collaborative will to potentiality is revealed. Students will thus feel a much stronger trust to exercise their will to potentiality within and beyond the learning environment, as they recognise that the teacher has similar endeavours, and needs and wants their contribution so that he or she may re-imagine and re-create his or her interrelationships in the world. (Curzon-Hobson, 2002, p.269)

As learning stories are told by both students and lecturers, an 'authentic' type of listening is also vital. During the process of exchange of learning narratives it's essential that both parties believe that the other is listening and that this exchange is genuine. If this happens, the will to potential and trust are generated.

> Trust provides a sensation of collegiality that rebels from the bland acceptance of the ideas and values of the 'public' and challenges each student and teacher to formulate, discover and test, through dialogue, their personally transforming relationships to knowledge, self and the other.
>
> (Curzon-Hobson, 2002, p.268)

Corrigan and Chapman's paper on trust published in *Radical Pedagogy* in 2008 emphasises the measurement of trust, empowerment and motivation using a number of different statistical 'scales'. This paper concludes that self-disclosure by academic staff as a strategy for developing trust leads to students who are more motivated to learn and more empowered. So, when I spoke honestly with students I collaborated with on the project about my lack of traditional performance skills and training, this self-disclosure, and its genuine nature, empowered them and unlocked their will to potential.

Endings

Bakhtin and Potential

Previously in this writing I have explored a number of different Bakhtinian ideas, in particular dialogue and heteroglossia; Bakhtin also writes a great deal about potential. It is another one of his key concepts.

> [W]hat constitutes my inner self-confidence, strengthens my back, lifts up my head, 'directs my gaze forward' is the knowledge that 'the real centre of gravity of my self definition lies in the future'.
>
> (Bakhtin in Morson and Emerson, 1990, p.196)

For Bakhtin, potential is a core value. Any self must have an element of potential. If not, it is bounded and finalised. 'Such wholeness demands no risk and requires no self that exploits potential... it allows for no self at all'. (Morson and Emerson, 1990, p.228) Heteroglossic languages are central to the growth and realisation of potential. As multiple languages and complex beliefs interact and hybridise, potential is realised. In monologic writing this is almost impossible. David Lodge, in his book *After Bakhtin*, identifies what he describes as 'a puzzle or a paradox' (Lodge, 1990, p.90) at the heart of Bakhtin's writing. If 'language is inherently dialogic, how can there be monologic discourse, on the postulated existence of which Bakhtin's literary theory depends?' (Lodge, 1990, p.93) He goes on:

> One answer might be that in writing, as distinct from oral speech, the physical absence of the addressee from the context of the speech act makes it possible for the addresser to ignore or suppress the dialogic dimension of language, and thus create the illusion of monologic discourse.

Lodge describes what he calls 'the typical scholarly article or book': these, he states, function as an argument with received discourses or the writing of others, but they don't actually engage in dialogue with these other writings. Most scholars present their writings as facts, avoiding terms such as 'I' or 'you', preferring consensual terms like 'we' or 'the reader'. Scholarly discourse for Lodge 'aspires' to the condition of monologism. They try to have the last word on a subject. They want mastery. They are not interested in dialogue with the reader. This is completely at odds with Bakhtinian notions such as unfinalisability. Principally monologic discourse is about writing as opposed to speaking. It is a mode that is evident in scholarly writing, and those academic forms that mimic this, and forms the encratic spine of university life. These forms descend from publications in our library, are mimicked in our PhD writing, theses, dissertations and essays. These are all monologic and singular.

Lodge notes that there 'is a tendency in Bakhtin to assimilate everything that's progressive, life-enhancing and liberating in writing to the concept of the novel'. (Lodge, 1990, p.95) Clark and Holquist echo this: 'Bakhtin assigns the term "novel" to whatever form of expression within a given literary system reveals the limits of that system as inadequate, imposed or arbitrary. The canonical genres are then associated with whatever is fixed, rigid, and authoritarian'. (Clark and Holquist, 1984, p.276)

So, genres are about rules and regulations and systems. Those forms that can be described as novelistic are constantly reiterating themselves, redefining themselves, reviewing themselves. They are not fixed; they are in motion. They fight against rules and conventions. For Clark and Holquist, these can be represented by two traditions: the heteroglot and the monoglot. Monoglots like sticking to convention, they like stability and systems. They are resilient and strong. Heteroglots are more open to difference, more self-conscious, more sensitive to otherness, more absorbent.

A single language, like academic language, can only develop when provoked, or challenged, by another language. This is a good way of looking at my own resistance to writing. My problem is probably with the monolithic authority of scholarly language; the essay, the dissertation and the thesis with their monological voices, singular and authoritarian. This type of language has no ability, or desire, to change in formal terms. It has no self-consciousness and no inherent reflexivity.

When I encouraged (art and design) students to work scriptovisually, or creatively, their submissions became more reflexive and heteroglossic. The formal structures became dialogic. The students began to use languages in plural. To realise or develop the potential of a language, 'outsideness' is required. (Morson and Emerson, 1990, p.310) This provocation is generative and produces unfinalisable, or interminable, systems that have an unlimited potential that is characterised as 'risk exhausting' and as generative of even more potential. In this situation, languages themselves become reflective and begin to see themselves. They lose assumptions of indisputability and incontestability, they evolve and they are certain that they have the potential to evolve further.

This way of working has also been explored in this (my) PhD work. *Performing Tangier* was about creating layers of collaboration. I wanted to generate as many collaborative moments or events or opportunities where different languages were able to inflect one another as possible. Academic language was in dialogue with the language of practice. Teacherly language was in dialogue with learner language. Rebekka language was in dialogue with Vinca language. And so on. This situation allowed all these languages to become reflexive, to evolve, to mutate, to see themselves, to take risks, to achieve potential and to see more potential in the future. This project was an exploration of my own will to potential and an exploration of how I might unlock the will of my students. It represented multiple deliberate, self-conscious, messy and risky attempts to create the perfect environment for dialogism and hybridisation.

The Will to Monologise

In the spring of 2010, I presented the first part of the first chapter of this thesis at the CLTAD conference in Berlin. At this point I was about here in the writing and I was stuck. How could I conclude this writing? Where was all this heading? My supervisors were asking me the same question. I was beginning to think that I would have to conclude with inconclusiveness, unfinalisability and failure. Perhaps that would be the only possibility; but that was a bit depressing. I presented my paper, with PowerPoint slides of the diagrams that I had made from Alison Shreeve's paper; I didn't get into the very confusing and messy second half to chapter one. I wanted to talk about context and supercomplexity, and about identityness and about failure. I had quite a big audience. At the end of my paper I said 'Any questions?'

'It's all a bit po mo isn't it?' said one voice in a sea of faces.

'What?' I said.

'It's all a bit po mo, we've moved past that now, haven't we?'

I genuinely didn't understand what he meant. Most of the Barnett references, in my conference paper, were from the 1990 book. Was he criticising me for that? Saying my references were out of date? Why was he saying 'po mo' not 'postmodernism'? Was that phrase 'po mo' a reference to outdated trendiness or a, somehow, old-fashioned take on postmodernism?

In spite of the fact that I have done it loads of times, presenting at a conference is still a nerve-wracking experience. This was new work; this was this work and this was its first public appearance. There were plenty of familiar faces in the room, and that fact, instead of being reassuring, made me even more nervous. I asked him to explain what he meant. Then he did one of those questions that wasn't really a question. It was long, really long; it felt like about ten minutes, it was probably three or four, and it didn't appear to have a question in it. I was trying really hard to concentrate, taking him seriously, but I was tired, I hadn't slept well, I had had a long journey (two flights) the day before. I could feel myself going red, and I was getting hotter and beginning to sweat. Then suddenly, I realised that he didn't want to talk about my research really; it was a monologue, about craft and skills, and managerialism, and stuff he was interested in. I had presented this stuff in a formal academic monologic way. For me the questions were the most important bit: they were the point at which this research could come alive, where it could be animated, in dialogue, where other voices and languages could be allowed in evolve it. But that wasn't what was happening. One monologue had prompted another. No hybridisation here. Depressing.

'Erm, excuse me', said a woman's voice from the back.

'Yes', I said, relieved, hot, exhausted, not understanding, feeling stressed.

'Um, well, um, why?' she said.

I was thrown again.

'Why, what?' I snapped.

'Well, why do this?'

I began to speak; I'm not exactly sure what I said. I didn't understand the question, I didn't answer the question, but my answer went on for a long time.

Afterwards I was disappointed. I wanted debate. I wanted people to be interested, ask intelligent questions, and perhaps mention other work that could help me finish this thesis. A reference would have been nice. At the very least some nice comments.

It took a while to sink in. I mean, it took a while for me to process what had happened. That woman. At the back. What she meant. A few hours probably. I hadn't been in the right frame of mind. That man had annoyed me. No, disappointed me. I had high hopes. It was after lunch when I realised what she meant. The woman in that conference session, sat at the back, who I had never seen before, had actually asked the right question. Why do this work? Why try to understand academic identity? Why think about disciplinary pedagogy, about heteroglossia, about practiceness? Why would I want to do it? Why should others do it? Does it help? Why can't we just get on with it and try and be good at it?

I'll start to try to answer this final, and most important, question autobiographically. When I went to Tangier, I set out to explore academic identity. I wanted to think about disciplinary pedagogy and about practice as research. The project was specifically designed to do that. I was also exploring research-informed teaching. This was a central idea as I had involved these two master's students in my practice as research. They had already engaged with my research, so they had previous experience of teaching informed by my research, but this was much more collaborative than before. I wanted to work with them to develop them as practitioner researchers. I also wanted this to be a piece of research that I could be proud of and one that would fulfil the aims of this PhD work. A tall order and very high stakes.

I was also aware that I was interested in *Performing Tangier* as a potential space for developing my own academic identity and the students' identities. In order for this complex experiment to work, I would need to destabilise myself, to allow my various academic and practice-led languages to be altered. By this I mean that I needed to take risks and to do things differently; this could fail. This approach is in contrast to the way in which we normally present our lecturer identities and the way that we plan our teaching and project work. Before going to Morocco, I took the project to our ethics committee at the University. 'What if it all goes wrong?' they asked. 'That could jeopardise your PhD and then how will you be able to assess these students fairly?' I reassured them that the activities in Morocco were only 30 per cent of the module mark and that their reflexive seminar presentations (70 per cent of their mark) would be double marked. I also made sure I appeared confident that it would succeed.

So, what should I call this, this particular way of teaching, of working with students, while simultaneously developing one's own academic identity? It needs a name. Initially I'll call this 'risk-activated practice as research-informed teaching'. This approach could be transferable given the right conditions. This is also something that has more in common with performance pedagogy where the artist-led project is standard, and members of academic staff often write, direct and publicly show work in professional contexts. Risk and trust were the preface to this work and they were the main reason it worked.

In the final section of Nicolas Bourriaud's book on relational aesthetics he includes a series of notes on what he describes as possible extensions of relational aesthetics. He calls these 'cohabitations'. These are, generally, short and relatively underdeveloped ideas. In this section he refers to Guatarri's determination to produce 'subjectivising machines'; he briefly mentions Cooper's assertion that madness is not solo activity but a product of interrelationships; and describes images in temporal terms, as a moment in time. These ideas are all fascinating, thought-provoking and potentially could have relevance to this project. However, it is his (again brief) discussion of the 'engineering of subjectivity' that I would like to explore. Bourriaud says that, during the 1990s, collective forms of intelligence emerged. And artists began to work in networked modes. He describes how artists look for interlocutors, expert conversationalists who can mediate audiences. Here Bourriaud is implying a tripartite system of artist–interlocutor–audience. However, in this system, the interlocutor needs to be fluent in the language of audience and the language of artists and may therefore function as both audience and artist simultaneously. There has not been any detailed work on this.

I would like briefly to return to the notion of the university as supercomplex. Barnett's writing on this was produced in the 1990s as a response to, and as an acknowledgment of, change in the university sector. This change has continued and there are more and more frames in play. The university is still recognisable as supercomplex, but a consideration of academic identity is about locating the individual in this space. It is possible to view this highly complex space as having certain drivers, desires and rhetorical norms, which are repeated so often and in so many different languages as to generate a frame so large that it is impossible to avoid. In universities there exists a level of Bakhtinian 'will to monologise'. This will is an action against supercomplexity, an attempt to make singular the confusion that surrounds us. It is a method for consensus. If we can all agree on what a lecturer's role is, what a 'good' student is and what a university is, then life becomes much easier. This monologic desire permeates everything: quality issues, the student experience (singular), assessment debates, debates on plagiarism, job specifications, mission statements, ALT strategies and learning guides. A desire for a correct way of doing things, a benchmark, a standard to work to is very attractive. We end up giving papers and lecturing in a singular voice; student fora and debates are summarised and bullet-pointed to make them more digestible; academic writing at all levels is valorised for its objectivity and analysis. Everything needs to be written, described, spoken about and idealised in the singular. This is 'good practice'; a singularity. It's easy to describe, it's easy to share and it's safer.

But what about risk? What about the way that risk and trust unlock potential in identities? What about the mess that this inevitably makes and the possibility of learning through failure? In the university, because of this desire for singularity, this will to monologise, risk becomes much more difficult to engineer. We become safer. Trust becomes less mutual and moves towards a monologic declaration from the lecturer to the student. 'Trust me' we say. We ask questions about how we can encourage risk taking in our students, how we can support real deep learning and paradigmatic shift. This won't happen unless we take risks too; and without mutuality our desire for risk taking falls on deaf ears.

More than fifteen years ago, when I was a very new lecturer, I remember saying to my students that a central tenet in analysis was always to look for binaries and for hierarchies. This is a kind of meta-binary in the university. A voice that loudly declares 'Simple good, complex bad'; or maybe 'Simple doable, complex impossible'. So, what is the best way to express the complex simply? To make it doable, palatable, partially digestible. There is an 'ideal' formula of trust + risk = potential, which we must be encouraged to access. This formula is the formula for a pedagogy of potentiality.

Conclusion

There's a long tradition in both art and performance of manifesto writing. From the Futurist manifesto in the early part of the twentieth century onwards these documents are a rallying call, a call to arms, and a statement of will. For Tristan Tzara (*Feeble Love & Bitter Love*, II):

> A manifesto is a communication made to the whole world, whose only pretension is to the discovery of an instant cure for political, astronomical, artistic, parliamentary, agronomical and literary syphilis. It may be pleasant, and good-natured, it's always right; it's strong, vigorous and logical.
>
> (Tzara, 1920, p.1)

The manifesto assumes that a particular problem is curable. That the loudest oppositional voices are not as loud as it's voice. It's an arrogant form. It shouts. It's monologic in extremis. I will finish this text with a manifesto.

A Manifesto for Academic Identity

1. Be suspicious of simplicity.

2. Risk + trust = potential. This is the pedagogy of potentiality.

3. Identity work is ongoing work – always and necessarily unfinalisable.

4. In the university our encratic language is critical language and we have been apprehended by it.

5. Some pedagogic sites need heat adding some need cooling down. Make sure you have methods for both.

6. Unlimited potential is 'risk exhausting' and is generative of even more potential.

7. 'Authentic' listening is vital.

8. In universities, there exists what I will describe as a 'will to monologise'. This will is in many ways an action against supercomplexity, an attempt to make singular the confusion that surrounds us. It is a method for consensus.

9. Pedagogy is a 'state of encounter'.

10. Identity is semi-permeable.

11. Beyondness is about complex academic relationships, about academic identity development, characterised by exchange.

12. In collaborative and heteroglossic spaces (particularly at postgraduate level) it becomes difficult to work out who's who and what's what; students look like academics, academics look like students.

13. In the mist, making and writing become intertwined; diagrams become drawings; drawings became diagrams.

14. An involvement in practice, and an engagement with the processes of practice, allows for the development of knowledge.

15. We are all hybrid.

References

Anderson, L. (2006) 'Analytic Autoethnography', *Journal of Contemporary Ethnography* 35(4), August 2006, pp.373–95

Bell, D. (2008) 'Is there a doctor in the house? A riposte to Victor Burgin on practice-based arts and audiovisual research', *Journal of Media Practice* 9(2)

Bourriaud, N. (2002) *Relational Aesthetics*, Dijon: Les Presse du Reel

Burgin, V. (1986) *The End of Art Theory: Criticism and Postmodernity*. London: Macmillan

Casey, K. (1995) 'The New Narrative Research in Education', *Review of Research in Education* 21, AERA

Corrigan, M., & Chapman, P. (2008) 'Trust in Teachers: A Motivating element to learning', *Radical Pedagogy* 9(2), Spring 2008

Curzon-Hobson, A. (2002) 'A Pedagogy of Trust in Higher Learning', *Teaching in Higher Education* 7(3), pp.265–76

Denzin, N. (2006) 'Analytic Autoethnography, or Déjà Vu all Over Again', *Journal of Contemporary Ethnography* 35(4), August 2006, pp.419–28

Denzin, N.K., & Lincoln, Y.S. (eds) (2005) *The Sage Handbook of Qualitative Research*. Third edition, Thousand Oaks, CA: Sage

Eisner, E. (1991/1998) *The Enlightened Eye: Qualitative Inquiry and the Enhancement of Educational Practice*. New Jersey: Prentice Hall

Finley, S. (2005) 'Arts Based Inquiry: Performing Revolutionary Pedagogy' in Denzin, N.K., & Lincoln, Y.S. (eds) (2005) *The Sage Handbook of Qualitative Research*. Third edition, Thousand Oaks, CA: Sage

Guha, E.G. (1967) *Proposal for the development and testing of new theories and methods of evaluation in field contexts*. Submitted to the U.S. Commissioner of Education for support through the Bureau of Research. Bloomington, IN: Indiana University and the National Institute for the Study of Educational Change

Holman Jones, S. (2005) 'Autoethnography: Making the personal political' in Denzin, N.K., & Lincoln, Y.S., *Handbook of Qualitative Research*. Third edition, pp.763–92, Thousand Oaks, CA: Sage

Lodge, D. (1990) *After Bakhtin: Essays on Fiction and Criticism*. London: Routledge

Moriarty, B., et al. (2008) 'Freire and dialogical pedagogy: a means for interrogating opportunities and challenges in Australian postgraduate supervision', *International Journal of Lifelong Education* 27(4), pp.431–42

Morson, G., & Emerson, C. (1990) *Mikhail Bakhtin: Creation of a Prosaics*. Stanford, CA: Stanford University Press

Schön, D. (1983) *The Reflective Practitioner: How Professionals think in Action*. Aldershot: Ashgate Publishing Ltd

Seale, C. (1999) *The Quality of Qualitative Research*. London: Sage

Shreeve, A. (2009) '"I'd rather be seen as a practitioner, come in to teach my subject": Identity Work in Part-Time Art and Design Tutors', *JADE* 28(2), pp.151–9, London: Blackwell

Spry, T. (2001) 'Performing Autoethnography: An Embodied Methodological Praxis', *Qualitative Inquiry* 7(6), pp.706–32

Tierney, G. (1998) 'Constructing Knowledge: Educational Research in Gay and Lesbian Studies' in Pinar, W., *Queer Theory in Education*. New Jersey: Lawrence Erlbaum Ass.

Tierney, G., & Lincoln, Y. (1997) *Representation and the Text: Re-framing the Narrative Voice*. New York: State University of New York Press

Tzara, T. (1920) 'Feeble Love & Bitter Love, II', in Tzara, T. (1981) *Seven Dada Manifestos and Lampisteries*. London: Calder Publications

•••

How much truth would be too much truth? Maybe all truth is good but not all truth is good to tell. Like many before me and despite the hard-line ethical fundamentalism of scholars such as Martin Tolich, (Tolich, 2010) I write this book with knowingly partiality, leaving out much of that which autoethnography so plainly allows. And I do so for two simple reasons: because in research, as in writing and as in reading, not everything matters equally; and because whilst this is a book about autoethnography and memoir, it makes no claims for full autobiographical disclosure on my own part, whether real or seeming.

That said, the issues facing me here are not radically different to those facing *de facto* autoethnographers. And indeed, because in other contexts my work has been knowingly autoethnographic, it may well be the case that, whilst this badge has been partly removed from my lapel during the writing of this book, some of those instincts remain.

Certainly I am aware that at least some of my observations and opinions ('insights' feels like too grandiose a term) will be as likely to caution aspirant autoethnographers against their form as to inspire them; and that I will seek to persuade readers through the structure of paragraphs, sentences and chapters as much as through any claims to impartiality, objectivity and those traditional staples of academic work. Certainly I am aware that no clean line exists between who we are and what we write and that no clear boundary separates the researcher from the researched. I am aware too that in my use of the personal pronoun I am invoking Romy Clark and Roz Ivanič's elegant arguments about the political conventions of self; and that in referring to their work as *elegant* I am adding nuance to fact. (Clark and Ivanič, 1997) And isn't that what writing always does? And isn't that what makes our occasional distrust of claims for writerly truth so compelling? Because we know that writing changes everything; just as we know that the self both is and is not a fiction; that despite a writer's best claims to authenticity, there is never anything authentic in the words we read. Certainly I am aware too, after Roland Barthes at least, that whilst autoethnography's implicit and often explicit claim is that this is just me writing my story within the particular complexities of my life, the subject who writes today is never and can never be the same subject who acted yesterday; and we do not need to locate ourselves as disciples of French post-structuralism in order to know this.

Like reading, writing is never even remotely free from discourse and my own words that make up this book are far from innocent. Edward Said would see this complexity as 'worldly', as being in and of the world rather than being particularly sophisticated. The ways in which we write are rooted as deeply in the things we have read as in the things we think and if when we write we locate ourselves within a huge conversation with everyone else who has ever written we are also engaging in the construction of the ways in which we are asking to be seen. This is the 'love-me' which Barthes sees as being present within all writing and which brings into the light the vanities we attempt so redundantly to conceal behind academic terminology; behind a tone of disinterest that amounts to hope disguised as an attitude that asks, and often *pleads*, 'Am I knowledgeable enough for you?' (Barthes, 1989, pp.40–1) When taken to extremes, the values and practices of academic writing, those values of rigour and complexity, nuance, accuracy and argument, awareness of the field and the right type of name dropping can make disciplines accessible to only small groups of specialised readers.

In her book *Stylish Academic Writing*, Helen Sword analysed 1,000 scholarly articles from a wide array of disciplines before coming up with some tactics used by those writers she regarded as 'stylish' academics. Sword's argument is that stylish writers aim to tell compelling stories, avoid jargon, provide readers with aesthetic and intellectual pleasure and write with originality, imagination and creative flair. In her survey of stylish writing, Sword noticed extensive use of first-person anecdotes, catchy openings, concrete nouns, active verbs, the use of apposite and illustrative examples, references that show broad reading beyond a subject specialism and a prevailing sense of humour. (Sword, 2012) In a similar vein, William Zinsser cites warmth and humanity as important parts of nonfiction writing. (Zinsser, 2001) All of which is good news for autoethnographers and memoirists who know instinctively that every research outcome tells a story and that a story without reader engagement is no story at all.

Zinsser's book is noteworthy on many levels. One of its most significant moments comes when the author shows a penultimate draft of his work followed by the final version. With this deceptively simple device, Zinsser exposes his own writing to critical examination, which reveals much about his own processes of self-editing as well as his levels of confidence and maturity. The lessons in Zinsser's comparison are profound: we see first and foremost that the author practices what he professes; and we see that he is as prone to inflating his sentences through useless verbiage as the rest of us. What Zinsser illustrates beautifully is how his own writing comes to be as tight as it is in its finished form. In showing us that words do not often have an untrammelled journey from mind to paper, Zinsser provides a valuable lesson for us all.

Zinsser's book provides something of a checklist for writers. (Ibid., pp.10–11) Distilling this here is no substitute of course for reading his work; nevertheless, within the context of this chapter, his views merit inclusion:

> Prune out every word that does not perform a necessary function.

> Strip each sentence to its cleanest components.

Learn the small gradations between words that seem to be synonyms.

Improve the rhythm of sentences by reversing the order of words.

Vary the lengths of sentences.

Make our first sentences our best, in order to capture the reader.

Take care too with a paragraph's last sentence, as it is a springboard to the next.

Make each of our sentences lead naturally into the next.

Make our paragraphs short, because readers think in segments.

Read our work aloud to see how it sounds and re-edit in light of this.

Prune out redundant adjectives.

Prune out adverbs.

Understanding is about knowing what to do next, whilst skill is demonstrated through knowing how to do it. As my own writing no doubt demonstrates, *understanding* Zinsser's words and *valuing* his views does not automatically mean that we have the skills to develop his advice in and through our own practice; but, as Elmore Leonard is to novelists and David Mamet is to dramatists, William Zinsser remains one of the autoethnographer's very best guides.

Writing is directed to a certain end and, in so far as we attempt to articulate our views in a language that will be deemed acceptable by the readers we desire, we exercise a relatively controlled discourse, even when we pay homage to our readers' abilities to write their own meanings into our words. Writing is the negotiation of controlled intent amid the knowledge that readers will always go their own sweet way and that all our attempts to seduce and coerce, educate and fool are subject to the very same readerly interference that we also might champion. All of which is to say that awareness of this is what helps us to distinguish writing from typing.

We cannot imagine that which we cannot first remember, and all memory is an act of imagination and *ergo* of invention. Words can do many things and, within the pages of this book, notions of ineffability will be given little or no line space; but we know that words can only do their best and that even the best words fail to record experience accurately. In failing as accurate records, words can occasionally do much more than this. Perhaps the finest six-word example in English remains Ernest Hemingway's extraordinary idea for a story: *For Sale: Baby Shoes, Never Worn.* That Hemingway considered this to be his finest work makes absolute sense. Like much that is great in art, these words achieve maximum impact from minimal means. They paint a picture and that picture invokes a truth rather than trying to reproduce one. The words 'wedding dress, tear-stained' do something similar.

It is important to remember how this relates to autoethnography and memoir, for we know that truth is a slippery concept and, for those of us who cannot write like Hemingway or paint like Picasso, our attempts run the risk of reducing the truth of experience to something both literary and banal, rather than channelling it into something purposive. Questions of truth go hand in hand with authenticity: another word that, as we have already seen, is often glued to autothenography and memoir without much regard for why. The question of what it means to write with authenticity should be laced through every autoethnographical text, just as it will fuel the contents of this book.

Because my writing in this book is generally based on published work in the public domain, I am faced with few of the ethical questions that autoethnography frequently encounters. Nevertheless an engagement with ethics will also run through this book, rather than being dealt with solely in the chapter on ethics approval as it is often determined by university boards. Like Kristina Medford, I know that the difference between truth and truthfulness is considerably less evasive than the difference between truth and fiction, (Medford, 2006, p.853) just as I know that writing an objective account of reality is not remotely possible, and that written text can be a lazy machine for dissemination. (Eco, 1994, p.49) I know too that the charges of self-indulgence that have been brought against autoethnography stem from critiques of self-showing over self-knowing and that the type of solipsism that offers the argument (whether hidden or overt) that there could be no thoughts, experiences, and emotions other than the thinker's own marks much of the egocentricity of the autoethnographer. In its diluted form, solipsism is a fact of life inasmuch as one can never know other minds in the way that we know our own; and knowledge of other minds exists on the basis of certain inferences that we make from what evidence of external behaviour is directly accessible to us. In John Locke's view, all that we can know directly is the existence and contents of our own minds and all insights into other people's thoughts are indirect and analogical, inferences from our own deeply held perspectives. (Locke and Sigmund, 2005) But if autoethnography is to function as more than a diary of the given writer's thoughts and if autoethnographic research is to have any purposive validity then a frame of critical thinking and external views is as inevitable as it should be desirable.

I don't care what you say anymore, this is my life
Go ahead with your own life, leave me alone.

Billy Joel

CHAPTER TWO

Are You Talking to Me?
Where Autoethnographic Conceit
Becomes Autoethnographic Deceit

Memoir and momoir; research, pseudo research and me-search; narcissism, solipsism and misdirection; Jimmy's World; James Frey and Oprah Winfrey; insider ethnography; definitions and suggestions; personal identities and dominant cultures; interviews, data collection and note taking; selective memory and confirmation bias; Nazar Jabour's case study

When we read a memoir, we are justified in thinking that we are discovering the real person behind the story. This is what Philippe Lejeune refers to as the 'autobiographical pact', the reader's understandable and implicit belief that the author, protagonist and narrator of a memoir are one and the same. We readers tend toward a similar belief that the 'I' of an autoethnography exists both within and outside of the text: that autoethnography, as we generally understand it, reveals the researcher to us alongside the researched.

Recent studies of authorship, however, have invited us to re-imagine the traditional idea of the author as originator, external to and in control of the text s/he has created. Barthes' suggestion that writing is the destruction of every voice, or every point of origin, reveals a cautious approach toward texts that look to reveal their authors, precisely because, as Barthes would have it, the author is never anything more than the instance writing, just as *I* is nothing other than the instance saying *I*. If one's identity can never be fully realised in print, this does not prevent our attempts at achieving that very same thing; perhaps for no greater reason than that we come to understand ourselves as much through the stories we write as the stories we read.

We can think of auto-narratives as *creating* the subject whose name is on the work's cover, to the extent that even when we imagine the real person behind an autoethnography (the writer) this is simply another story for us (the readers) to tell ourselves. We see this clearly in the autoethnographies of the great and the good in their fields, where the works are marketed in such ways that the author is no less of a construction than the text: in this way the autoethnographical author is created by a text and not the other way around. If we can ask what we could ever really know of Saul Bellow or Bill Bryson, we can equally ask what most of us know of Carolyn Ellis or Amanda Coffey, Kip Jones or Deborah Reed-Danahay. We know them as characters within their own published narratives and, as with most protagonists, the edges are smoothed and the virtues enlarged.

Partly because of this, autoethnography attracts exponents and deriders in roughly equal measure, with neither telling a fully legitimate tale. Edges blur between forms and one writer's autoethnography is another's personal essay, and another's autobiography, and another's act of creative nonfiction and yet another's memoir. We could argue that memoir merits a chapter in its own right rather than being collapsed alongside autoethnography, yet a stand-alone chapter could distinguish the genre more greatly than would be genuinely meant. Ubiquity has led to a demise in quality which, if not quite inevitable, is singularly unsurprising. Me-search has become so much more dominant than research and memoir's never-need-to-leave-the-house-or-office ease of access to subject material and its plugging into the current trend for the Mystory of trauma and the Momoir of family disclosure has seen a huge increase in publication.

A qualitative distinction should be drawn at the outset between the work of writers such as Blake Morrison and the 'read how I have survived against the odds' outpourings of countless online and in-print publications. For skilled writers, and where those writers are telling a story worth the reading, memoir is an incredibly powerful genre. The flipside of this is that memoir can be used to shortcut imagination. Everybody has experiences of life, every parent has stories about their children, each orphaned child has a tale of grief to recount. No matter how heartfelt these memories might be, it is not always easy to see where the line is drawn between indulging our growing sense of victimisation and writing something that offers some form of empowerment as well as empathy. Neil Genslinger's tongue is only partly in his cheek when he writes:

> There was a time when you had to earn the right to draft a memoir, by accomplishing something noteworthy or having an extremely unusual experience or being such a brilliant writer that you could turn relatively ordinary occurrences into a snapshot of a broader historical moment. Anyone who didn't fit one of those categories was obliged to keep quiet. Unremarkable lives went unremarked upon, the way God intended.
>
> (Genslinger, 2011)

Letting somebody know that you share their position is not the same thing as empowerment and in many online cases empathy is skewed into the type of contemporary indulgence that sees every day as a victory over the travails of ordinary life. The *Momoir* (a term copyrighted by Linda Clark in 2002) is, as Patty Sotorin explains, enjoying a near-manic rise in popularity:

> There is a wiki called *The Momoir Project*; online zines like *Literary Mama*, *HipMama* and *Brain Child*; an annual Mother's Day contest for 6-word momoirs like 'Better mom when someone is looking' and 'Puppies would have been much easier'… and lots of mom blogs with names like *True Mom Confessions.com*, *Tales from the Mommy Track*, *The Mommy Blog*; *Adventures from the Wonderbelly of Motherhood*, *Offsprung: Your Life Didn't End When Theirs Began*, *Mommy Logic*, *The Momtrap: Digging Myself Out Since 2004*, *Diary of a Playgroup Dropout*, and *PlainJaneMom.com*'…
>
> (Sotorin, 2010)

As with autoethnography, many recent memoirs involve people writing about their experiences of drug abuse, sexual abuse, child abuse, rape, incest, anorexia and chronic illness, experiences which, as Patricia Clough notes, are 'symptomatic of the trauma culture that has been most outrageously presented in television talk shows.' (Clough, 2000, p.287) This is, I would suggest, a form of false trauma. Not false in the sense of invention, but false in terms of the survival-speak that such forms seek to peddle in. Wrapping the desire to be read and heard (no more, in fact, than the desire to be published) in the need to speak something worth saying, false trauma turns experience into opportunism in a way that is more about manufacturing a platform than managing a pain.

As will be discussed presently, wallowing in this moral low ground is in no significant way redeemed by adopting the supposedly ethical stance of changing key names and details.

Acknowledging the way that the woe-is-me of victimhood is turned into the I-will-survive of the Ellen DeGeneres or Oprah Winfrey guest slot puts a frame around the validation we give to almost anyone with a half-inspirational story to tell. Cancer victims are applauded for having the condition, divorcees are applauded for loving again and the obese are whooped at for losing some weight. Whether this is described in print or in the echo chamber of online social media, the results are often insular, narcissistic and self-affirming. In a climate such as this, where stories are both the effect and the cause, there is little wonder that the memoir is such big business, with innumerable titles, increasing daily, on every online book site. We do well, however, to consider the fact that, while a commercial publisher's intended market is the general public, a vanity publisher's intended market is the author.

In the light of these aspects, this book will look to provide value through its more measured appraisal of autoethnography and memoir; seeing these as valuable and inevitably here-to-stay research methodologies and outcomes which nevertheless have their share of problems, many of which are self-inflicted and/or self-invited. On a very clear level then, *Remaking Memory* continues to set its stall out as a critical and cautious rather than fully *convinced* guide to self-narrating practitioners.

Readers of this book are likely to be reasonably well-versed in the ideas of autoethnography. Notwithstanding this, and as a relatively recent term, 'autoethnography' is in need of some clarification; some sense of what exactly it might mean in terms of methodology, intent and application. Overlaps with ethnography are inevitable as are those with biography and autobiography, postmodernism, memoir, narrative and storytelling, research, subjectivity, trust and the ethics of disclosure; and these links can and do lead to confusion. In striving to offer some clarification, this chapter will move also towards a note of caution, a note to self perhaps as much as to any reader; a note that in some ways might be seen as something of a contradiction in its acknowledgement of autoethnography's potential failings and self-indulgent, even narcissistic qualities.

In this context, narcissistic autoethnography finds its home in the construction of predominantly personal narratives: those stories by researchers who locate and regard themselves as the research subject and who then go on to write evocative stories of their experiences. These are often the most difficult forms for self-writing to accommodate. This is because they are largely reliant on experience reading as its own analysis. In the weakest examples they also offer diary-like description of the researcher–writer's life as surrogate for a re-telling that provides an adequate informing of our understanding of a particular cultural context. It can be hard to distinguish these stories from autobiography. In these cases autoethnography can be used as little more than a relatively research-friendly term, as something that sounds more academically legitimate than autobiography but which has more in common with drawing the reader into the researcher's own life than using one's culturally located experiences as something that opens a door onto wider understanding. Determining this will always be an act of subjective response: doubtless, this paragraph will have done disservice to those who intend their writing to have a higher purpose and yet have produced a text that reads (to me) as something rather more base and self-serving.

As ever, in this book the intention is to poke a critical and concerned stick at the nest of self-writing to see which ways the hornets fly; if indeed they fly at all.

Sometimes the wings flap furiously but nothing takes flight. In a work on father narratives and autoethnographic exploration, Bryant Keith Alexander tells us that he is not yet ready to tell his story. It is a story, he says, that resists its own telling because it might reveal too much of Alexander to the reader as well as to himself. (Alexander et al., 2012) In the same article, Claudio Moreira asks whether he has the courage to 'go further… to explore the impossible pain of finding the origins of myself in the Father?' (Ibid.) Explaining this to us, Moreira writes 'Yes, my story resists its telling even when it is already being told.' hari stephen kumar continues in the same vein, informing his readers that he lives in a state of tension between courage and cowardice, ruptured by treason and tradition (and I suspect between the urge to stay silent and the desire to be published). The article's concluding statement that 'We three men, separated by the materiality of difference… have found psychic connections through the articulation of lived experience that provide each other comfort and refuge in our process of becoming better men' does little to strengthen autoethnography's claims, acting instead as a licence to write about not writing in a work that threatens to speak only to itself.

Whilst many scientists are understandably and not at all unexpectedly cautious when it comes to autoethnography, its main critics are often those closest to home. Thinly veiled hostility regularly comes from researchers working within the humanities and also within the methodologies of traditional social science. From the perspective of those who emphasise the desire for objectivity within social research, qualitative researchers in general and autoethnographers in particular are often referred to as 'journalists, or soft scientists' and their findings are termed unscientific, or only exploratory, or entirely personal and full of bias. As Denzin and Lincoln (2012) have argued, a great many quantitative researchers regard the materials produced by the softer, interpretive methods as innately unreliable, impressionistic and not objective. This view is further identified by Garance Maréchal, who suggests that the early criticisms of autobiographical methods in anthropology were based on concerns as to 'their validity on grounds of being unrepresentative and lacking objectivity'. (Maréchal, 2010) Maréchal reminds us that the emotionally evocative approaches of autoethnographers have been taken to task by seemingly more analytic researchers on account of their 'lack of ethnographic relevance as a result of being too personal.' (Ibid.)

Criticised for being biased, navel-gazing, self-absorbed or emotionally incontinent, and for hijacking traditional ethnographic purposes and scholarly contributions, autoethnographers have always been subject to assassination as a result of friendly fire. The nature of autoethnography lays it open to the critique of excessive subjectivity, narcissism and solipsism. The critique is damning because, whether by design or accident, it does much to render the method itself as a diminished practice, along with the narratives its processes produce. Clearly when there is an overemphasis on the self in isolation from the wider social context and setting, or when there is an over-reliance on description that is divorced from analysis, critics from any field of practice are justified in questioning autoethnography's worth. In such cases as these it is legitimate to label the practice as a problematic form of qualitative inquiry and research.

Lest my own concern that the 'auto' in autoethnography sometimes assumes an overly large role appears too much like attack disguised as critique, it is tempered here by recognition that no methodology exists without flaws and that no one approach can be all things to all people. This much is true, or True with a capital T. A lower-case and less-emphatic truth exists in this book's reluctance to function as an unequivocal endorsement of autoethnography's claims. Whereas zealous advocates feel comfortable describing autoethnography in the language of born-again hagiography, this book will continue to tread a middle ground. It will do so not through any sense of being undecided so much as an attempt to resist the urge to rhetoric over reason.

At a time when a researcher's methods have become seemingly more important than the subjects they are used to scrutinise, and methodology wars are fought as passionately as they are, it is prudent to step back for a moment and reiterate what it is that this book is about. In doing so opportunity is taken to locate autoethnography, life writing and memoir as what they are: ways of discovering and ways of describing. That many of the theorists and practitioners cited in this book commonly refer to themselves as autoethnographers ultimately does no more than muddy the waters; for whatever autoethnography is, it is not at its best when it reads as a club one can join or, as is increasingly and more accurately the case, as a careerist bandwagon one can climb aboard. To call oneself a feminist, postmodernist, structuralist or Marxist rightly suggests an overtly politicised way of viewing the world and it does so in ways that denote causality between viewpoint and description, between seeing and telling. Whilst working through autoethnography (or memoir come to that) is in no way an apolitical choice, it is a choice and its value lies in its fitness for purpose. One intention of this book is to prepare the ground for autoethnographical research that is ethical at the same time as it is applicable in the real world; in other words, that the ethical dimension is not so single minded as to destroy a project before it begins. A co-intention is to function as a critical guide for those authors, researchers and educationalists who find themselves increasingly drawn toward autoethnography as a process of extending social and sociological understanding in ways that seek to expose rather than conceal the researcher–writer's own agenda and role.

In the 1970s, autoethnography was quite narrowly defined as being about insider ethnography, inasmuch as it was assumed to refer to studies of the culture of a particular group of which the researcher was her or himself a member. In recent years the principles and applications of autoethnography have evolved in such a way that any precise definition is well-nigh impossible. No wonder, really. In relativist times all things slide toward an absence of fixity that makes certainty a casualty of the age. Not all certainties are bad, not all certainties are wrong and there is a place for exactitude. But when even the researcher's reality is up for grabs, certainty starts to fall through the fingers like sand. Steve Grand argues that we are not permanent enough, even in life, to regard our acts of memory as in any way *embodied*. Inviting his readers to think of an experience from childhood that they remember clearly, Grand sets us up neatly, albeit with a high degree of existentialism:

> After all, you really were there at the time, weren't you? How else
> would you remember it? But here is the bombshell: you *weren't* there.
> Not a single atom that is in your body today was there when that event
> took place.... Matter flows from place to place and momentarily comes

together to be you. Whatever you are, therefore, you are not the stuff
of which you are made.

(Grand, 2003, p.19)

So much for memory then as relating to events we can reliably claim to have
lived through, leave alone remembered and re-told with any accuracy. Like an
original broom that has had three replacement shafts and nine replacement
heads, we may well no longer be the stuff of which we believe we are made.

As it is elsewhere in life, truth in nonfiction is an often-messy business. The
history of truth writing is rife with examples of dishonesty and the following
are a few from a long list. The journalist Janet Cooke wrote a front-page feature
in the *Washington Post* called *Jimmy's World*. The article went on to win her a
Pulitzer Prize in 1981 and the film rights were sold for $1.5 million US. The
only problem with the story was that it was a complete fabrication. More than
thirty years later the story of Cooke's hoax is still taught in journalism schools
worldwide. Cooke's story focused on Jimmy, an eight-year-old boy with a heroin
habit, who had been introduced to the drug by his mother's live-in boyfriend.
But Jimmy did not exist. And by definition, neither did the mother or the live-in
boyfriend. These details did not stop Cooke from describing Jimmy in rich and
emotive detail, telling her readers that the child was 'a precocious little boy with
sandy hair, velvety brown eyes and needle marks freckling the baby-smooth skin
of his thin brown arms.' (Prince, 2010) To give Cooke the benefit of a fleeting
doubt, her story of Jimmy may well have conveyed a wider truth about the
conditions that existed in many inner-city parts of the USA, even though it did
not actually tell the truth at all.

The bottom line, however, is that different forms of work make different
claims for truth and, whilst we know and accept that different newspapers,
magazines or similar publications have different political agendas, we do not
expect journalists to play fast and loose with the truth. By the same token
readers are within their rights to assume that a memoir is not the same thing
as a parable.

If Cooke now reads as a writer of fiction masquerading as a journalist she is
not quite alone. In 2003 the reporter Jayson Blair was outed as having misled
readers of the *New York Times* with a series of bogus dispatches, fabricating
comments, concocting episodes and purloining material from other newspapers
and online services. Blair used these techniques to write about sniper attacks in
Washington and the anguish of families grieving for loved ones who had been
killed on active service in Iraq. When Blair's previous articles were exposed to

scrutiny, it became clear that he had invented quotes, created names, lied about places he had never visited, claimed to have interviewed people he had never met and regularly lifted details from other reports and publications. When he was challenged, Blair told his editors that he had downloaded a number of news stories and that he had subsequently confused them with his own journalistic notes. Not overly burned by his public outing, nor seemingly distressed that two of his senior editors lost their jobs because of his actions, Blair wrote the self-justifying book *Burning Down My Masters' House: Life at the New York Times* (2004). Stephen Glass is another disgraced American journalist whose lies were at the expense of the magazine he was employed by, in this case the *New Republic*. Glass was exposed as a serial faker and fired by his editor, before going on, like Blair, to write a novel about his experiences: *The Fabulist* is the story of a character called Stephen Glass who is fired from his job as a reporter for telling journalistic lies. And so, like someone claiming innocence in a court of law and then writing from the cell about their guilt, the dishonesty of fiction presented as fact is transformed into a kind of after-the-event truth.

And it is not just these few rogue journalists who tamper with the truth at their professional peril. Herman Rosenblat's book *Angel at the Fence* is a love story about a girl who threw apples and bread to the author over a German concentration camp fence. Not true. And whilst Rosenblat had indeed been an inmate of Buchenwald and other camps, the invented love story he placed at the heart of his tale was enough to discredit both author and publisher, Berkley Books, part of the Penguin Group. Rosenblat's publishers had managed to secure him high-profile guest slots on Oprah Winfrey's daytime television show. Winfrey herself has some previous form when it comes to being swept along by the myth of memoir: she had championed the author James Frey, who went on to admit that he had embellished his bestselling memoir about his battle with drug addiction, published in 2003. Winfrey had made Frey's nonfiction memoir *A Million Little Pieces* her personal selection for what had by then become the world's most influential book club. Frey's recounting of his years as an alcoholic, drug addict and criminal was lauded in an edition of Winfrey's programme called *The Man Who Kept Oprah Awake At Night*, with the presenter choking back the tears as she described how much she loved and was moved by the book. Frey's book, which sold 3.5 million copies and sat atop the *New York Times* nonfiction bestseller list for weeks, was widely regarded as being inaccurate, dishonest and manipulative, none of which prevented Winfrey from publicly supporting Frey's follow-up memoir, *My Friend Leonard*. Like his earlier work, this book roared up the *New York Times* nonfiction list and Frey's work, translated into 30 languages by 28 publishers, remains incredibly popular.

It is worth noting that the original manuscript for *A Million Little Pieces* was first touted to publishers as a work of fiction but Frey's publisher Doubleday/Random House went with a re-versioned manuscript, presumably believing that all of the fictional elements had been excised. As Errol Flynn was fond of saying, 'why ruin a good yarn with a crippling regard for the facts?' (Flynn, 1961) Maybe so and maybe not. Writing in *Vanity Fair*, Evgenia Peretz puts the current hunger for memoir in some sort of context:

> On the one hand, memoirs have often been afforded a certain poetic
> license to stray from absolute truth in the interest of storytelling.
> On the other, they have the appeal of the real. Over the years, the
> marketplace hungered for more of both.... It was inevitable that one
> day the mixture would blow up in someone's face.
>
> (Peretz, 2008)

For his own part, Frey claims not to care if people call his work a memoir, or a novel, or a fictionalised memoir. 'The thing on the side of the book', Frey tells us, 'means nothing. It's just a story. It's just a book that was written.' (Hylton, 2007) The late Norman Mailer told Frey that memoir was by definition a corrupt form of literature: 'That's why a writer writes his memoir, to tell a lie and create an ideal self. Everything I've ever written is memoir', (Castro, 2008) whilst HarperCollins' publisher Jonathan Burnham insists that publishing professionals 'all know that the genre of memoir is a uniquely strange one, where many writers have played with the truth or reshaped the truth or have their own vision of the truth which can never be judged in any final court.' (Ibid.)

A Belgian writer, Monique De Wael, recently revealed that she had invented her tale of survival as a Jewish girl searching for her parents accompanied by a pack of wolves in Nazi-occupied Europe. De Wael, it emerged, was not even Jewish. Margaret B. Jones' memoir of being raised in poverty by a black foster mother and selling drugs for gang members in a Los Angeles gang was exposed as a lie after her sister contacted the publisher. And so it is and so it goes. Where veracity is involved, we pay our money and we make our choices. Alain de Botton is a more than usually reliable guide when it comes to negotiating the route between the artist's abbreviations of what reality actually is into something that we actually want to read. For de Botton this involves the:

> curious phenomenon whereby valuable elements may be easier to
> experience in art... than in reality.... Artistic imaginations omit

and compress, they cut away the periods of boredom and direct
our attention to critical moments and, without either lying or
embellishing, thus lend to life a vividness and coherence that it may
lack in the distracting wooliness of the present.

(de Botton, 2002)

De Botton's feeling is that any writer who gave too many unnecessary details
would be too maddening to read, and he is doubtless right. But a lie by omission
is never quite the same thing as a lie by invention and lies in print have a way
of catching people out. For students engaged in autoethnographic research, the
particular rigours and requirements of academic honesty only add to the perils
of straying too far from what happened into the righteously tempting desire for
what reads well on the page.

Sebastian Junger's book *The Perfect Storm*, which details the sinking of the
fishing vessel *Andrea Gail* in 1991, shows us what can be achieved with care.
Whilst the book has sometimes been accused of factual errors and one-sided
research, Junger's opening words do much to set his stall out as a writer whose
concern is accuracy rather than connected invention. Junger tells us that he
'toyed with the idea of fictionalizing minor parts of the story... to make it more
readable', but that ultimately 'No dialogue was made up.' (Junger, 2007)

Ethnography means writing about a culture and writing about its people.
Autoethnography then is the writing of a people of which the writer is him- or
herself a member, the people writing the people; much like in autobiography,
where the author and protagonist are models of each other. Where the *bio*
of autobiography provides one focus, the *ethno* provides another, suggesting
a concentration on one's reading of a group of which one is a part, rather
than holding up a mirror to one's self. In practice the overlap is messier than
this and the manners of narrative are not bound by strict rules of definition.
Nevertheless, and particularly within research, autoethnography is generally
thought of as a means of shedding light on society through one's involved
participation and is not about using that society as an opportunity to write
primarily about oneself. Complicated though this often is, it remains a key
distinction between autoethnography and autobiography.

Whilst no-one would deny the predominance of white, middle-class
members of staff at the majority of Western universities, Abraham P. DeLeon
is somewhat disingenuous in his belief that these same universities would be
unlikely to value his cultural experiences. (DeLeon, 2010) Universities embrace
arts and humanities research outcomes much more strongly than they value

particular methodological approaches and, if one's cultural background fuels work that is disseminated appropriately, no vice chancellor is likely to raise an objection. My own early cultural experience was of being a white working-class male within a community that favoured physical prowess and loyalty over academic success and an interest in the arts, and which was tolerant, forgiving and even supportive of anti-social behaviour: a sexist, violent and often racist environment. This was my world until I was well into my twenties and the values instilled in those years (by my immediate social surroundings rather than my family) as well as those discarded have had an impact, large or small and for good or ill, on every aspect of my professional life: which is not the same thing as making a career out of the route from that life to this. We carry our experiences with us whether we choose to or not and the probability that the bulk of my colleagues come from quite different class backgrounds and that the attitudes encountered in my own early world would not be particularly appreciated in my current reincarnation as an education professional has resulted, at least as far as I can see, in no marked impediment to my career.

As researchers and writers, it is not ultimately who or what we are, have been or aspire to be that are significant so much as what it is we do with those factors: how we develop what matters to us into material that will matter to other people. It is understandable that DeLeon felt the need to distance himself from his cultural roots in order to negotiate a new form of identity, but his confession of a sense of 'anger and shame that [he] decided to turn to the dominant culture in which to find and situate [his] sense of personal identity' (ibid.) appears overblown. In my case, the aggressive attitudes I was raised with were so patently at odds with academic study that something had to give; but what gave was not any sense of who I was so much as what I was doing for a living. In other words, I was aware of moving into a different world that was not necessarily a *better* one. For some people social class is made up of a set of ideas and values they hope can be shed and grown anew like a skin; for others it can feel as deep set and unchanging as sexuality, and perhaps even more so. Class is a complex thing and who we are is not defined by the work that we do. Working in a university, learning a few new words and realising that prejudice is wrong does not mean that one's roots are necessarily torn up and replanted in a middle-class pot.

Autoethnography is the peg on which so many researchers are hanging their work that it is not always easy to separate those who believe that knowledge is built from lived experience from those who see the documenting of the minutiae of everyday life as an act of easy tenure. University lecturers and researchers are more inclined to describe themselves as learning practitioners than at any time in the past and this is evidence that the idea of lifelong learning is more than a sound bite; but there is a gap between one's own learning and the value this might have for a wider public. Despite the vast majority of university research being both sound and well-intentioned, universities have also become home to a pendulum of something close to pseudo research. At one extreme of the swing is research without outcome, whilst at the other we find outcomes that have been arrived at seemingly without any research at all. The rise in a focus on outcomes, where investigation is redundant without result, has been harnessed to the rise in academic publishers and so our shelves groan under the weight of books from authors in search of tenured contracts; when we leave the library and head to the theatre or gallery we see work in progress, and whilst these might be examples of research (on many unfortunate occasions, I fear they are not) they tend in my experience to be often quite alarmingly light on significant outcomes. Practice-led research thus gives us plenty of practice in lieu of research, we quickly lose track of the academic books with their vocabulary that disguises their core of emptiness: the boxes get ticked and everybody wins their battles in an increasingly pointless war.

Autoethnography invites us to read it as a form of resistance and we perpetuate this further by locating ourselves as methodological outlaws, unloved and unwanted, misunderstood and misaligned. There are parallels in my own background fields of theatre and performance studies where postmodernism, postdramatic theatre and then practice-led research were seen initially as resistant. That they were then and remain today resistant to a mainstream majority is not in doubt; but within their own fields of operation they quickly became more than accepted: they became *expected*. Hard to locate one's work as in any significant way 'outside' when it is inside the same corridors of power it purports to resist.

Because questioning autoethnography has come to be seen as opposing it, few balanced arguments emerge. One is either for or against and publishing in one of the journals that has been set up as a home for autoethnographic research means largely toeing a positive line. Sara Delamont opens her 2007 conference paper 'Arguments against Auto-Ethnography' by labelling it as deliberately provocative when in fact her views are eminently reasonable – reasonable inasmuch as using an educational conference as a platform from which to challenge a particular perspective is the absolute norm. Yet such is the seeming vulnerability of autoethnography that reason is excused as provocation even in the moment of utterance. Delamont's paper's position (provocation?) comprises the following:

Autoethnography is essentially lazy.

Autoethnography is experiential rather than analytic.

Autoethnography abrogates the duty to collect and analyse data.

Autoethnography is self-indulgent.

Autoethnography is almost impossible to write and publish ethically.

Autoethnography has a focus on the powerful.

(Delamont, 2007)

Delamont is as entitled to her views as anybody else and in fact they can be boiled down further: laziness, self-indulgence, reliance on experience and a lack of data analysis are each aspects of the same critique, which leaves issues of ethics and power to address. Delamont sums up her laziness argument by saying that 'our duty is to go out and research... not sit in our homes focusing on ourselves', (ibid.) leaving the two more difficult suggestions to speak for themselves. And is it the case that autoethnography focuses on the powerful? We saw in Chapter One that Jill Taft-Kaufman's view is entirely oppositional to Delamont's, and my own experience of university supervision and examining leads me to side with Taft-Kaufman.

In writing about identity, our communicative acts always embody projections of the self, even if these are carried at a subconscious level and that self always says something about one's relationship to the culture it describes. Nazar Jabour's astonishingly raw accounts of life as an Iraqi refugee artist draw the subconscious out into the light and blur the line between encounter and research, process and product. The following section comes from Chapter Three of the exegesis that accompanied Jabour's creative work on Iraqi Nights and goes some way toward articulating how he sought to negotiate group work within a highly personal method of investigation.

Iraqi Nights

Part One: The Methodological Processes

Nazar Jabour

The methodology of Participatory Action Research (PAR) conceptualised as practice-based research in performance applies to the entire research project and to the documentary film interviews and performance processes. In *Performance as Research: Research by Means of Performance*, a discussion paper by Alison Richards, the focus is on the processes:

    a) By rigorous reflection and investigation

    b) By the clarity and specificity of… [the] research questions, and

    c) By the openness of… [the] processes to question and evaluation
       by others.

The central hypothesis of my research emerged from the collaboration of participants, through their input, continuous analysis and discussion. I transcribed what we discovered through creative thinking during the study of the data. In this project, the data was not interpreted by me as researcher only by the Australian participants.

Ethnodrama and ethnotheatre employ the traditional craft and artistic technique of a theatre production alongside the researcher's interpretation of the data; and the goal is to investigate a particular facet of the human condition for the purposes of adapting those observations and insights into a performance medium. Simply put, this is preparatory fieldwork for theatrical production work.

I provided an ethnographical account of the transcripts, not as readymade plays or scripts for acting but as raw materials for making a performance. Johnny Saldana describes the relationship between the written script and the data as:

> written script consists of dramatized, significant selections of narrative
> collected thought interviews, participant observation field notes, journal
> entries, and/or print and media artefacts such as diaries, television

broadcasts, newspaper articles and court proceedings. Simply put, this *is dramatizing the data.*

(Saldana, 2011, p.196, emphasis added)

I collected the data but I didn't dramatise it; I didn't turn it into a writing script but kept it as a box of stories. I played multiple roles such as participant, participant observer, facilitator, co-creator with analytical input to the historical background of the narratives and finally directorial assistant to the participants.

The Australian performers were the key elements to closing the distance between me and the audience as they were English speaking within their own communities, in their own voices, with their concern about the narratives. They were the key players in an artistic response to history, stories and events in performance, and I sought at all times not reduce their voices to my own sense of reflection and analysis.

An ethnodrama is 'a written, artistically composed arrangement of qualitative data' (Saldana, 2011, p.196). I neither arranged nor thought consciously about the presentation of a drama but presented transcripts as raw material to the participants to engage thoroughly and collectively on how to respond to the stories and engage with them in social and creative manners. I agreed with Saldana's notion that 'you [must] find a new way of telling an established story by transforming it from one medium to another while maintaining the integrity and the spirit of the piece'. (Ibid., p.197) The transcripts of interviews with the Iraqi artists were not established stories but oral narratives: their stories told in their own words. The transcript was not something that 'turns notes from the field into texts that are performed' (Denzin, 2005, p.23) but rather the experiences of Iraqi memories and stories brought to life as the participants/performers spoke about their lives. The transcripts exemplify hidden and hitherto unheard voices of people situated in place and time: Iraq between 1979 and 2012.

I collected data in the form of video footage instead of on audiotape as a way of recording people's own voices, their presence, and their vocal and facial expressions while they narrated their stories. I did so because performing data is an immensely powerful way of presenting research.

Alison Richards emphasises the importance of performance as research for local knowledge and the position of the researcher, which, she argues:

include[s] the position of 'outside' observer... as one valid perspective
from which research into performance might be undertaken. I would
also argue that a background in at least one discipline of performance
practice is of enormous benefit, in conveying some of the crucial detail
of 'local knowledge' to anyone wishing to undertake performance
research.

(Richards, 1995)

The local knowledge comes from a refugee artist's life and the ways artistic
experiences are fused into performance autoethnography.

This practice-based research project utilises the methods of Action Research
(AR) in the first investigation, the filming of the Iraqi narratives, and PAR in its
creative process of the performance. Australian social science researcher Bob
Dick provides a basic but useful definition of AR, which I reproduce here in full.
He describes it as:

action using a cyclic process, repeated cycles with continuously
refining methods, data and interpretation in the light of understanding
developed in earlier cycles. It is thus an emergent process which takes
shape as understanding increases; it is an iterative process which
converges towards a better understanding of what happens. In most of
its forms it is also participative (among other reasons, change is usually
easier to achieve when those affected by the change are involved) and
qualitative.

(Dick, 2012, emphasis added)

The *Iraqi Nights* performance experiment follows the cycle of PAR methods in the
plan/action/reflect/re-plan.

My project uses this cyclical research process to develop the creative responses
of Australian performers. Through a dialogue we were sharing the present of
our lived experiences in performance making, arriving at a dialogue created by
Australian participants through processes of reflection and engagement with the
diverse Iraqi memories.

In my research, I explain the process by giving an example of this process and
an example applied to the entire process of making the performance. I focused
with the participants on finding the meanings in relation with each other's views

from an artistic point of view about the impact of historical events on artists' narratives rather than engaging in the social and political conflicts. The process begins with what I have provided the participants with: a selection of external research materials such as books of poetry, music and artworks. The process was collaborative and open ended inasmuch as it invited the participants' own understandings rather than imposing my own perspectives upon participants.

It is based on individuals understanding their own options, or lack of options, and their views of the controlling dramatic structure. The main concern was to find ways of communicating and connecting Iraqis' stories to Australian audiences through working with Australian participants. The cycle of action, found and refined and restarted again and again was based on exploring creative ways of maintaining the quality, content and stylisation of the narratives. It was a creative process with an analytical approach to data collection. Each individual brings their own understanding to the notion of what might constitute a true story.

Ming-Fang He writes:

> Understandings of our cross-cultural lives and cross-cultural identities are not easily obtained through conventional ways of thinking. Rather, understandings are achieved by thinking about cross-cultural lives and cross-cultural identities narratively and making meaning… in relation to people, time and history changing.

> (He, 2000, p.515)

Such understanding of history and time is the central key in the process of exchanging knowledge and the experiences of those involved directly and indirectly. He explains:

> there are two kinds of inquiries: *stable inquiry* and *liquid inquiry*: Stable inquiry lends itself to fixed research phenomena, questions, purposes, objectives, methodologies and outcomes. The knowledge obtained in one inquiry is sustained without any change in subsequent inquiries. In liquid inquiry, knowledge produced in one inquiry is changed in subsequent inquiries. This change involves revision of the meanings of the terms of inquiry and their relationships.

> (He, 2000, p.516)

The process of flow in my project has increased understanding and opportunities to reflect on findings, change direction and refine the performance with the new knowledge discovered early in the process. A liquid inquiry is an open process of flow of information and changes of direction which continue forever, an open-ended dialectic between continuity and change in the process of cross-cultural narratives in performance.

The dynamics and the fundamental of the groups using PAR is 'the commitment that all participants actually do research for *themselves*' (McTaggart, 1991, p.170) to improve their own vision, individually or collectively.

I worked with PAR in the creative process in the following ways:

1: As a facilitator, I provided the participants with documentary film including the transcripts and Chapter One of the thesis as a starting point for discussion before and during the rehearsal times.

2. I opened conversations about the narratives, history and personal experiences.

3. I worked on aspects of creative interaction and reflection on what we learned about the issues and the narrative.

4. I created an environment for sharing personal and engaged in a dialogue about found materials.

5. As a dramaturge, I worked with the performers on the potential meaning and links between each selection of segments or story.

6. I worked with the group on additional relevant external materials such as Iraqi writers', poets' and artists' webpages. We engaged with what we found in the first step and built upon it for the next step. (Plan-action-find and re-define.)

7. Individually and collectively, we worked on our own understanding of the sequences.

8. We agreed on the dramatic order of segments/narratives.

   • As a director, I worked on workshops, training and rehearsals in conventional ways, including lights and set etc.

- I directed the performance for public as final step of the research project. To this end I used McTaggart's Participatory Action Research (PAR) model that the participants 'can learn from their own experiences and make this experience accessible to others' (McTaggart, 1991, p.170) in the way that participants connect their voices to the Iraqis' narratives. The participants were free from the first meeting to make their own minds up about the Iraqis' memories.

These examples illustrate the process of working with participants, using a room as a constructed site in the *Iraqi Nights*.

I engaged with participants in the process of performing Iraqi stories in ways that would allow the participants to be themselves and see their own memory in relation to other people with similar remembered experiences. I began the process with photographs, video footage, music, visual arts and books of poetry with real people involved in everyday life in Iraq.

I shared the photographs and video recording of Iraqi people at work, in the street, gathering around food, sitting together at nights, women and youths gathering in the markets.

I presented to the participants a holistic and complex picture of reality as a way of generating access to the distinctively cultural ways of living and behaving.

Throughout this process, I integrated Iraqi culture with my own personal life experiences in and during my life in and outside Iraq.

I created a conversational style of answering and responding to questions arising from my prolonged and/or intermittent contact with the project's participants.

The stories and creative illustrations became the tool to communicate and connect with participants and to cross the various cultural and intentional bridges between us. The aim was to reflect one universe, with people living in different locations but with the same primary concerns to live in peace and with love; to aspire to our own shared humanity where there are no genuine barriers between us.

I created an atmosphere for a safe and respectful environment that generated an open gate towards our feelings, thoughts and emotions. What we see and how that can be related to us collectively and individually was something that the *Iraqi Nights* performance sought to explore and express.

It followed subsequently that the personal emotions and empathetic responses arose during our conversation around what it might mean to be in someone's position during a difficult time, and where difficulty is a central part of everyday life. Again, theatre's ability to deal with the concrete reality of live bodies onstage and the metaphorical presence of acted 'others' was central to this. The images and music, video footage and daily life stories of Iraqis alongside artists' works guided us to live in a similar but innately *creative* environment, which always resonated in our present. The key question is where we stand in the stories we tell and depict and what, if anything, we can do about it.

As in traditional acting terms, to tell other stories is to become the other within a performer with one's own voice and concern to what s/he understands and how in some ways to *become* the person rather than to function as a character only. Other people's stories are our stories, we can feel it even if we have not experienced it yet. What if it was someone you knew, your friend or me, the one you were talking with during the rehearsal to make a performance for your friends and families?

We moved towards lived experience in depth in order to try and understand our selves in similar situations. This process opened the gate to one's own feelings and interpretation to a story and to the ways in which those stories occupy our/their minds.

I became the owner of the story from a creative and humanitarian perspective. This process led us to resolve the location and space between nation, culture and personality. I witness a story, I carried in my memory, I become the carrier of the story; I am a story, not an actor *telling* a story.

In the *Iraqi Nights* performance, the elements of participatory cultural aspects were focused on the collaboration in terms of communication, coordination, community (grass-roots artist), social and artistic interaction among participants. We have made decisions based on feelings, hunches or 'gut' instinct. Our discussions in this instance generated more artistic and expressive ideas.

Additionally, we made decisions that were not necessarily based solely on data, but rather on opinions, speculation and personal observation that lead us to create and circulate new self-made meaning to personally related stories in the performance.

This collaborative and interactive movement started, as performer began to use the data information and collaborative understanding with their own families and community members' comments and reflection. During the process and period of rehearsal and afterwards we were able to embrace the need to work, interact, and contribute together in new ways to provide information along with community support for the project as an example of community cultural action.

Part Two: The Creative Process of *Iraqi Nights*

In conversation with Umberto Eco, Robert Wilson stated that an artist recreates history, not like a historian, but as a poet. The poetic point of view that Wilson mentions can encompass personal history without having a direct description of a story. A world without official records, labels and names created both linguistic and artistic stylisations of a story. What can a refugee poet do!? What follows is my departure to the last remaining step in trying to answer this question.

I was invited to produce *Iraqi Nights* at Full Throttle Theatre Company in Townsville by the manager–director of the company, Madonna Davies, so I moved from Perth to Townsville in Queensland on the opposite side of Western Australia.

I worked with a cast of seven performers, five young women, one in her mid-forties, a man in his 80s and myself. We were working together as a small family, eating together and sharing our personal stories.

The set for the *Iraqi Nights* performance is an empty space with nine white frames, the size of a door, representing the Iraqis that I have interviewed. There are two data projectors, one projected on the ground with the film footage of Iraqi exiled artists and the second projected on a white screen showing multi-layers of images. One mirror is placed on the stage as title for the last room. The mirror simplifies things: What do you want to see? How you want to see yourself? This creates images of the self rather than reflecting how you look.

I used the mirror in the production of the *Iraqi Nights* to extend this process to the audience as they looked into the mirror while characters revealed their narratives.

The *Iraqi Nights* collaborative process built on re-constructed Iraqi memories by Australian participants. Their engagement and shared views constitute the practice of building a historiographical narrative in performance. The creative hypotheses emerge in collaboration with the participants at the various stages of workshop and rehearsals.

The performers shared with each other what they knew about Iraqi memory, culture, faith and arts, and where all aspects are resolved and shared in a beautiful and peaceful manner with them as the actors become the first audience. We started solely and then collectively searching for further details about the stories through libraries and the internet. Each participant retained the right to choose what meanings they see in the Iraqi narratives, poetry and artwork. There wasn't any clash between my suggestions and other participants' input and we were acting like a family supporting one another.

How can we make sense of ourselves and our experience of others?

The participants' understandings emerged in shared conversations about their relationship with, and the reactions and the responses of their memories to, the Iraqi memories. How does Australian participants' understanding or thinking about war differ from that of Iraqis at war?

Reflecting on this issue brought knowledge of their Australian history at war, and the history of the first generations arriving in Australia. The participants become themselves, voicing their own concerns, and they become their voices.

Telling and retelling is the essence of engaging in dialogue about our memories of cross-cultural narratives and events. It is a dynamic process of negotiation between participants' views of memory.

Iraqi Nights is an event presented, not in a series of logical plot, conventional dramas or continual narratives, but as a rug of dreamatic sequences in memory. The narratives in *Iraqi Nights* are poetic and open-ended, situated within open process and nameless characters. The Iraqi narratives and performances were my vehicle in the process of cross-cultural narratives and dialogues towards a passage of hope, and the love to communicate one's own experiences with others.

My dreamatic interpretation comes alongside Kantor, who accepts a reality that was wrenched out and separated from the everyday as the first element of creative process, extracting the event from internal and external memory in a space/room. The rooms may be filled with a gesture, a light, a frame, a picture, poetic verses, body movement or stillness, mime or dance, sound or vocal, rhythm or breathing sounds; it can be anything that looks to discover, as in a mirror, the secrets of biography.

The performance of *Iraqi Nights* is a room of imagination, a room of memory, as Kantor recalled his childhood room. The rooms of memory are the rooms in all human cultures and the stories. The rooms are rooted in space and time, the past, present and future of our memories in micro-realities and in the arts.

An Iraqi night is a room of memory in the minds and lives of Iraqi artists and people, on the one hand, and a room of imagination in the minds of Australian participants on the other. To me as an artist, the Iraqi memories of historical events are lived experience and the concept of performance differs from a performer attempting to narrate a story. The tension between imagination and memory is neither about the effects of the room nor the aesthetic means of presentation, but rather, rises from the revisiting/tracing of events in the perception of history and in the lost and hidden memories.

In the *Iraqi Nights* performance, I developed with participants the segment titled 'The Books' (based on my experience of returning to find my books had been used as cooking fuel). I further explored the reality of starvation, not only as experienced by Iraqis inside Iraq, but also as my experience of not having food outside Iraq.

The workshop, rehearsal and the concept of making a performance with members of a particular community were the tools towards further conversation about refugees and exiled artists' experiences.

The following excerpts from my journal represent key moments in the creative practice of *Iraqi Nights* to reflect on my roles and as *knower experiences*.

In the process, the participants are accountable and responsible for what they in their own turn carry for their audiences.

The participants begin to understand that what was happening to others can easily happen to all of us, and it is at this point of understanding that other stories become our stories. It is a process that actually began to enhance one's own faith in a sense of self. In engaging with the reality of other lives, the participants' own lives became understood and valued on a new level.

I focused on the final moments of human life, what you want to say to save someone's life. We moved far away from traditional notions of acting in order to become the personal carriers of a story and from here, we were able to voice our own voices and develop the conveyance of genuine concern in our telling.

This is not about seeking to become the owner of the story only but to have the honour to tell a story that impacted in terrible ways on the well-being of a community. This in part is one of the main essences of collaboration that helped to connect us with each other through our stories in the open space and time of rehearsals. This collaboration helped empower participants not only to think critically about events happening in our lifetime and our lives but also to have a direct response to the event in our heart and mind towards others.

In order to find participants, Madonna Davies (director and manager of the theatre) and I started to send emails to people involved in the community and professional theatre workers. On Friday, we invited the public to see the film (footage about the Iraqi narratives) for the first time in Australia, and I was interested to find out how the people would see it and what questions they would ask.

Two Australian women (aged 40 and 59) spoke to me. One said: 'Australian people are numb, and this work needs to be exhibited outside Australia because it would receive great respect.' The second one said: 'I think this footage needs more editing; it's too long to see someone talk face-to-face on camera for 15 minutes.'

The young people in the audience saw things differently; they said, 'You brought us something about the life of Iraqi people which we don't know much about', and they thanked me for sharing with them the film footage and the information.

I used the footage to find more participants and as a way to meet people. On the night of the first film exhibition, I found four interested students from James Cook University who said they would like to be part of the project.

The first night of showing the footage was my first experience of interacting with public views about events that took place in memory. I respect all public and artistic opinions and the more I know, the more I learn about their immediate perception, and in the same way that memory is immediate.

References

Denzin, N.K. (2005) *Performance Ethnography: Critical Pedagogy and the Politics of Culture.* London: Sage

Dick, B. (2012) *'What is Action Research?' Action Research and Action Learning for Community and Organisational Change.* Available from: http://www.aral.com.au/

He, M.-F. (2000) *A River Forever Flowing: Cross-Cultural Lives and Identities in the Multicultural Landscape.* Charlotte: Information Age Publishing

McTaggart, R. (1991). 'Principles of Participatory Action Research', *Adult Education Quarterly* 41.3, pp.168–87

Richards, A. (1995) 'Performance as Research/Research by Means of Performance', a discussion paper Presented to the Australasian Drama Studies Association Annual Conference, Armidale NSW. Available from: http://www.adsa.edu.au/research/performance-as-research/performance-as-research

Saldana, J. (2011) *Ethnotheatre: Research from Page to Stage (Qualitative Inquiry & Social Justice).* Los Angeles: Left Coast Press

•••

Autoethnographic inquiry employs the autobiographic materials of the researcher as key data. It tends to differ from other self-narrative writings such as autobiography and memoir inasmuch as autoethnography has (or *should have*) a default focus on cultural analysis and interpretation of the researcher's behaviour, thoughts and experiences in relation to others in a particular society. Whilst the boundaries between definitions are fluid, we can say that in many cases autoethnography is ethnographical in its methodological focus, cultural in its interpretive focus, and autobiographical in its content focus.

There are some pitfalls we need to be aware of when using autoethnography in research, the chief of which is the tendency to adopt the term as a statement of blind belief rather than as an informed methodology. No single methodology is without flaws and every decision is also a loss. If lived experience has long been accepted as informing one's research and research agenda, autoethnographers still need to exercise considerable critical caution when it comes to collapsing feelings into findings and assuming that one's own experiences have *ipso facto* value as research. Examples abound to show what happens when autoethnography strays from its research focus; the result of which is that it can be drawn towards elaborate narration at the expense of socio-cultural analysis, insight and interpretation.

Autoethnography is at once ethnographical and autobiographical. Placing the terms in this order creates a more acceptable research slant than putting the more self-indulgently 'autobiography' first and yet autoethnography, if it has to have much worth to an external reader, has to highlight the ethnographical character of its inquiry. Autoethnography has an inevitable concern with the cultural connection between self and others in the society being studied: without this being made central, autoethnography is no more than a sixty-dollar term for the 'this happened to me today' aspects of autobiography, memoir or diary, and these are much more difficult terms to sell as research. Like ethnography, autoethnography pursues the ultimate goal of cultural understanding underlying autobiographical experiences.

To achieve this ethnographic intent, autoethnographers undergo the conventional ethnographic research processes of data collection, data analysis/interpretation and report writing. They collect field data by means of participation, self-observation, interview and document review; verify data by triangulating sources and contents; analyse and interpret data to decipher the cultural meanings of events, behaviours and thoughts; and they write autoethnography. Like ethnographers, autoethnographers are expected to treat their autobiographical data with critical, analytical and interpretive eyes in order to detect the subtle cultural undertones of what is recalled, observed and told to them. At the end of a thorough self-examination within its cultural context, autoethnographers look to gain a cultural understanding of self and others. Autobiographical narratives will add live details to this principled understanding, but narration should not generally be allowed to dominate autoethnography when such is submitted as evidence of university research.

The initial step of research involves collecting data, which continues throughout the research process with different intensity at different points. And data collection engages memory directly. As we will see in this book's final chapter, memory is both a friend and foe of autoethnographers. Whereas memory allows researchers to tap into the wealth of data to which no-one else has access, our memories also select, shape, limit and distort. Memory fades as time goes, blurring the vitality of details. Annie Dillard recognises this type of blurring as 'smooth[ing] out details, leaving a kind of schematic landscape outline'. (Clandinin & Connelly, 2000, p.83) Omitting certain aspects and exaggerating the significance of others is an inevitable part of research. Confirmation bias might not be quite so inevitable but it is something that we often struggle to avoid, not least because we rarely recognise it in ourselves and in our own work; and because self-knowledge falls some way short of the demands of self-editing.

The fact that I know that my own work is shot through with confirmation bias does not mean that I can easily defend against it, nor is it something that other people can necessarily edit out of my work, or anybody else's. Indeed, one's *entire work* is often illustrative of bias and to exclude it would be to reduce a dissertation or report to its title alone. What an edit might do is encourage a different kind of subterfuge. When this occurs we often end up concealing our beliefs behind the vocabulary of objectivity. We do this when we search cynically for a reference in support of our views in the hope that acting thus we align ourselves with other and often more established beliefs. This is not necessarily about pointing the reader to a rich source of linked information so much as offering up an act of magician's misdirection. It is a shabby trick and one that many of us (young students too) have practised so often that it appears as second nature, something we do without always being aware of wide reading as a screen behind which the ordinary nature of our thoughts can take comfort and pause.

The *a posteriori* use of academic references is used to lend a veneer of intellectual credibility to that which might otherwise be seen as a diaristic report of events as they were encountered and the feelings that these encounters gave. Naturally enough one's writing will come after the experiences it describes but this sense of writing from what comes later is not enough to justify the Google search for references that will be made to read as influences before the fact. Readers may not always be aware of this, but sometimes we/they are, and name dropping in a final draft in lieu of theoretically framing one's research from the outset can be painfully obvious on the page: an act of immoral manipulation if not quite academic dishonesty.

Writing about experience will always change *that* lived moment into *this* written one, and no amount of writerly control can eradicate that. In fact, the more one seeks to exercise control the more one will add layers of alteration. As we have seen, placing ethnography ahead of autobiography is a powerful determinant on the way we read a sentence and the choices writers make (or actors, musicians, designers, photographers, artists) cannot avoid failure in their attempt at conveying unvarnished (untarnished?) truth. Whatever approach an autoethnographer uses in an attempt to write the truth (sic) of what happened, the taking and keeping of field notes is obviously considered useful. I hesitate to use the term 'vital' here. Notwithstanding the reminder from Clandinin and Connelly that field texts (i.e. any recorded data) can return 'the reflecting researcher to a richer, more complex, and puzzling landscape than memory alone is likely to construct', (ibid., p.54) it may be the case that the vagaries of memory and recall form an integral part of the research process and that any form of notes is the last thing the autoethnographer needs. This does happen from time to time and yet this relatively rare occurrence aside common sense dictates that one should keep a record of significant moments, especially when the research will subsequently make claims for authorial and/or academic honesty.

The difficulty within autoethnography is that moments of significance are not always apparent in the moment; and because no researcher can keep an accurate record of all that takes place, it is important to develop a sense of any event's potential importance to one's work. This can lead to tension between confirmation bias and genuinely investigative research. If, as Sher Doruff has suggested, research is not always so much about a re-search as it is a combination of *res*, the thing, a circumstance, a physical emotion, and *arch* as a point of entry, one can configure research as a process of circling circumstance until a way in is found. Accordingly, research becomes a port of entry into a thing that matters and into an area of concern. Perhaps it is in this responsiveness to the moment of insight that avenues of inquiry lead best or most creatively to new knowledge; and perhaps this type of knowledge is impossible to predict. But if it is impossible to predict then how might the researcher know what to record? Not everything can be noted, we know that much. We know too that the things we note in the field and the ways in which we note them start to predict and limit any subsequent writing up. The fields we investigate then read in key ways as crime scenes. Like detectives, we do not necessarily know what will emerge as significant, perhaps not even until a case comes to trial, and if we assume one outcome too soon we start to build a profile that can blind us to alternative views. Significance is as likely to dawn on us slowly as it is to arrive in a blaze of insight. Significance is also something we create through the act of our own writing. The fact that this is inevitable does not mean that we should not be aware that our writing is always an activity in pursuit of persuasion.

Tessa Muncey warns us that 'Memory is selective and shaped' and that it 'is retold in the continuum of one's experience.' (Muncey, 2005) Memory can create past experiences just as easily as it can censor other experiences out. Fusing memory with field notes and external data from sources such as interviews and published documents can provide ways of enhancing the accuracy and validity of autoethnography at the same time as it goes some way toward tempering (never, I would suggest, fully *eradicating*) the researcher's own conscious or subconscious bias. The ways in which any given researcher chooses to record data are not overly important. As with writing up the work, choices are personal and not always recognised by the chooser. Heewon Chang's 2008 book *Autoethnography as Method: Developing Qualitative Inquiry* is particularly strong in its sections on the taking and collating of field notes and, whilst I do not wholly share Chang's focus on traditional qualitative research, all autoethnographers would benefit from reading her work.

Interviewing is a near-vital technique of data collection for the autoethnographer. Through interviewing, researchers can sometimes gather information that may be unavailable from observation and/or participation. James Spradley has published a number of interview techniques that informed his work, and his taxonomy of questions as Descriptive, Structural and Contrasting make for extremely useful reading despite the specificity of his approach. (Spradley, 1979) For autoethnographers, interviewing allows people from the target culture to express themselves in their own words. Interviews carried out by autoethnographers are generally open ended and unstructured, conversational even. Interviews of this nature are generally the ones that allow the researcher the greatest flexibility to pursue lines of questioning based on what emerges from observing a culture and standard thinking is that they do not generally involve predetermined questions, as the autoethnographer might not know in advance what will be the most important issues to explore. In informal conversational interviews questions arise from the immediate context in which the interview occurs. In practice, of course, this type of freestyle spontaneity is a bit of a myth. Researchers ask leading questions. They always do, and an interview remains an interview even when it is described as a conversation: its purpose is to elicit information to a particular end.

Sometimes we can see this most clearly when researchers try their hardest to convince us of the opposite fact. Shane Hall's paper on interview techniques pull us in one way at the same time as its coded language shows us something else:

> Questions should be clear and phrased in understandable, appropriate
> language that is free of cultural biases. Interviewers should treat
> subjects with respect and work to establish a rapport; after all, it is
> an interview, not an interrogation. Researchers should ask follow-up
> questions to add detail, even if using a set of predetermined questions.
> Interviewers also should listen and observe carefully. When possible,
> tape record interviews to ensure accurate quotations. In addition,
> researchers should take notes during interviews to highlight key

points. Shortly after the interview, review the recording and check
notes for accuracy.

(Hall, 2010)

Terms such as *establish a rapport* and *taking notes to highlight key points* reveal
the realities of interviewing, despite Hall's best contrary efforts; whilst asking
questions which are free of cultural bias seems like a stretch too far, not in the
sense of this as an ideal so much as in its easy view that wanting this to be the
case will lead to *ipso facto* achievement. Because our own perspectives may so
easily obscure the value of any qualitative data it is important that we do not
fall into the trap of believing that what we write stands somehow outside of
ourselves. To call for acknowledgement of one's own partiality, bias (including
cultural bias), intent and agenda might seem like asking for an endless act of
self-reflection and qualification, but what better way to deal with mistruth than
to out it? What better way to record something accurately than to acknowledge
that the accurate recording of human behaviour is doomed to relative failure,
albeit failure that is oftentimes glorious?

We are all familiar with Hollywood hyperbole such as 'This film is based on
real events' and 'This is true story', and when we've finished our popcorn we share
the outrage of those whose stories have been manipulated and misrepresented.
The 2012 film *Argo* angered the Iranian government not because of the film's
politics but because its portrayal was presented as 'true'. *Argo*'s director, Ben
Affleck, who also played the role of a CIA agent in the film, claimed the work
faithfully depicted what happened and yet historical evidence shows his account
to be somewhat naive. The issue is not that a particular film presents a false
view of events, for how could it not; the issue is that the fiction is presented as
true. Cinema and television's re-envisioning of reality tends not to be something
that is taken with a pinch of salt by a knowing public. Just the opposite, as big-
and small-screen lies quickly assume the status of definitive truth: Meryl Streep
makes a British public fall half in love with the most divisive prime minister in
living history; Helen Mirren's portrayal of Queen Elizabeth II humanises an
otherwise distant monarch; and Mel Gibson's William Wallace has an affair
with Princess Isabella of France who falls pregnant to him, despite the fact that
she was three years old at the time and living in France. Of course, screenwriters
are in the business of creating clean and coherent plots out of the messy realities
of life; and of course, in order to give viewers the reassurances we desire, writers
seduce us into believing that the narratives we take comfort in are actually true:
but when fiction begins to read as fact, because it is more plausible, pleasurable

or profitable, the way back to reality is long. The huge increase since 2000 in US films based on real-life events has been as remarkable as the parallel increase in published memoir and reality television programmes. Such is the nature of zeitgeist.

Perhaps it always was. Shakespeare's depiction of Richard III as a hunchback with an emaciated arm and a hunchback has little or no basis in historical fact. A painting of the King shows him with uneven shoulders, but there are strong indications that the portrait was altered after completion to conform to the image made popular by Shakespeare's play. The line between propaganda and creative malpractice is rarely clear and this is how lies become accepted truth. The pressures of persuasion are less evident with autoethnographers than with playwrights, screenwriters and actors but they are still there.

In all varieties of ethnography, the collection of primary data is carried out through fieldwork, to the extent that fieldwork is absolutely synonymous with ethnography. As a sub-genre, autoethnography is about more than methods, it is also grounded in ways of using these methods. Objective facts of reality shift through the ways they are studied and the human factors of politics, prejudice, economy and personal agenda legislate against ideas of the neutral or dispassionate observer. Autoethnography's location of these factors as *present* rather than rendered absent through forces of will is a given of good research practice. Tony L. Whitehead recognises this when he suggests that 'In recording field notes, ethnographers not only continuously record their notes on the host community, but they also need to keep records on his or her reactions and feelings regarding their field experiences. These personal notes should be periodically analyzed in relationship to interpretations about the host community, or *the Other*.' (Whitehead, 2005) For Whitehead, as for many of us, this process is about reflexivity, and its role in controlling confirmation bias is hugely important.

Fieldwork inevitably locates ethnographers in the world of their host communities and autoethnography takes this a step further through its part-concentration on the researcher's experiences within these communities, rather than on the ways in which these groups are being observed. Under such circumstances it is well-nigh impossible to have any sense of the impartiality usually demanded by research. Autoethnographers would claim, with no small justification, that the absence of the researcher's neutrality is itself a valuable thing, suggesting that whilst autoethnography can never lay claim to being the most rigidly controlled form of research, its strengths lie in exactly the opposite direction. This much is certainly true, and the path toward reflexivity is often also the path toward honest declarations of interest, but engaging with this journey does not mean that researchers can pick and choose honesty as it suits. Autoethnography is about making inferences, reading and writing significance into some actions and events at the expense of others. This is personal and this is political. It is never remotely neutral.

The goal of data collection is usually to collect information in such a way that the researcher imposes only a minimal amount of their own bias on the material gathered in. Autoethnography issues a challenge to this, not least because the primary source of data is the researcher's own experience. Autoethnographers are privileged researchers, then, inasmuch as the material they are dealing with is never too distant to find; a second privilege comes in the way that autoethnographic research tends to be written up and disseminated. The writing style is often deliberately engaging and deals with narrative, the subject matter (people, always people) is also one that many readers can engage with; which is to say that specialist knowledge of the subject matter is not generally required. This opens autoethnographic research findings up to a wide and varied readership, just as the methodology invites many people to carry out the research. According to Robert J Nash and DeMethra LaSha Bradley, 'scholarly personal narratives' free researchers from the straitjacket of impersonal writings and 'touch readers' lives by informing their experiences'. (Nash et al., 2008) The unique voice of the autoethnographer is what readers respond to: what matters is that this voice remains the voice of research accuracy rather than that of a storyteller lacing a narrative with a handful of facts. It is this, ultimately, which separates research from me-search.

CHAPTER THREE

Ethics

Ownership and appropriation; Copyright Acts and cultures; acts
of witness; rebuttal; name-changes; university ethics committees; the
architecture of power; verfremdungseffekt; mimesis and simulacrum; New
Guinea Watermen, Yves Klein's Methylene Blue, Tearoom Trade and
knockout punches; Kate Rice's case study

Addressing the ethics of writing narratives that consider *what happened* means asking ourselves some questions; and the way we answer these determines how we view our work's ethical quotient. We have to ask whether it is possible to make any watertight distinctions between autobiography, autoethnography and story, and whether different forms carry different ethical responsibilities. We have to ask what experience any one person can say truly and exclusively belongs to them. We have to wonder whether research observation can so change the event being studied that it loses its *a priori* currency. We need to know the extent to which any one person can give or withhold the rights of any others to tell their stories, or stories they might feel are very culture specific. We need to know in what sense the essence of somebody's identity or experience might be privileged to the extent that others might be seemingly prevented from writing it. We read often enough about the rights that certain people have or do not have to tell certain stories, and we need to know whether, in the context of our own work, these beliefs hold true.

Commencing the writing of this book whilst being employed at an Australian university served to concentrate my mind on Australian issues, and where ethics are concerned that concentration often falls on Indigenous matters. In Australia it is the case that when research projects involving traditional stories are published the copyright almost always ends up with the non-Indigenous author. This is due to the requirements of the Copyright Act 1968 that the work must be original, that it must have been reduced to material form and have an identifiable author. As Terri Janke eloquently points out, the Copyright Act as it currently stands is unsuited to protecting Indigenous culture because its legal focus is on individualistic commercial concepts rather than notions of communal ownership or the cultural integrity of a work. Janke argues that because Indigenous stories are passed through generations by oral means rather than in writing, this legislates against re-telling from outside of the source culture. (Janke, 1996, p.14) Effectively these stories are so 'owned' by one culture that members of another group have no automatic right to tell them. Whilst on the surface this sounds reasonable enough, it highlights a situation that cuts to the heart of research into cultures other than one's own.

No reasonable person would deny that the rights of Indigenous Australians have been suppressed for too long and that something needed to give, and it is worth noting some of the historical background that lends weight to Janke's views. During the time of British settlement, Australia was regarded as being uninhabited. Aboriginal and Torres Strait Islander people were thought to be part of the flora and fauna of the country rather than human beings, and indeed it has become a common (though contested) belief that the lives of Indigenous Australians were governed under the Flora and Fauna Act. Certainly, Aboriginal and Torres Strait Islander people's rights did not exist under British law as it was first imposed in Australia. Almost unbelievably this state of affairs lasted until the 1967 Australian Referendum.

Up until this time, Aboriginal and Torres Strait Islander people in Western Australia, the largest state in the country, remained under the control of the 1905 Aborigines Act. This Act had given the Chief Protector of Aborigines the powers of legal guardianship over all Aboriginal people under the age of 16. This power held sway over any legal rights of parents. In theory and often in practice, this meant that the Chief Protector could remove the children of Aboriginal and Torres Strait Islander parents from their family as he saw fit and without any significant rights of appeal.

Under the Act, children, particularly those of mixed descent, were regularly removed from their parents and placed in white foster homes, missions, orphanages and hostels. These children have come to be known as the 'Stolen Generation'; children who never found their way home and suffered trauma as a result of this policy. Parents were often not told where their children were, while the children were regularly told that their parents were dead.

Social, educational and financial disparities between Indigenous and settled Australians still exist. Indeed as Pat Mamajun Torres notes, over the last two centuries Indigenous Australians have provided copious information for research theses, books and governmental reviews but few have ever benefited personally. According to Torres this is because those same people who have provided specialised information to authors have not been seen as co-authors, writers or owners of the information or the copyright holders. (Torres, 1994, p.25) True enough, but if one can step back from the politics of the situation, might it not be reductive to assume that stories belong to participants rather than chroniclers? Certainly copyright that is linked to ownership of experience rather than authorship is often problematic. When John Mortimer chooses to write about his father, copyright goes to the son because he is the author of the tale, not his father, the subject. (Mortimer, 1971) Joint copyright deals are manageable, as in the case of the book *Jandamarra and the Bunuba Resistance*: the book's author holds joint copyright with the Bunuba people and all of the book's royalties feed back to them; but more usually, the one who holds the pen is deemed the owner of the story.

Australian Aboriginal art is perhaps the oldest continuing tradition of creative expression in the world and much of the most important knowledge of Aboriginal society in Australia has been conveyed through different kinds of storytelling, including oral narratives in speech and song as well as those that were either performed as dances or painted, initially on rocks. Indigenous Australians traditionally used art as a means of communication or expression in a variety of forms including wounds cut into their bodies, known as scarification. The symbols of their artwork were expressions of their beliefs, just as the Dreamtime and Dreaming stories were records of specific events. Whatever Indigenous artists drew, engraved or painted onto such surfaces as sand, earth, rock, trees or wood had significant meanings for them. These forms of Aboriginal art were often sacred because of their connection to spiritual beliefs or because they were accessible only to initiated adults. Other stories were non-sacred or secular and these, for example, served to record major events such as great battles, hunting expeditions or the arrival of Europeans who would soon transpose Aboriginal narrative forms and contents into Westernised words.

Cultural ownership is a precarious thing, yet stepping away from its issues places us in no less complex waters: it is fairly standard practice in edited academic publishing that chapter contributors receive no royalties, whilst editors do. As with *Jandamarra and the Bunuba Resistance*, bespoke deals can be struck but ethics often places a distant third to convenience and expeditious legal concerns. (Pedersen & Woorunmurra, 2000)

In his 2003 work *The Borrowers*, Thomas Keneally refers tellingly to his experience of writing *The Chant of Jimmy Blacksmith* and of various authors writing under assumed Aboriginal identities. In a conclusion that is pertinent to this book's chapter, Keneally suggests that:

> whoever can get to the research and turn it into a book... owns it.
> Women can write about men and vice-versa, both well and badly and
> should be permitted to. Jews can write about Gentiles, and vice-versa.
> But the question of ownership of the story in the profoundest, morally
> right sense is the most vexing in the greatest cultural divide of all,
> the divide between sedentary and nomadic cultures. Here one should
> tread carefully, for in the indigenous cultures still left living, tales are
> more than mere tales.

> (Keneally, 2003)

The key question in Australia as elsewhere and for academic autoethnographers as much as for the writers of memoir is this: do we need to get permission from the community which owns a story in order to re-tell and sometimes make gain from it? In a perfect world, the answer might well be 'yes'; but in the real world it might also be 'no'.

This question arises for some beyond the allegedly truthful realms of autobiography, autoethnography and memoir. In Paula Fleming's *The Ethics of Tragedy: Plot Victims are People Too!*, we read the following response to fictitious suffering:

> In the critically acclaimed 1988 mainstream novel *The Bean Trees*, by
> Barbara Kingsolver, a toddler is raped. The novel focuses on an adult
> woman's maturation process as she becomes the accidental adoptive
> mother of the toddler. The emotionally and intellectually stunted
> toddler is a mere prop, a catalyst for development in the protagonist.
> Later in the book, the child is threatened by a child molester in the
> park. Again, the consequences for the child are not dealt with, as the
> story focuses on the emotions of the adoptive mother. *This is wrong.*
> Infant rape victims – even fictional ones – deserve to be more than

props in the lives of their adult caretakers. Also, aside from the vague
concern any decent person has for the well-being of an abused child,
we never feel a compelling, sharp, driving fear for this child's welfare.

(Fleming, 2005)

Ethics depends on the position from which we are viewing, and also from
the time. Would Nelson Mandela have needed permission from his Robben
Island guards before he could tell his story, if indeed the story he told could be
said to have been his to tell? Does a victim of crime need permission from the
perpetrator? Does an abused child need permission from the abuser before s/
he is able to talk? Does an ex-wife need her former husband's consent in order
to write about their marriage and subsequent divorce? Do I need permission
from my brother or my school friends before I write about our childhood?
Do survivors from the attack on New York's Twin Towers need permission
from other survivors or family members of the dead before they can recount
their tales of escape? Does Sir Alex Ferguson need David Beckham's pre-
publication approval before he can write about dressing-room rows and private
conversations? Strange and strangely empty world if all this is the case. Of
course, gaining permission is usually the best and safest option, just as letting all
concerned have pre-publication/pre-submission approval is considered desirable,
but such does not always happen, not least because issues of positive ethical
consideration can morph all too easily into issues of pedantic ethical control.
We are all of us agents of research and agencies of documentation, caught up in
endless experience and reportage, and to suggest that there might be some one-
size-fits-all ethical coversheet for autoethnography seems to be almost as naive
as it is desperate.

The book you are reading is defined by all of the words between the covers, as
well as the way it looks and feels and the price that it costs. Despite any seeming
chronology for the reader, my own writing, at least up to now, has been carried
out before I have received the five case studies that also make up the between-
the-covers content. Whilst I am familiar with the interests of the contributors,
I have no sense of what exactly they will say or how they will say it. I made a
decision to accept their work sight unseen. When their copy arrives it will be
fed into the structure of the book, and all that I will do is determine in which
chapter and at what point a particular case study will best fit and perhaps write
a sentence or two that takes the reader from my train of thought to somebody
else's. The contributors each know something of my work but they will not
have sight of the overall book that their words will appear in (and to a large

extent, be judged by) until the book goes on sale. They have not been involved in determining where their sections will appear, nor how that will impact on the ways that their words will be read. Is this an unethical act on my part? As a concept, it did not feel unethical to me and, in reversed circumstances, I have happily contributed to other people's books without having knowledge of much other than my own section; and yet now, seeing these words appear as I type them, it feels dictatorial and controlling. Despite its inclusion of what I hope will be the strength of diverse voices (if indeed our voices differ at all), this book is not created by a committee. Is this view fair and/or ethical? We can write endlessly about empathy, but our stance is ultimately determined by where in the debate we are currently standing. And that place is *somewhere*. It is not some ethical nirvana of neutrality that only exists as a concept.

Within this book, the order in which case studies appear will have some impact without being in and of itself overly *significant*. Elsewhere in the world, the order in which events are told can be more important even than the things they describe. Curious though it might be, we have a strong inclination to believe the first version of events that we hear. Secondary versions, especially when they run counter to the first, tend to be regarded with a greater degree of scepticism. Tellers of second versions can feel on the defensive, as though their rebuttals are tantamount to evasion. Part of this is because a rebuttal almost inevitably means calling the first teller a liar, whereas the first version utterance carries no such claim: one is merely stating an as-yet unchallenged version of events. This lays down a base line of evidence. We may cling to the belief in innocence until guilt is established but, outside of a court of law, guilt is often established without waiting to hear the accused person's view. This is a recognised aspect of divorce involving children, where the parent living with the child is commonly regarded as Jesus and the other parent as Judas.

Telling stories is a fundamental part of being human and few if any stories exist without implications for someone, somewhere. Narrating lives then, narrating real lives, is not just something people do, it is part of what people *are*; and this chapter's concentration on ethics does not negate a wider belief that the legitimate freedoms afforded to and by autoethnography within the university sector are being rapidly subdued by ethical zealots. These zealots exist within the very collective of researchers that would benefit most from being afforded intelligent licence rather than evasive control.

A clear case in point comes with the changing of subjects' names to protect their privacy. Few people would argue with this as a point of principle, but the principle is often quite shamefully faux. Autoethnographers, like memoirists, are often happy in their zeal to be seen as ethical to change the names of their subjects, be they sons, daughters, colleagues or members of any given social group, at the same time as they are unwilling to publish under pseudonyms that might more accurately and honestly protect their subjects. Is it just me or does this point to something utterly hypocritical, and absolutely unethical: as the triumph of vanity over care and responsibility? If I write about my son in a way that has the potential to cause him harm or embarrassment then changing his name in print from Jake to Rory does little to protect him when my own name is on the spine and cover of the book and when he is my only son. Of course, to change my own name means I do not then get to gaze lovingly at my name on other people's bibliographies; but if my intention, my *ethical intention*, is to tell a story that needs telling rather than to develop my own career, then wouldn't an authorial name change do at least part of the trick? Yes, it would, and plainly so. But such happens only rarely. There is no way for us to be absolutely certain about the ethical positions we adopt, and in the absence of absolute certainty, all we can do is the best that we can. But increasingly this 'best' refers more to career advancement and authorial vanity than to narrative authenticity or a genuinely ethical concern, and few hypocrisies are worse than those of the self-serving memoirist who will happily change every name but her or his own.

I do indeed have a son called Jake; and I have not checked with him whether it is okay to use his name in this book. The first he will likely know of this is when he has the book in his hands. I also have three daughters, Danielle, Eva and Isobel, and I do not feel that typing their names here violates their trust. If I were to reveal specific details of my children's lives then things would be different. But how different? Ultimately, events from their childhood that I might feel are completely harmless to report could cause my children a certain discomfort or/and delight, just as certain writers referenced in this book's pages might feel that the ways in which I have selected their words might have skewed their original intent. When we write, we trust our judgement. Without doing that and without the risk of getting things wrong, we would only ever write anodyne work. The flipside of this, where everybody named in a book was approached pre-publication to see if they agreed with the way they were being represented, would mean that no book ever made it to the shelves.

In short, ethically sound work does not follow causally from adherence to the tick-box, cut-and-paste schema of ethics application forms any more than ethically unsound autoethnography follows automatically from impatience with the language of care. Care is not generated through the filling out of forms and care is not guaranteed by the researcher's familiarity with the terminology of ethical propriety. As with any creative and organic pursuit, autoethnography can go wrong. And when things go wrong, people can be hurt, trust can be violated and damage can be done. Like art, autoethnography is messy and its manners are occasionally bad: it does not always do as we expect. There is no autoethnography without this risk. There is no human or social interaction without this risk. There is no love without this risk. No marriage, no parenting, no friendship. Having supervised my share of postgraduate students who have worked through autoethnographic processes, my conviction remains that ethics committees exist in no small part as a consequence of the paranoia universities have about any trace of bad press sticking to them. From a committee member's perspective (and I have sat on and chaired my share of these committees), it is hard to shake the feeling that the awarding of ethical approval rewards i-dotting and t-crossing at the expense of research that might actually need doing.

Somewhere along the way trust between universities and their research students has been lost and, within this context, replacing trust with compliance never feels quite right. In fact, it feels more than slightly unethical; a reminder to the researching student that power resides with the institution rather than the individual.

Power is as power does and art institutions are no less instruments of control than universities. Seguing into the field of theatre provides a mirror to autoethnography's resistance to the norms of research behaviour. It is no accident that site-specific performance originated as a development of the site-specific artwork movement that began in the late 1960s and early 1970s. The Mummers Plays and Christian Passion Plays of medieval England were site-specific, and history is filled with examples of theatre from all over the world that was either designed for, or recontextualised by, its location in non-theatre buildings. Within the context of this chapter, the emergence of site-specific work is seen as a reaction to the dominance of twentieth-century theatre buildings and is not taken to mean that theatre outside theatre buildings is a new concern. Recognising art galleries and theatre buildings as sites of power and (usually state) control, performance looked to create forms that were designed to exist in non-mainstream and non-dedicated places where the work could be conditioned by its environment and architectural or geographical location and histories. At the centre of the site-specific movement was an attempt to take theatre away from what was perceived to be the affected and pretentious atmospheres of standardised public spaces and to relocate them in a wide variety of outdoor and indoor venues. A prime purpose was/is to make the public aware of the artistic merits of ordinary buildings and spaces that have always been of interest to ordinary members of society but which have been passed over by the elitist and institutionalised artists of the past. Site-specific performance often then involves a more or less political decision to work against the dominant discourse of theatre, its buildings and its traditions.

A growing number of terms have arisen from 'site-specific performance'. These include 'site-determined', 'site-referenced', 'site-conscious', 'site-responsive' and 'context-specific'. A useful definition of the form has been given by Patrice Pavis, cited in Mike Pearson's *Site-specific Performance*. Pavis suggests that:

> The term refers to a staging and performance conceived on the basis of a place in the real world (ergo outside an established theatre). A large part of the work has to do with researching a place, often an unusual one that is imbued with history or permeated with atmosphere: an airplane hangar, unused factory, city neighbourhood, house or apartment. The insertion of a classical or modern text in this found space throws new light on it, gives it an unsuspected power and places the audience at an entirely different relationship to the text, the place and the purpose for being there.
>
> (Pearson, 2010, p.8)

Perhaps the single greatest contribution of site-specific performance as a hybrid art form to site-specific work as a whole has been the radical transformation and re-constitution of the concept of audience and of how audiences are invited to experience live performance. When site-specific art first emerged as a twentieth-century conceit, it appealed to spectators primarily because of the novelty of the form and viewing experience. Nonetheless, site-specific art, whilst appearing novel in itself, did not make any profoundly novel contributions to the nature, identity and constitution of its audiences. Site-specific work has not yet developed a distinctive critique or paradigm, despite its pioneers being often as articulate in print as they are in performance. The breakthrough achieved by modern site-specific performance is that it seeks to draw its audience into an intimate participation with that performance. In this way the audience becomes an essential part of the performance itself.

The aim of site-specific work is for spectators to reach an enhanced empathy and understanding with the performance that they have witnessed. In this sense, site-specific performance represents an evolution towards a level of greater spectator involvement and identity. The philosophy that underpins this has much to do with a reaction against the perceived snobbery of traditional theatre and its tendency to promote the values and aims of elite members of society above the aspirations of the ordinary citizen. Site-specific performance, then, can be said to be an equalising art form: it holds as a basic philosophical principle the belief that the members of the audience are of equal importance and significance for the meaning and successful execution of a particular performance as the performer, director and writer themselves. As such, site-specific performance argues that the greater the participation and sense of involvement of the spectator, the greater will be the efficacy of that performance upon both performer and viewer.

This reconsideration of audience by site-specific performers strives for a sense of collective audience identity, a knowing group of spectators that constructs itself as an interpretative body via a cumulative framework of experiences. The extent to which site-specific performance achieves this intensive audience self-interrogation is perhaps unrivalled in all twentieth-century performance art forms.

Site-specific performance also raises the notion of the importance of the community in which a particular performance or art exhibit takes place. For many companies, site-specific theatre is work that takes place in the living space of a particular community and is enacted alongside and within the working life of the community. Thus there is, in theory at least, an experiential authenticity that is unique to site-specific theatre.

In all forms, the architecture of power is permanence: palaces, government buildings, galleries, state theatres, monuments, statues, universities: all symbols of quality and greatness. Bertrand Russell has defined power as the production of intended effects, as the accessibility certain groups and people have towards the means of production. A more basic articulation of power is that some voices are heard and other voices are silenced. Autoethnography allows hitherto silenced voices to be heard, but our act of hearing is filtered through the researcher's voice; and perhaps the very act of speaking and being heard (being *published*) denies the very authenticity of the experience it describes. When the researcher moves from the act of research to the act of writing, focus shifts from responsibility to the researched towards a relationship with the reader; and if I write that last idea differently, perhaps concluding with a question mark, the writer–reader relationship shifts accordingly. The points at which the researcher looks up from the page of field notes or out from memory and types words on a screen may not be easily defined but they signal changes in intention, and these change meaning. We decide what is important for the reader, even if that is at the expense of what was important for the research. When things go well, this marriage of experience and articulation can be relatively untroubled, but it is always there. This is the ethics of writing, the necessity for ornament and for editorial control, the ways in which writers seek to determine the ways in which their words are encountered, and in giving form to ideas we cannot but change those ideas. It is what writing does and no amount of ethics-speak can control it.

Would that it were even this simple: in the act of research, we are already writing what we see into our minds, so that one researcher sees a freedom fighter where another sees a terrorist; one sees a hospital, another sees a birthplace; one sees evasion, another sees attack; and one sees an instrument of control where another sees an example of empowerment. Empathy, like autoethnography, is just a word until we use it in particular ways – and even then it is as much about missing the mark as hitting it. Writing is always about transformation; and changing what happened into what we say happened is an inevitable and, I would suggest, an ultimately ethical act. It is in the nature of writing that its manifestation seduces us into forgetting that what we read is just ink on a page. Exposing the frames around the work, as Brecht did with his *verfremdungseffekt*, succeeds more as an act of showmanship than of authenticity as we no more give back our willingness to lose ourselves in the act of spectatorship because the stage hands are in view than we pull back from immersive reading because we can see where the book ends and the hand that holds it takes our gaze.

Practice as Research and Ethics Review

Kate Rice

The inclusion of creative practice as research in the humanities represents a fundamental shift in our understanding of what constitutes knowledge within the academy. Formal structures appear to struggle to accommodate this rupture. Practice-led research has been caught in a blanket definition of 'research involving humans', originally conceived for medical science. Creative work undertaken in a university setting is now subject to ethics committee review under the *National Statement on Ethical Conduct into Human Research.* (National Health and Medical Research Council et al., 2007) Ethics review is structured around the core values of research merit and integrity, justice, beneficence and respect. (Ibid., p.13) While these values are undoubtedly relevant to artistic practice, they are applied in the *National Statement* according to a much narrower understanding of research. The scientific, medical conception of research in the *National Statement* is 'premeditated, time limited, discrete and external to the researcher'. (Langlois,

2011, p.144) Despite efforts that have been made to broaden the framework to accommodate the humanities, 'the underlying conceptual architecture… remained the same'. (Ibid., p.143) Ethics review committees are obliged to structure their operation according this conception of research. The result is a process that does not easily embrace research that sits outside the medical model. This process has attracted criticism for being not only inappropriate but also potentially damaging to political research (Langlois, 2011), biography writing (Hill, 2007), criminology (Winlow & Hall, 2012) and anthropology (Van Den Hoonaard, 2006). As with research in these disciplines, artistic practice is frequently spontaneous, ongoing and personal to the researcher. This creates particular challenges for the artist whose creative research comes within the scope of the *National Statement*.

Creative Practice as Research

I developed an interest in writing about real events through professional practice. *Sweetest Things* is a play I wrote based on a criminal case of a sexual relationship between a male high-school teacher and a female student. When I began researching *Sweetest Things* under the auspices of Deckchair Theatre Company in 2009, I did not follow any formal ethics process or protocol. I did what appeared ethical to me at the time, based on previous experience gained on similar projects. I was open and honest with those I approached about the project and I promised confidentiality. After a long period of negotiation, the girl agreed to be interviewed and through her I was able to interview her friends, family, teachers and professionals associated with the case. I spoke with the teacher but, after several conversations, he declined to be involved.

Moving into the university context for my next project enabled me to develop my interest in writing about real events and more fully address issues of ethics and authenticity. *Monologue for a Murderer* is a play script based on a high-school shooting that took place in Germany in 2002, and forms the practical component of my PhD in creative writing. When I began my PhD work I was confronted for the first time with the need to have my process approved by an ethics committee. The definition of human research in the *National Statement* is to be 'understood broadly'. It includes participants 'being observed', researchers having 'access to their information'. (National Health and Medical Research Council et al., 2007, p.8) This definition includes research where an artist uses or is informed by contributions from other people to create their work. In performing arts practice, this would most often apply to workshops with volunteers or actors, collaborations with other artists or surveys of audiences. It also applies, as in my case, to artists creating work about real people or events.

The *National Statement* states that 'Research with more than a low level of risk… must be reviewed'. (National Health and Medical Research Council et al., 2007, p.8) Review of research involving no more than low risk may be done at a departmental level and is less demanding than full ethics review. (Ibid., p.79) 'Low risk' is defined as research 'where the only foreseeable risk is one of discomfort'. (Ibid., p.18) 'Discomfort' is defined as 'less serious than harm' (ibid., p.100) and 'harm' is defined as including 'physical harm, anxiety, pain, psychological disturbance, devaluation of personal worth and social disadvantage'. (Ibid.) I initially applied for ethics approval for research with a low level of risk. My proposal was to follow the process I had applied in the research and writing of *Sweetest Things*: I intended to interview participants about their experiences of the shooting in Erfurt. My application was rejected and my proposal was escalated to full ethics review. The initial assessment committee felt that interviewing volunteers about their traumatic experience and writing about them for public presentation entailed a foreseeable risk of harm rather than mere discomfort.

The ethics application required me to describe what I was going to do, assess the ethical issues of representing real people, identify and address the applicable laws and issues of researching in Germany, describe my recruitment process, procedure, the risks of harm, and how I would reduce the risks, how participants would consent, how their privacy would be protected and what the interviews would be like. The intention is to heighten awareness of ethical issues and integrate the core values of integrity, justice, beneficence and respect into the fabric of the research project. However, I argue that in the case of artistic practice, the review process does not necessarily achieve the intended result.

These are Strangers

The welfare of my potential participants was being protected by a faceless committee. My values, my respect for people, my ability to monitor and negotiate relationships – effectively my personal integrity – was reduced to a written document to be judged by people whom I would never meet. In my previous projects, these judgments on my character were the province of those I approached to contribute. I had made myself vulnerable to volunteers and convinced them to trust me. It felt strange for this natural process to be interrupted by strangers. I was now trying to convince the wrong people.

On previous projects I had to start by convincing potential participants of the value of my project and my own personal integrity. This had involved making contact through letters, emails or telephone conversations and then meetings in person before the participants agreed to participate. At every stage I was aware that I was adjusting my language and responses according to the evolving relationship. For example, I would match the tone and style of my writing or speech to suit the people I was communicating with. I would anticipate their concerns, address issues as they arose, and be mindful of who they were and what their experience had been. Importantly, the process of seeking and gaining a mutual relationship of trust was never cynical or formulaic. It was instinctive, and in a constant state of flux, like the development of any relationship. To write this down in a form before any of it happened, and convince a stranger that it would be respectful, seemed to be a betrayal of a relationship that didn't yet exist. My personal integrity had been reduced and was being judged by my ability to describe a version of its external appearance in writing to someone who ultimately had nothing to do with anyone involved in the project.

My ethical integrity is most clearly expressed in my personal interactions with other people. The process effectively removed my personal, embodied presence from the forum in which my ethical integrity was to be judged. I acknowledge that the power of personal charm is open to abuse, and could be used by researchers, as it is by politicians and salespeople, to win confidence where it is undeserved. But I would argue that written documentation is just as capable of being used to manipulate a desired response. Skilled writers write convincingly. Researchers will write for the benefit of the committee, and take time to write carefully and revise. They will research previous applications and write accordingly. The skill in this is not necessarily indicative of one's ethical integrity.

In artistic work, I believe that the ethical integrity of a research process is best measured by the researcher's ability to respond in person to those with whom they will be engaged. A written appeal to disinterested academics is borne out of a conception of research in which the personality of the researcher is irrelevant. In artistic work, it is paramount.

This Project is Closed

The ethics application required a detailed description of the project, the end result and the process I intended to follow to get there. In accordance with the *National Statement*, my research could not begin before it had been judged by the committee to be ethically acceptable. (National Health and Medical Research Council et al., 2007, p.8) In the past, I had begun my projects with some inspiration, a very vague sense of a destination, and an equally vague idea of how I might get there. My process was always in a constant state of development, whereby every interaction with a participant had the potential to influence the final outcome, or even change the course of the entire project. For example, in *Sweetest Things*, I had hoped to write a play in which both the girl and the teacher had substantial input. The teacher refused to be involved. In the end, his refusal to be involved became a scene in the play and turned into a crucial thematic point: his character was a construction, a gratifying invention of the playwright in the same way as the girl was a gratifying cypher for him. I couldn't possibly have known this from the start. Nelson notes the inherent contradiction in attempting to squeeze academically acceptable methodology out of artistic inspiration, which 'fits in no paradigm but its own'. (Nelson, 2009, p.25) He describes the difficulty artists may have in describing their process where it is 'so heavily steeped in the unknown, beginning in unknown intentions and enjoining unknown abilities to imagine'. (Ibid., p.47)

In creating and describing the project on my ethics form before I had even begun it, I effectively created a ghost of an artistic project. I pinned down a procedure that was intended to be flexible and responsive, and described it in concrete terms. This description was then the basis for a thorough analysis of the risks and benefits arising from the procedure and a description of how the risks would be managed in practical terms. I based the procedure and practices on my earlier work, but in doing so, I was pre-determining what would happen. A creative development process that had formerly been characterised by responsiveness and fluidity had become concrete and linear. The requirement to pre-determine the research procedure in such detail makes open-ended research projects impossible. (Van Den Hoonaard, 2006, p.266)

Writing in defence of ethics review of social science, Hedgecoe argues that researchers have to define their work in advance in order to obtain funding in any case, and therefore writing an ethics application should be no different. (Hedgecoe, 2008, p.880) However, when funding artistic practice, state and commercial arts funding practices are a more relevant model. When applying for project funding, artists are generally not required to set out their process in detail in advance. Rather, they demonstrate their ability to create a project based on a broad outline and an existing body of completed work. For example, the Australia Council selection criteria for funding new theatre works are: an artistic rationale; artistic and professional skill; contribution to diversity; and logistical planning. (Australia Council, 2013) An artist's ability to produce a work is thereby judged by existing circumstances from which a process will evolve, rather than by the process itself. This reflects an understanding of artistic practice that is fundamentally different to scientific practice: there is no formula for creating it. The procedure I had so carefully planned and analysed for ethical issues would not necessarily lead to the creative outcome I was looking for, and I would not know until I had tried. In artistic work, analysis of practice that has not yet occurred runs a serious risk of becoming redundant as the practice develops.

Even worse, it affects the shape of the work before it starts. This is not simply a matter of researchers adjusting their work to address ethical concerns: it changes the nature of the work being done. Van Den Hoonaard writes that at his university, open-ended, observational ethnographic research projects are declining in number while interview-based research projects are on the rise, because the latter are more closely aligned with the medical scientific model. (Van Den Hoonaard, 2006, p.263) In my case, the shape of the work was impacted and an open-ended, flexible, responsive project was deliberately re-modelled into a linear, pre-determined process so it could adequately address the requirements of the ethics committee.

I then had to wait for months while my application disappeared in the bureaucracy. This time lag effectively prevents researchers from responding quickly to current events and taking advantage of unexpected opportunities. (Langlois, 2011, p.146) Of more relevance to artistic work is the inevitable shift in perspective that occurs over the passage of time as the work develops. In theory, my research was planned but not yet begun. In reality, the planning process was just part of a longer thrust of creative energy that had begun long before, endured through the process of writing my application and then continued to percolate while I waited for the result. I continued to read, reflect on my ideas and experience events that influenced how I felt about the project. Nelson describes artistic method as 'unscholarly, unaccountable, possibly arbitrary, resting on taste, flattering big ideas, vanity, maybe snobbery, indulging in an altogether unwarranted sense of superiority'. (Nelson, 2009, p.50) By the time I had ethics approval to do the work I had said I would do, I no longer wanted to do it that way. While the inspiration for the project had not changed, my belief in how to realise it artistically had. As an artist, it would now be nonsensical follow a method that I was no longer interested in pursuing to achieve an end that I no longer felt was desirable.

However, in the interests of avoiding further delay, and with the knowledge and approval of my supervisors, I did not re-apply for ethics clearance. The complicated approval procedure, intended to facilitate my ethical awareness as a researcher, therefore bypassed the most crucial ethical decision I made about the project: the decision not to interview participants at all.

The Extraction of Ethics

Anthropologists Chenhall, Senior and Belton draw a distinction between procedural ethics, or complying with formal requirements, and ethics in practice, or what actually happens during the research. (Chenhall et al., 2011, p.13) They illustrate the point with a case in which ethics approval was sought and obtained, consent forms signed and returned, but the participant in question avoided the researcher. (Ibid., p.15) The researcher rightly judged that the participant did not want to do the research any more. This was something that occurred within the fluid, ongoing negotiation between the researcher and the participant. Within that relationship, the prior approval or disapproval of a remote ethics committee was entirely irrelevant.

Winlow and Hall warn that the bureaucratisation of the process threatens to turn ethical responsibility for a project into a box-ticking activity that requires no further thought once approval is gained. (Winlow & Hall, 2012, p.411) Ethical issues arise organically within the course of an ongoing relationship. To deal with them administratively prior to the existence of that relationship is potentially to abrogate researchers' responsibility to be responsive and engaged with ethical issues throughout the course of a project. While the process is intended to embed ethical issues within the design of a project, in practice, it extracts them as something to be dealt with separately before the real work even starts. It therefore encourages researchers to deal with ethics as a planning hurdle which, once cleared, is removed from contention within the project. Ethical issues that arise subsequently, such as the issue above with the reluctant participant, are then left dangling outside both the administrative process and the plan for the project. This potentially devalues researchers' capacity to make ethical responses and judgments in the course of the project, where such decisions have a tangible impact. Rather, it is only researchers' ability to anticipate and plan in writing that matters.

Even worse, the procedure inevitably places more emphasis on the representation of ethical process than the reality of it. (Winlow & Hall, 2012, p.413) Winlow and Hall write about ethics committees in the context of the collapse of modernist certainty. In the absence of a firm, communal understanding of right and wrong, embodied in broad principles of the church or the government, small task-oriented bodies provide practical guidance in the shape of administration rather than ideology. They describe how the entire process is therefore a product of a society in which ideals have disappeared:

> the surface image of rigorous oversight is useful… but it masks the hollowing-out of faith in and commitment to the process of doing ethical research, and its replacement by a world-weary, cynical engagement deprived of the very substance that would make the process real and valuable.

> (Winlow & Hall, 2012, p.412)

Looked at in this way, the process is exposed as a sham that can only ever have the appearance of facilitating genuinely ethical research. It also suggests that the only path to genuinely ethical work is through faith, and that this has been lost forever in the postmodernist world.

Risk and Benefit

The *National Statement* states that the 'likely benefit of the research must justify any risks of harm or discomfort to participants' (National Health and Medical Research Council et al., 2007). The researcher and the committee must therefore identify and judge 'benefit' and 'harm' against each other. The conception of 'benefit' and 'harm' as mutually exclusive and quantifiable in advance presents a particular challenge when applied to research that falls outside the traditional scientific model.

Langlois points out that 'for a series of types of political research… causing harm (or at least discomfort) may be the whole point'. (Langlois, 2011, p.150)

The same may be true in creative work. Bolt, a member of the University of Melbourne Arts Ethics Committee, bemoans the rise in 'safe' project applications and encourages artists to continue to conceive of risky work. (Bolt, 2012) She uses Marina Abramovic's performance *Lips of Thomas* as an example of artistic work that would present a problem for an ethics committee. In this performance, the artist carries out repeated acts of physical violence against her own person. Its outcome is unknown and the risk of harm is high. She points out that the benefit of the artwork in this case, or its artistic value, is in the unknown, or unknowable quality of the experience as it unfolds and in the harm it causes to the performer and the audience. The oppositional qualities of 'benefit' and 'harm' are therefore inextricably interwoven where the art itself sets out to test the boundaries of human endurance. Investigating whether such a project has ever gained ethics approval in the context of university-based practice as research is beyond the scope of this paper. In any event, I believe the application process itself would discourage researchers from applying.

While *Lips of Thomas* is an extreme example, a complicated interplay between benefit and harm can arise in any artistic work that involves other people's lives and experiences. The *National Statement* is oriented towards instances where a participant may be directly, tangibly harmed or made uncomfortable during the research process. For example, where participants may become distressed during interviews or feel vulnerable to misinterpretation or misrepresentation of sensitive material. Much more intangible, yet no less significant, is the potential for harm or distress on publication of research in which a person's life is represented. This potential is exacerbated in artistic works, which are intended to reach an audience beyond the academy.

In *Sweetest Things*, the girl's accusations against the teacher were clearly damaging to him. In our initial conversations, he made similarly damaging claims against her. He was initially willing to participate in the project, but only if I did not speak with her. It appeared that there was no way to deal with this story without causing harm on publication to one of those involved in it. Hill, quoting James Walter, suggests that in biographical writing 'harm is inevitable' (Hill, 2007, p.226) because any representation of a person's life is bound to conflict with the image that person holds of themselves. The potential for harm is compounded when researching events involving conflict, injustice or trauma, and it is particularly these events which invite artistic attention.

When writing *Sweetest Things*, I knowingly defied the wishes of one of the central participants in the story by continuing with the project. I have also proceeded to write *Monologue for a Murderer* without seeking the direct consent or contribution from anyone involved in the shooting. These people would still be defined as participants in my research. A participant is 'anyone who is the subject of research' (National Health and Medical Research Council et al., 2007, p.101) and this could 'include those who may not even know they are the subjects of research'. (Ibid., p.8) The statement also stipulates that ethics review may be necessary where 'the conduct of human research… has an impact on the lives of others who are not participants'. (Ibid.) The consent of the participants is considered in the *National Statement* to be a central requirement to any research (ibid., p.19) and there is no allowance for a participant's involvement without it.

The *National Statement* acknowledges the breadth of ethical issues and contexts that may arise, and that it is not a comprehensive set of rules but a framework for heightening ethical awareness. (Ibid., p.13) The difficulty for creative work is in conceptualising a clear dichotomy between 'the risks to the participants' and 'the potential benefits of the research'. (Ibid., p.13) In creating work that includes unaware or non-consenting participants, the only means by which potential harm can be addressed is in the artistic work itself. Within an artwork, it is possible to make ethical dilemmas manifest, acknowledge the ambiguity of conflicting points of view and to take responsibility for one's own artistic agenda. For example, artists Hélène Cixous and Ariane Mnouchkine 'physicalized the ethical negotiation between self and other' (McEvoy, 2003, p.224) in their production of *Le Dernier Caravanséril*, based on interviews with asylum seekers. Scenes were performed on rolling platforms that actors pushed in and out of the performance space. Authorship and representation, submission and resistance were manifested in this theatrical device. In my work, I similarly attempted to expose ethical issues through the practice itself. I theatricalised the absence of the teacher's voice in *Sweetest Things* by turning his character into a cypher. I attempted to leave space for ambiguity in the girl's accusations against the teacher by choosing which ones to dramatise and which to present as testimony. In *Monologue for a Murderer*, I have attempted to chart a navigable line between fact, memory and fiction in order to manifest the ethical difficulties of representing events which I did not personally experience.

Concepts of harm are further complicated in artistic work where the artist's experience is intrinsic to the project. Artistic research inevitably involves the personal experience of the artist being brought to bear on the process of generating, judging and refining the work. This is even more pronounced in memoir, autobiographical or ethnographical work where the artist takes a visible role in the created work. Tamas identifies the harm that her research causes her, and notes with some irony that 'my won trauma may offer grist for the mill... without having to get clearance from an institutional ethics review board'. (Tamas, 2009)

While 'harm' caused by creative practice as research is problematic to identify and address, 'benefit' is no easier. An artistic work may have tangible, direct benefits for its maker, where there is financial compensation or a therapeutic benefit in self-expression. An artwork may also be of particular benefit to a community, where it gives voice to oppressed minorities, exposes difficult issues or celebrates a shared culture or history. However, the benefit of a work will primarily be measured by its artistic merit. This is a contested concept, which exists in a constant state of flux and varies according to the audience and the context in which it is received. The impossible challenge in the context of ethics review is to identify and judge the artistic merit of a work before it exists.

What to Do Instead

The question remains: is there an external process by which ethical considerations can be embedded into artistic practice as research? In the postmodern absence of a unifying communal ideology, what is the best way to heighten awareness of ethical issues, encourage dialogue about them and facilitate genuine ethical engagement? Langlois suggests a process whereby researchers are required to undergo ethics training and report regularly to a committee on ethical issues arising within their research. (Langlois, 2011, p.152) He agrees with Chenall's position that 'formal ethical approval should be a process, rather than a one-off event'. (Chenall et al., 2011, p.17) I believe that creative practice-led research projects would benefit from the active involvement of an ethical advisor. The advisor would meet regularly with the researcher, discuss ethical issues as they arise, and provide perspective and guidance where required. They would also be available to meet with research participants and mediate between the researcher and participants if necessary. The current model maintains an artificial distance between the researcher, the research process and the mechanism by which its ethics are judged. An ethical advisor would enable dialogue about ethics within the creative research process itself, allowing researchers to genuinely engage with the ethical issues their work provokes.

Conclusion

I believe that the core values of the *National Statement* should be central to any field of endeavour. Unfortunately I do not believe that these values are nurtured by the current university ethics review process when applied to artistic work. Rather than fostering them, the current process artificially extracts ethical issues from the organic process of creative work and artistic identity. It imposes a closed, pre-determined structure that undermines artistic process and excludes engagement with ethical issues arising in the course of the work itself. It imposes a binary equation between 'harm' and 'benefit' which is not useful when considering artistic intentions, nor does it accurately reflect the contradictory spectrum of possible responses to artistic production. I believe that an embodied, personal, involved approach to ethical concerns is appropriate to the embodied, personal and involved nature of creative practice-led research.

The girl at the centre of *Sweetest Things* came to opening night. She later thanked me for the experience and, through the generosity and enthusiasm of her response, I felt confident that this project had merit and integrity, and was just, beneficial and respectful. Some time later I received an email from the teacher. He had found an extract of the play online, and wrote 'your play is based on lies and deception, and false information... your professional integrity... shows very little or none at all.' It is possible that if the project had been subject to ethics review, it may never have been written. For me, to repress this story would have been the unethical choice.

References

Australia Council (2013) *New Work: Eligibility and Selection*, available from: http://www.australiacouncil.gov.au/grants/2013/theatre-new-work [accessed 8 August 2013]

Bolt, B. (2012) 'Back and beyond the sublime: Catastrophe in contemporary art', in: *CREATEC Symposium 2012 – Catastrophe and Creativity*. Perth, Western Australia

Chenhall, R., K. Senior & S. Belton (2011) 'Negotiating Human Research Ethics: Case Notes from Anthropologists in the Field', *Anthropology Today* 27(5), pp.13–17

Hedgecoe, A. (2008) 'Research Ethics Review and the Sociological Research Relationship', *Sociology* 42(5), pp.873–86

Hill, D.T. (2007) 'Ethics and Institutions in Biographical Writing on Indonesian Subjects', *Life Writing* 4(2), pp.215–29

Langlois, A.J. (2011) 'Political Research and Human Research Ethics Committees', *Australian Journal of Political Science* 46(1)

McEvoy, W. (2003) 'Finding the Balance: Writing and Performing Ethics in Theatre du
    Soleils' *Le Dernier Caravanséril', New Theatre Quarterly* 22, pp.211–26
National Health and Medical Research Council, A.R.C., Australian Vice-Chancellors'
    Committee (2007) *National Statement on Ethical Conduct in Human Research.*
    Australian Government: Canberra
Nelson, R. (2009) *The Jealousy of Ideas: Research Methods in the Creative Arts.* Ellikon: Fitzroy
Tamas, S. (2009) 'Writing and Righting Trauma: Troubling the Autoethnographic Voice',
    Forum: Qualitative Social Research 10(1)
Van Den Hoonaard, W.C. (2006) 'New Angles and Tangles in the Ethics Review of
    Research', *Journal of Academic Ethics* 4, pp.261–74
Winlow, S.H. & Steve Hall (2012) 'What is an "Ethics Committee"? Academic Governance in
    an Epoch of Belief and Incredulity', *British Journal of Criminology* 52(2), pp.400–16

• •

A principal argument from the ethics perspective (not the same thing at all as an ethical argument) is that transformation involves an act of deception, which is why an increasing number of ethnographers insist on the right of research subjects to be offered both sight of any written report and the freedom to veto publication. Fearing the possibility that something might be produced that does not tell the truth, we are taken back to Plato's well-worn objections to mimesis. For Plato, the imitations of the artist (our autoethnographic researcher) confuse spectators or readers about what is real and what the source of reality might actually be. Art becomes about artifice and artificiality, which by definition takes us further away from the very reality it purports to describe. If description is no more than the shadow of experience, as Baudrillard's simulacrum made overt, then Kant's demand that we 'Do not lie' would deny all claims for truth in any writing.

All production involves the presentation of something dressed up as something else and all production is in this way an act of deception, but no more so than saying 'I love you' is a tame deceit in relation to the emotions those words spring from. We cannot imagine anything we do not first remember and we cannot remember something other than through an act of imagination. Memory is re-made and re-imagined all the time; true or false, trusted or doubted, it is the mind's reproduction of prior experience, and the twenty-first century's fetishism of authenticity holds no real sway here.

A research report, or thesis, might blur the line between the twin realities of original experience and subsequent articulation but few would believe that words on the page are accurate reflections of lives lived, and this ethics of readership falls beyond the gaining of research approval. Back in the 1930s, long before the term was in use, Gertrude Stein put her finger on the pulse of autoethnography and we do well to remember her words:

> There are many that I know and they know it. They are all of them repeating and I hear it. I love it and I tell it. I love it and now I will write it. This is now a history of my love of it. I hear it and I love it and I write it. They repeat it. They live it and I see it and I hear it. They live it and I hear it and I see it and I love it and now and always I will write it. There are many kinds of men and women and I know it. They repeat it and I hear it and I love it. This is now a history of the way they do it. This is now a history of the way I love it.

> (Stein, 1995, p.58)

Autoethnography is often used in the area of health, where ethics has a unique and delicately weighted currency. But ethical concerns are no less finely balanced elsewhere. Ethics is after all concerned primarily with human relations, and autoethnography, in writing about people, not only describes the nature of these relations but also requires and presupposes a position from which the knowledge about human relations can emerge. An individual self is always and already in a particular world, surrounded by and constituted with the other; in this sense the researching/writing self stands in an inherently ethical relation to experience, and autoethnography is never innocent.

Carolyn Ellis infamously ruffled the feathers of a community she had inveigled herself amongst when between 1972 and 1981 she carried out research into a kinship network in the North American Chesapeake Bay area. The community of so-called Guinea Watermen made Ellis welcome over a prolonged period of time and, although they had been aware that she was a doctoral student, the results of Ellis's research – published as an award-winning 1986 book, *Fisher Folk* – contained enough to make the community regard Ellis as a traitor who had been masquerading as a guile-free guest. Ellis herself came fairly clean about the ethical mess she created (and professionally prospered from) in a 1995 essay in the *Journal of Contemporary Ethnography*, and her acknowledgement about the tangled forms that research deception can take has done much to tighten things up in terms of what contemporary ethical concerns will look to allow. (Allen, 1997)

Time moves on and it is never easy and perhaps never even proper to judge the deeds of the past by the attitudes of today. Nevertheless, when Ellis secretly tape-recorded her seemingly off-the-record conversations with the watermen and their families, it is hard to see a way that she might have thought this was an acceptable aspect of sociological research. Despite the contrition shown in 1995 and subsequently, Ellis is adamant that her acts of deception were necessary: 'I know I did [the Guinea kinship] an injustice… but I couldn't have done the study any other way. My study was predicated on my getting close to them, and if you're constantly reminding people that you're not one of them, you can't do that.' (Ibid.) And Ellis is not alone in this view that the end can often justify the means: Erich Goode believes social scientists should have the freedom to trade 'less-than-complete honesty versus getting the information' one needs. (Ibid.) If these positions of ethical fluidity have become less common in recent years then issues of the deception of subjects remain and likely always shall. The old term for this was 'situation ethics' and certainly we have ample evidence of sociologists who have entered groups such as Alcoholics Anonymous in order to write articles and books. Whilst there is no real evidence pointing to the harm this might do to research subjects, it does speak to a shifting sense of ethical concern, driven by an absence of personal integrity aligned to professional gain; and this makes for a dangerous combination.

Richard Leo wrote unashamedly of having consciously reinvented his identity in order to gain the type of admission into police interrogation rooms that would aid his University College Berkeley dissertation, claiming a form of evidentiary privilege one would normally associate with representatives from the legal and medical professions. Likewise, Laud Humphrey published *Tearoom Trade* after presenting himself as gay and gaining the trust and confidence of his subjects. In order to discover their names and addresses, Humphrey took the registration numbers of cars belonging to the men he was studying and interviewed them some time later, in their family homes. No model for best practice and no real surprise that Humphrey was later hospitalised when a Professor of Social Theory in his Sociology Department at Washington University tried to punch some ethical sense into him. The punching professor's name was Alvin Gouldner. Two versions of the assault are in circulation. In one the reason given is that Humphrey had mocked Gouldner in public, which provoked the attack; the other is that it came as a result of the tearoom incident. The consensus appears to be that the mocking acted as a catalyst on simmering rage at Humphrey's earlier deceit. In either case, there is some doubt over the extent to which Humphrey told the truth about his research, his sexuality and his role as passive observer or 'lookout'. (Fabio, 2007)

Thankfully no fisher folk punched Carolyn Ellis, but the backlash left her scarred and it appears to be one of the reasons she moved away from ethnographic fieldwork toward a concentration on the autoethnographic self. With the naiveté of relative youth and inexperience, Ellis had hoped that the people whose lives she was re-telling (and I would suggest *re-making*) would not read her published book because they would simply be unaware of its existence. To a certain extent, Ellis had to hope that this would bypass the need for any real concern for the type of deductive disclosure that happens when groups or individuals become recognisable in written reports: when knowledge that the writer has a son reveals 'Rory' to be a pseudonym for Jake.

In a prime example of the biter bit, some autoethnographers feel that the main person in need of protection is the one who carries out the research. In her article *Do Thyself No Harm: Protecting Ourselves as Autoethnographers*, April Chatham-Carpenter says that she will 'walk the reader through the choices [she] made in an attempt to protect [herself] as a researcher in the process of publishing an autoethnography about anorexia'. (2010) Chatham-Carpenter lets the reader know, through an author's note, that italics are used in the article to convey her inner voice or thoughts. On the face of it this seems a peculiar indulgence, for is it not the case that the entire article is made up of the writer's voice, and that separating a voice into 'outer' (non-italics) and 'inner' (italics) means nothing when each appears in public? Is an inner voice still something we can regard as inner when we write it? Be that as it may, Chatham-Carpenter's inner voice has this to say, and we can borrow her italics to use it here:

> *Oh, how I've grown to love and hate that word 'autoethnography'. I love the method and how it allows a person to be free of the constraints of typical academic writing, but I hate what it has done to me (or rather what I have not been able to get it to do for me). No publication, no finished research project, nothing to show for all of the hours and hours I've worked on this project over the past 7 years.*

(Ibid.)

Clearly Chatham-Carpenter has a story she wishes to tell and she has determined a form through which she can tell it: a form allowing her to '*do an autoethnography about [her] experiences with anorexia... so others can know what it felt like to live the hell [she] had experienced*'. But to suggest that autoethnographers struggle to get their work published *because* it is autoethnography smacks of self-delusion. Any and all of us in academic employment have a familiarity with publishers' rejection slips that is as necessarily weary as it is wearily necessary. It goes with the territory of writing that not every journal and, at times, not *any journal* will want to publish our work. In my own experiences of rejection and acceptance, my feeling is that editors and review boards tend to get things right. Like Chatham-Carpenter I have sometimes struggled over several years to find a home for a certain piece of writing. After a while, and seven years seems more than long enough to me, it seems safer and more honest to assume that one's work is flawed rather than convince oneself that there is some form of publishers' conspiracy against autoethnography.

Ragan Fox cites the refusal of a journal, in his case *Qualitative Health Research*, to publish one of his articles because his work was an autoethnography – 'Are Those Germs in Your Pocket, or Am I Just Crazy to See You?' – and in fairness, the rejection email he quotes from is surprisingly dismissive. But he overcooks his argument slightly in his double-bluff commentary that he is:

> especially frustrated by journals that won't even consider
> autoethnography, a mode of inquiry that is beloved by scholars from
> historically marginalized groups. I, for example, understand why gay
> men are drawn to narrative-based studies. Quantitative reasoning
> has resulted in Kinsey scales and other objectifying discourses that,
> for decades, provided the proof of the truth of anti-gay animus. I
> won't suggest that all people who deny the worth of autoethnography
> are homophobic. That's not a claim I believe. I will, however, argue
> that the marginalization of that specific mode of cultural criticism
> is intimately connected to the same sort of routinized, systemic
> impulses that devalue and dismiss many of the people who author
> autoethnography.
>
> (Fox, 2013)

Fox is a fine writer, thinker and performer, and he is as naturally entitled to his views as anyone; but linking a distrust (or perhaps just somebody's dislike) of autoethnography with the marginalisation of its authors is a stretch too far. As Nigel Karuth points out, however, there are examples of prejudice that are simply too difficult to ignore. In 2005, a student of Karuth's, Marilynn Loveless, produced *Mrs Shakespeare: Muse, Mother, Matriarch, Madonna, Whore, Writer, Woman, Wife – Recovering a Lost Life*. As Karuth describes it, 'at Loveless's graduation, the Acting Dean refused to read out the title of her PhD; perhaps he considered it un-academic.' (Karuth, 2011)

Almost all research students in the arts and humanities are in the fortunate positions of being able to choose what they write about and how. Inevitably, a proportion of academics will be driven to research things that matter to others more than to the fulfilment of their own careers, and Chatham-Carpenter (writing here with her outer voice) is honest enough to write that she took the risk of writing about her own condition 'in order to be successful professionally' and that the benefits of subsequent publication outweighed the costs to her personal life.

Ellis and Chatham-Carpenter present similar views on the toll autoethnography can take on the researcher. Ellis has asked whether the 'pain involved for me as the storyteller [is] too much to make the storytelling worthwhile'. (Ellis & Bochner, 2000, p.275) As we will see in the next chapter, that looks at ways of performing autoethnography, research all too often benefits no-one so much as the researchers themselves; and no matter how earnest our claims of giving value, my suspicion is that more university research in the arts and humanities is carried out in pursuit of tenure than to make the world a safer place – or, as my own university at the time of writing this chapter has it on its web pages, to 'Make Tomorrow Better'. Better, yes; but better for whom?

Autoethnographic writing is compared and contrasted with realist writing, the former being seen to be accorded with several advantages when writing the self. Culture flows through self and *vice versa* and there is little argument that that this flow can be captured particularly well in autoethnographic works. Well, but not easily. Adopting the multi-faceted role of a researcher, informant and writer, autoethnographers can be tempted to claim full responsibility for their stories without hesitation. D. Jean Clandinin and F. Michael Connelly suggest asking the question of narrative inquirers, and by default autoethnographers: Do you own a story because you tell it? And if we attempt to tell a story with integrity, how do we balance that with subject confidentiality? (Clandinin & Connelly, 2000) The principle of protecting the confidentiality of subjects is always relevant to autoethnography, but since the identities of characters are invariably revealed through their actions within the communities described, it is extremely difficult to protect identities from people who are intimately connected to these known characters. Autoethnographers, like all researchers of human subjects, are driven to adhere to ethical principles of confidentiality despite our knowledge that publication leads to revelation. The best way to maintain the confidentiality of research subjects is not to publish one's findings to any but the smallest community of readers, and yet any research findings of worth demand to be shared. Ethical confidentiality thus wrestles with accountability (particularly where research is funded from the public purse), significance as opposed to secrecy, and academic career development that is inextricably linked to publication. Indeed, whilst university careers often revolve around books being read by particular people and thus, in the curious circularity of academia, cited in particular texts, the wider the readership the more significant one's research might seem to be.

There are some logical rules of thumb when it comes to ethical autothenography; but it is in the nature of research, particularly when one's approach or outcomes are seen as 'creative', that the edges blur and one person's ethical dilemma is another's ethical imperative. For example, we would usually say that when conducting research autoethnographers should be aware of the potential impacts of the research on the people they study. It would follow from this that if the seeking of new knowledge will negatively impact on the people we will be studying then we should probably not undertake the study at all. But at what point might this negative impact be justifiable? The artist and academic Neal White proposed a project that drew on the May 1959 opening of Yves Klein's exhibition *Le Vide* (The Void) at Gallery Iris Clert in Paris. Klein's exhibition featured a white gallery space within which special blue cocktails containing a mixture of gin, Cointreau and methylene blue were served to the guests. (White, 2012) As Klein intended, the cocktails caused the urine of drinkers to turn blue for the planned run of his show. Klein had famously created his own shade of ultramarine, International Klein Blue (IKB), and in effect the gallery goers creating the colour that Klein was known for every time they urinated became the very *private* art that these people had gone to the *public* gallery to see.

Methylene blue as a stain has been subsequently established as toxic. White's intention was to recreate the event as an experiment to establish what might be the safest or least toxic dosage of methylene blue in an alcoholic cocktail required to turn urine blue. The setting of White's trial was a gallery where the visitors would become consensual participants, 'informed self-experimenters' in White's terms. In a managed process of consensual participation, the visitor would be faced with a choice to consume an artwork that contained the ingredients of methylene. The project was proposed as a rational and logical approach to create a cultural experiment on the basis of a clinical trial under closely monitored conditions as well as functioning as a challenge to the limits and practices of ethics as articulated across art and science practice. In this way, White looked to engage with the politics of consent, belief and creative research. White's research proposal can be accessed online and it makes for compelling reading. What is interesting of course is the idea that subjects would be willing to self-experiment in order to partake in an event that could turn their urine blue through the knowing consumption of a toxic liquid. Now, this is clearly a project that has a negative physical impact on its participants that is definitely temporary and possibly permanent, but what about its values, and what about the free will of participants? If fully informed adults are prepared to take a reasonable risk then, one might ask, why not allow research to proceed? Isn't some negative impact, in some cases, potentially acceptable?

Generally speaking, more freedoms are afforded here to athletes than to those working in the arts. The noted performance artist Stelarc has found it almost impossible to have his own experiments on his body accepted by the ethics boards of the various universities he has been attached to; primarily, I suspect, because the frame around his practice is 'art'. Were he an athlete, changing his body shape through exercise or putting his health and safety at risk through extreme sport, it is likely that his research would have been approved as well as being more readily appreciated. It is one of the ironies of Stelarc's career (and one he is himself wryly aware of) that the practices universities prevent him from doing under their auspice are the self-same works that university academics are most keen to conduct their own research into and write about.

Following another ethical pathway, we might also say that when conducting research our autoethnographers and memoirists need to be open with funders, colleagues, the persons studied or providing information, and relevant parties affected by the work about the purpose(s), potential impacts, and source(s) of support for the work. Again, this sounds both admirable and logical. But creative research does not always follow predictable patterns and its trajectories are as subject to instinct and even accident as they are to design. Studying the impact of a caffeine-free diet and writing one's findings into a suitably end-noted report is one thing, but creative research (and I would suggest that autoethnography and memoir are *always* creative) is not likely to follow as predictable a line, nor is it likely to relate to an area with such a demonstrable set of findings. By its very nature, creative research cannot predict a potential impact with any great accuracy. Similarly, its entire purpose might shift during the research process. That many people (including at times this writer) struggle with creative research that is so open ended as to be often indistinguishable from creative practice is not quite the same thing as suggesting that creative research is only deserving of that term if it moves towards a pre-determined end. The distinctions between *practice as research* and *creative practice* might seem too slight to dwell upon, but if all creative practice is an *ipso facto* research project then the term 'research' becomes so elastic as to lose all of its function. It is axiomatic that creative research, or research by creative production, or practice-led research, or practice-based research, will nudge at the barriers of acceptability. At its most cynical (or pragmatic), we see academic *curricula vitae* amended so that one's previous projects are made to read as research projects when research, in the ways we commonly regard it, was not a key feature at all. At its most purposive, we are seeing the opening up of research into methods of enquiry that were hitherto closed off.

When it comes to the dissemination of findings or results we might also work to some fine-sounding ethical codes. We would argue that, when disseminating results of a study, autoethnographic researchers have an ethical obligation to consider the potential impact of both their research and the communication or dissemination of the results of their research on all those directly or indirectly involved. The research results of ethnographies should be disclosed to participants in the project if that research is subsequently to be observed by other people; and the approval of participants should be a given before any work that is significantly *about them* is broadcast, presented or otherwise published. But this might not always be possible and it might not always be in the best interests of the work. If a creative researcher is shaping work for public consumption then is it right that one of the work's subjects can veto or edit that work? For sure, sometimes it might be; and just as surely, sometimes it might not. We each seek to do no harm but the measures we take to ensure this are not easily determined as a one-size-fits-all and catch-all policy.

Gary Alan Fine claims that researchers are generally not as ethical as they claim and that 'each job includes ways of doing things that would be inappropriate for others to know'. (Fine, 1993, p.267) Fine points to the ways in which researchers tend to make idealised ethical claims which are based on partial truths and self-deceptions; and when we deceive ourselves about the ethical good of our work, it is hard also to adhere to external ideas of control. In the same way that we feel our truths are somehow more true than other people's, so we feel that our personal engagement with ethics creates its own frame of reference, which should be free from the need for pre-project approval.

Within the university sector, it is inevitable that researchers intending to involve humans as participants in their work must first receive approval from their institution's human research ethics committee. In conducting such research, all researchers are generally advised to read and abide by their country's code for the responsible conduct of research. The purpose of these codes is to guide institutions and researchers in responsible research practices and to promote integrity in research. Whilst they differ slightly from country to country, research ethics codes explain what is expected of researchers by the community they are working within. As such they are designed to assist researchers, administrators and the community with how to manage departures from 'best research practice' (notions of best research practice are innately restrictive and would almost certainly mean that White's post-Klein project would never be approved). Codes are written specifically for universities and other public-sector research institutions. However, all organisations involved in research within each code's country are encouraged to incorporate it as far as possible in their operating environments. There are almost invariably university ethics committees at faculty level and each faculty will generally appoint its own research ethics officer or representative.

Concerns amongst academic researchers about standardisation as censorship notwithstanding, it is fair to say that universities are committed to ensuring that their activities involving human participants are conducted in a way which minimises risk; maximises the public benefit of research; and appropriately manages personal data and respects the dignity, rights and welfare of all participants. Universities are likewise committed to the idea of research that is designed and undertaken in a manner that evidences accountability and quality, and which sets appropriate standards of conduct in line with current legislation. Most of us would agree that research is about aspiring towards communal and general good; about academic integrity and responsibility to one's discipline; about safeguarding the well-being of participants; about the careful management of data; and about appropriate forms of dissemination. But it is important that these categories are not seen to prescribe particular approaches. For example, the idea of communal or general good should not be taken to imply that all research should have an immediate applied value beyond the context of the research. There is a place for research where no such immediate or even long-term application can be reasonably demonstrated, just as there is a place for art that makes no claim for communal good. There are, for example, a number of plays considered to be 'political' which work effectively on many dramatic levels and yet singularly fail to evidence change in the minds of any members of an audience. Whilst it is legitimate to ask whether a particular research question is sufficiently interesting and valuable, it is restrictive to expect that notions of value will be shared across a subject area, department, faculty or any committee of appointed experts.

As with creative research, autoethnography is a relatively young discipline with distinctive characteristics. Whilst autoethnographers can learn a great deal about good ethical practice in research from more established disciplines, there also needs to be regard for the specificity of the subject domains and the particular research practices that are becoming established. Autoethnography can often challenge conventional responses to ethical issues developed in other disciplines, just as creative practice research involving audience participation, participatory projects and any work involving representation through performance will raise their own ethical issues. Ethics should never be seen simply as a matter of bureaucracy and compliance, despite the fact that these two aspects are increasingly the *lingua franca* of universities.

Engaging with ethics is part of autoethnography's coming of age. Ethical awareness and good knowledge of ethical practice in research in any discipline are key attributes of the informed researcher and we should all be able to articulate an ethical defence of our intentions and approach. Yet what this means for autoethnography has still to be fully determined. To what extent is it useful to embrace ethical guidelines developed in other, longer-established disciplines? Should we develop ethical guidelines that are generic to the social sciences or are our self-writing needs fundamentally different? To what extent do existing autoethnographic practices conflict with and challenge conventional approaches to research ethics? Is it the case, as Martin Tolich has posited, that autoethnography is in fact a form of journalism and thus generally exempt from the rigours of formal ethics review? If we are to take autoethnography seriously as a research approach then these are questions we have to address.

Universities are increasingly creating forms that relate specifically to autoethnography, memoir and creative production, and many of these are in the public domain, but a standard university ethics form will look something like the one offered in Appendix B. They are as impossible to avoid as they are difficult to complete successfully, but they are here to stay; and so acquainting ourselves with the types of questions that will be asked of our work allows us to second guess at least some of the criticisms or concerns before they arrive. For arrive they surely will.

Looking back at my own doctorate proposal from the mid-1990s, I see now that its original title (*British Theatre and the New Surrealism*) had nothing at all to do with my finished research, and very little, really, to do with the research I actually intended to do. At the time, I considered my written proposal little more than a bureaucratic exercise, something that would secure both registration and supervisor. In fact, after twelve months I changed universities, supervisor and the focus of the work without having to do much more than fill in a form with my name, address and confirmation that my fees would continue to be paid by my sponsor. A research proposal now is written much more as a contract, which, if not quite legally binding, describes the task the researcher is taking on and the ways it will likely be carried out in terms that leave room for manoeuvre but not for radical change. This is the case not least because any sizeable shift in focus requires a concomitant shift in ethics clearance. The language of a formal research proposal is often more authoritative than in earlier times, conveying the student's understanding of ethics as well as subject. It is a contract which is written in the future tense depicting a trajectory along which the researcher will travel in order to reach the sought after destination. Whilst some room is left for what the results might actually turn out to be (particularly in the case of creative and practice-led work), the structure leading to the outcome is not significantly negotiable.

And no thesis proposal is acceptable now without a research ethics form. This book's Appendix A provides guidelines for the completion of a research proposal form and its Appendix B is an example of a proposal form for ethics approval. This form is an inventive composite, rather than belonging to any one university. The terminology used shifts from one institution to another as it does from one country to another, but the gist of proposal forms remains the same and they are something all university researchers now encounter. It is generally accepted that all research coming out of universities needs to be granted ethical clearance before it can be carried out. Because of this, ethics forms have become a way of life and familiarisation with the types of questions asked (no less than the types of responses that are most likely to be approved) is necessary knowledge. If this makes the filling in of ethical clearance forms appear purely onerous and/or cynical, that is not the intention. In fact, relating our own research agendas to ethical concerns is a useful way of sharpening our thinking and reminding us that research involving people is not something we can rush into without due consideration for all concerned.

Oh, I believe in yesterday
Paul McCartney

CHAPTER FOUR

Rewriting Memory

Malcolm Gladwell and The Beatles; False Memory Syndrome; The Heart of a Humument; the written word as evidence; Michel de Montaigne, Elizabeth Loftus and Ernest Hemingway; Luis Buñuel and Ronald Reagan; Freud's memoire volontaire; how memory works; Steph Brocken's case study

Barbara Kingsolver's statement that memory is a complicated thing, a relative to truth but not its twin, has become so well-travelled that we can easily forget its potency; and yet memory is always at least partly inaccurate. Because of this it can only be used as the basis for relatively spurious claims for reliability. We know this at the same time as we choose to ignore it. We know that our memories are unreliable when it comes to knowing where we put our car keys when we walked into a room, yet we convince ourselves that our memories of events from decades ago provide faithful records of the past.

No matter how liberal the approach, study is an exercise in memory and we do our best to provide aids to memory without always knowing which methods might suit us best. Sigmund Freud wrote that 'If I distrust my memory... I am able to supplement and guarantee its working by making a note in writing', (Freud, 1963, p.61) and students worldwide are encouraged to take notes in lectures and classes, just as researchers in the field are advised to record their impressions while these are still fresh. This is logical enough. Many people find that, when they take good notes, they can remember things well enough and so rarely end up having to look back at what they've written. It would appear that writing something down helps us to remember it better. Conversely, not writing things down is seemingly just asking to forget. In ancient Israel, kings were required to write their own copy of the laws down. The physical act of writing was then, and is now, regarded as being symbolically powerful. As the words we write appear on the screen or on the page, they get pressed into our minds.

When I was a younger man, I was almost instantly forgettable in a few plays. I found the only way I could successfully remember lines was to copy them out in long hand as a way of etching another person's script into my mind. I use these words as opposed to describing myself as a young actor primarily because I am never sure how much one needs to have done something or to what level or to what professional gain before that person can be regarded as *the thing*: actor, athlete, writer, dancer, painter or whatever else. I have written the book you are reading now and a few other, but my various university contracts have allowed me the luxury of paid time to write; indeed, despite various heads of school preferring the carrot of *impel* rather than the stick of *compel*, my contracts have at times urged me quite strenuously to write work for publication. Without being in that privileged position, would I still be writing? On one level, I suspect not. All of which means I would never comfortably regard or describe myself as a writer, much less an author. This puts me a little out of sync with the position of many of my colleagues, as I came to realise when I rehearsed this argument in a previous title for Libri, *Blood, Sweat & Theory: Research through Practice in Performance* (2010). Cooking meals does not make me a chef any more than writing a poem to my wife makes me a poet; directing a play does not make me a director, any more than being in a play makes one an actor in anything but the flimsiest and most facile of senses.

Naturally enough there are exceptions and challenges to this. The world of description, and particularly self-description, is a complex one. People who commute to work each day on bicycles might legitimately call themselves cyclists but people who drive to work are not generally referred to as drivers, even though they might rack up a great many more miles each week than a van driver. Is a person who plays golf every sunny Sunday called a golfer and would somebody who plays bad guitar to an audience of none be called a guitarist? Fuzzy Logic (not the same thing as Fuzzy Thinking) gives us some answers. The concept of Fuzzy Logic comes from Lotfi Zadeh, a professor at the University of California at Berkeley. Fuzzy Logic works not as a control methodology so much as a way of processing data by allowing partial set membership rather than crisp set membership or non-membership. In Fuzzy Logic, unlike standard conditional logic, the truth of any statement is a matter of degree and truth claims are located on a scale of one to ten with values that indicate the amount of truth ascribed to a particular statement. In these terms, the bad guitarist is a musician to the value of one, perhaps, whereas Jimi Hendrix, Julian Bream or Django Reinhardt would rate as ten.

The opening lines of Bob Dylan's 'Blowin' in the Wind' ask how many roads a man must walk down before we can call him a man; and we might as easily ask (albeit with a marked reduction in philosophical gravitas) how many words a man needs to write down before we can call him a writer. Malcolm Gladwell's popularising of Anders Ericsson's theory of 10,000 hours of practice leading to expertise provides a benchmark, and Gladwell cites the early days of The Beatles, when they played in the clubs and bars of Hamburg, as a good example. (Gladwell, 2008) For Gladwell, these 10,000 Hamburg hours gave the band the time to practice (eight hours a session) that would turn them into exemplary musicians and songwriters. What is not quite so clear is whether those same 10,000 hours alone would have turned Joe Bloggs into John Lennon. Perfection might not be possible without practice, but practice alone is clearly no guarantee of perfection.

Ever since Kurt Schwitters claimed that anything an artist might spit out is art and Marcel Duchamp exhibited a urinal as *Fountain*, it has been hard to equate the term 'artist' with quality, and this line has continued through Andy Warhol, Jeff Koons, Damien Hirst and a host of others. This may be fine and good (or fine and bad) but what makes Schwitter's spitter an artist in the first place? What makes one human being an artist and another not? We can recognise a four-minute miler as an athlete and a plodding jogger as not because we make considered and relatively common judgements as to what constitutes athletics. The jogger on a racetrack is a non-athlete engaged in athletic pursuits whereas the miler remains an athlete no matter how slowed down the pace may become. The distinction is clear. Even when debates rage as to whether the throwing of darts at a board should be regarded as an Olympic event, we are not considering darts players as athletes, despite their level of skill, any more than we would use the term to describe snooker or chess players. An athlete then is defined by a degree of physical achievement aligned to potential and, crucially, this ability must be demonstrated often enough to impress the distinction upon us.

We instinctively work in a Fuzzy Logic sense when we describe a professional boxer as a 'journeyman'. There are countless such boxers and by definition their names are largely unknown and unheralded. The term refers to fighters who have adequate skill, relative to the profession they are in, but who, like Sylvester

Stallone's fictitious Rocky Balboa, have little or no expectation of winning fights against genuine title contenders. Writing is a different animal altogether. Many professional writers write badly, many amateur writers write well and, unlike life in the square ring, quality is no accurate barometer of career. Nevertheless, in a world of increasing immediacy, delusion and spin we would do well to rein in our predilection toward self-promotion. Perhaps False Description Syndrome is as deserving of its own acronym as False Memory Syndrome's FMS?

Or perhaps I am being overly restrictive. Perhaps too I am confusing my own insecurity, false pride or fake humility with a call for greater honesty?

Finding a few things out is not automatically the same thing as research, and research that does not lead in some disseminated way to advancement of other people's knowledge and understanding is not quite research in the way that a university will generally understand it. And at the considerable risk of sounding old school and even reactionary, this seems a perfectly valid position for universities to take. Opening up the idea of research to include autoethnography and memoir alongside creative production and thesis as a type of *Humument* has allowed artists and practitioners greater and more positive access to higher degrees by research than at any time in our past. And few of us would deny that this has been a change for the better. And yet… notwithstanding a university's implicit charter to break, make, re-break and re-make the seeming rules of art, learning and even some of the ways in which life is lived, limiting research to something more than sanctioned solipsism remains a good thing.

The term *Humument* refers to Tom Phillips' reworking of a relatively obscure Victorian novel, *A Human Document*. (Phillips, 1985) Phillips altered the fabric of the novel by applying paint, collage and ink to its pages and by selecting words on various pages in order to create a new river of text that flowed through the fields of newly created images, and then published the result as *The Heart of a Humument*. Phillips thus created a new narrative and new meanings from an original document, transposing his own work onto somebody else's and inviting readers to transpose their meanings onto Phillips'. My own introduction to *The Heart of a Humument* came in a core lecture during degree study at what was then called Crewe and Alsager College, later Manchester Metropolitan University. The passing years have only made me more grateful for my tutors' patience with a cohort of students (including the noted television writer and novelist Jeff Povey and one of the UK's leading experts in professional role play, Steve Harvey) for whom making sense of the legitimacy of creating original work out of extant material created by another person was a slow dawning but ultimately priceless experience.

My own academic struggles aside, Phillips' book was significant inasmuch as it drew together the genre of artists' books and the intertextuality of modernist and subsequently postmodern practice. And whilst my suggestion that research theses have become a type of neo-*Humument* might seem a stretch too far, there are numerous examples of PhD submissions where, in practice and in print, Phillips' model has been taken as standard.

We often need to write in order to know what we know; and there is good evidence that the act of writing itself helps us remember things better. What is interesting is that writing things down appears to help us remember the *important* things and that the better our notes are, the more likely we are to remember. Writing from notes rather than relying on memory is an aid to what happened, but it is just as obviously evidence of what we thought might have happened at the time; or even, as has been proven in the case of some police officers' notes, evidence of what we hope will be believed despite our knowledge that its contents are irregular and incorrect.

And of course this does not just apply to notes taken by police officers and of course it does not apply solely to attempts to delude. Diaries are widely thought of as being inadmissible as court evidence, but this is not generally the case and, despite being open to challenge on a great many levels, diary entries tend to read with the power of truth. The notebook of a girl who accused two young men of raping her was admitted as evidence for the defence when it was found to contain text, written after the alleged offence, stating that her only sexual encounters had been with a named boy who was not one of the individuals involved with the case. The court's decision was challenged on the grounds that sifting through a young girl's diary and reading a particular entry in open court to contend that the girl was a liar was a humiliating and embarrassing public fishing expedition into her sexual conduct. (Miller, 2012) During the Lockerbie Bombing trial, the judges reached a ruling, after legal arguments relating to how the item had been discovered, that the diary belonging to Al Amin Khalifa Fhimah was admissible in evidence and the diary notes were considered persuasive. (BBC, 2000) In 2006, Kenneth Emmanuel Dyers faced 22 charges relating to the alleged aggravated and indecent sexual assault of two girls, both aged 12, and diary entries from children involved were admitted as powerfully persuasive evidence for the prosecution. Dyers subsequently took his own life. (Goldner, 2006)

In 2000, a jury in California found a man guilty of first-degree murder for stabbing his wife to death with a kitchen knife. This particular trial was different from most other domestic violence cases culminating in murder. The husband was convicted using the in-diary testimony of his dead wife. In the first criminal prosecution involving a new hearsay exception for domestic abuse incidents, extracts from the deceased victim's diary were read out in court. In her diary, the victim described being beaten by her husband on several occasions. The exception to rules relating to hearsay was one of several new pieces of legislation that came to be known as 'O.J. Laws', that is, legislation springing up in the wake of the notorious O.J. Simpson trials. During Simpson's criminal trial, Judge Ito excluded certain portions of Nicole Brown Simpson's diary, which documented abuse and threats by O.J. Simpson. After the not-guilty verdict, the California legislature passed the new hearsay exception. (Grimes, 2010)

A popular family law website gives the following advice to its prospective clients:

> One of the most important things that you can do to assist yourself
> in any family law matter is to keep a daily journal. Daily journals
> are normally admissible as evidence in a court of law. However, their
> most important function is to refresh your memory as to events that
> happened on particular days so that you can accurately describe these
> events to other people such as your attorney or the court.

> (McCasland, 2012)

The idea here is that a description is accurate and *ergo* honest by dint of its having been written down. This is made clear in the website's subsequent section: 'By writing in the journal on a daily basis all of the events recorded in the journal will have more credibility.' (Gruske, 2011) The case concerning Nicole Brown Simpson was one of murder. If we can stand back for a moment from the tragedy of that event in order to concentrate on *writing* (no easy thing to do), it remains shocking to see the power given to words for no more reason than that they were once written down. Rae Earl, whose diaries were developed into the UK television programme *My Mad, Fat Teenage* Diary, suggests that diaries 'have a bilious authenticity that is impossible to replicate in memory'. (Earl, 2013) The real issue here is that nobody, including Earl herself, has any idea whether authenticity refers to the diarist's feelings at the time or to what events might have happened and in what ways. 'Feelings thrown down in a diary are raw, immediate and uncensored,' Earl tells us, with 'no thought given to anyone but the writer'. (Ibid.) But this is not always so, particularly at a time when careers are increasingly fashioned from making one's private thoughts and deeds public.

In terms of academic work, research notes are paid a similar amount of respect, standing as usually unquestioned confirmation that something happened at a certain time and in the way it was described. Many allegations of academic plagiarism (from the Latin word *plagium*, meaning kidnapping) have been dropped when a student produces hand-written notes transcribed from books and articles, as though this stands as axiomatic proof of innocence. Despite a disciplinary panel's knowledge that the notes could well have been written after the allegation was made rather than (as is always claimed) *before*, and despite the fact that the evidence for plagiarism has to be clear and abundant before any case is made, the production of notes serves to convince its audience that an honest and naïve mistake has occurred. More cynically even, the production of backdated notes might allow a disciplinary panel enough wriggle room to pretend to believe that no plagiarism has taken place; thus avoiding an appeal board's decision that the situation was only ever brought about by the failure of lecturers to explain things properly in Learning to Study 101.

Assuming they are made before rather than after submission, research notes are a means of recording thoughts and inspiration, providing ways of expressing ideas that one can return to and *remember* at a later period. But not all of the notes we make will be used and certainly not all of them will be developed into the prose of a subsequent thesis or otherwise autoethnograhic document. This means that some of the things deemed important at the time of their observation or soon thereafter fall away during the transition from experience to articulation. Events that took place at a specific time might be conflated just as a memoirist might resort to dialogue that is a creative composite because reporting the actual words spoken might legislate against the honesty the writer seeks. If written notes can take us back into corners of our memory that might otherwise have been simply forgotten, they can also provide information that might not be bettered by revision. Flawed though they are, first-version notes are often the closest we can get to records of our in-the-moment thoughts and, for all their polishing into paragraphs, subsequent iterations inevitably manipulate events into literary artifice.

If diaries document the life of their writer, research notes document the development of a particular set of circumstances; and just as poring through somebody else's notebooks would likely be a recipe for misreading and misinterpretation, so might the re-reading of our own notes expose nothing so much as the gap between what seemed of interest then and what fits our purpose now. Not all of the information that makes up research notes, of course, is written. We doodle and sketch, photograph and film, and these forms

– whether in the abstraction of pencil scratches that look to capture a mood or moment, or in video footage that seduces us into believing the accuracy of what we see – are equally problematic.

Whenever we commit images to film, we are organising a set of signs as a way of making a particular statement about how we see the world, and about the ways we want our ways of seeing to be seen by others. All recording onto film thus deals with the articulation and structuring of its makers' views of the world; and this applies no less to film we shoot as grist to the research mill than it does to film made to be shown to other people.

Sidestepping the considerable fact that the act of filming sometimes changes the nature of the thing we observe (especially when that *thing* is human activity), research film footage straddles fact and fiction in an always awkward fashion. What, for example, are the strategies by which our films make and record meaning? In representing observed events, how do we think about accuracy in relation to the things (or people) we choose to point our lens at? What gets unconsciously locked into research footage is the conceit of the real, a term built on a concept of something *not* being something else. Because the footage does not create a knowingly false image the implication is that it is somehow authentic; because one's footage is not a deliberate fiction, *ergo* it is a true record of events. We are brought face to face here with the idea of researchers insisting on the innocence of the camera's pure description at the same time as they embrace an autoethnographic research form that elsewhere exposes innocence and neutrality as the first casualties of integrity.

We can chase our tails to the point of insanity or stasis by clinging so tightly to the idea that if reality changes over time and context, to the extent that all permanent records will eventually become a lie, then no essays on the now are worth the writing; but of course, this would lead not so much to *ennui* as to the end of writing. But film images *are* problematic. The assumption we carry is that it is natural for us to understand pictures. Photographs and film footage read to us as representations of natural events, and we understand these representations on a level that we regard as intuitive, compared to the literary learning we bring to acts of understanding through reading. Photographs that have not been improved, corrected or edited (and this editing happens often now at source) are identified as *natural*; the natural is seen as the *real*; and the real, as we know, presents to us as the *true*.

The human brain is made up of regions that process different kinds of information. Some process auditory data, whilst others deal with visual information, emotions and verbal communication. We know that these regions overlap inasmuch as one can have an emotional response that is put quickly into words. When we make field notes we create spatial relations between the various bits of information we are recording. In numerous psychological tests involving students attending lectures, students who did not take notes remembered the same number of points as those students who took notes throughout. We can see from this that the simple act of taking notes did not increase the amount of information students remembered. In tests such as these, each group of students remembered approximately 40 per cent of the information covered in the lecture. What was important, however, was that those students who had taken notes consistently remembered a higher proportion of key facts compared to those who did not. The non-note-taking students remembered 40 per cent of points covered in the lecture, but much of this material was extraneous.

This suggests that when we write, and actually before the act of writing, we are putting some degree of thought into evaluating and ordering the information that we are receiving. It is quite probably this process, rather than the taking of notes in itself, that helps fix ideas more firmly in our minds. Research suggests that when we write something down, as far as our brain is concerned, it is as if we were actually doing that thing. In this regard writing seems to act as a kind of rehearsal for doing and it leads to greater acts of memory, or *memorisation*, in much the same way that visualising the performance of a new skill can improve our skill level and athletes' visualising of victory has become an accepted part of a sports coach's training technique.

Maybe so or maybe not. Plato, no less, wrote in *The Phaedrus* that the written word is the enemy of memory. In Plato's work Socrates tells the story of the god, Ammon, who offers King Thamus the gift of letters, which would give the Egyptians better memories. Thamus replies that Ammon's discovery will actually create forgetfulness in the learners, because having events written down will lead to the erasure of memories; the Egyptians would place their trust in the external written characters and lose the ability to remember for themselves. Thamus goes on to say that Ammon's words are not aids to memory so much as reminiscence and that words will lead not to truth, but only to its semblance. Might Socrates have been right? Might writing things down actually impede our ability to remember?

In 1927, Bluma Zeigarnik noticed that waiters who were serving her appeared only to remember orders that were in progress. As soon as the order was sent out and complete, they seemed to wipe it from their minds. Zeigarnik tested her ideas out under controlled conditions, asking groups of adults and children to perform various tasks. Half of the tasks were interrupted, to the extent that they could not possibly be concluded. At the end of the allotted time, Zeigarnik's subjects remembered the details of their interrupted tasks twice as well as the completed ones. For Zeigarnik, this was evidence of a state of tension: the human mind is driven to want to know what happens next. Its urge is toward conclusion. While other tasks are being completed, the mind will be remembering the ones it never got to finish.

Again, maybe so or maybe not. Michel de Montaigne knew a thing or two about writing and more than a bit about writing from his own past. For Montaigne nothing fixes itself more deeply in the mind than the wish to forget, so that the wish to forget invariably defeats itself. Like Montaigne, Ernest Hemingway is generally a good guide in terms of writing and in *The Strange Country* he reinvented his experience of losing a suitcase full of his work. Explaining why he finds it impossible simply to remember and re-write his lost stories, Hemingway's character cites his years as a newspaper journalist as the absolute cause: 'Because I had worked on newspapers since I was very young, I could never remember anything once I had written it down; as each day you wiped your memory clear with writing as you might wipe a blackboard clear with a sponge or a wet rag.' (Hemingway, 1987, p.612) If Hemingway's fiction here is as autobiographical as it often seemed to be then he is of the same belief as Plato. And these celebrated writers' thoughts are borne out by current research. Scores of studies suggest that people are far less able to recall information that they expect to be able to have access to in the future, remembering instead only where and how to find that information.

We have, it would appear, no accurate way of distinguishing which of our memories really happened in the ways we recall them and which are added images of events that never originally happened. We reconstruct what we think happened based on the images that our minds contain and construct; and whereas on a psychological level we might have confidence in our reconstructions, from any remotely scientific perspective most reasonable people would have to admit that their recall could not really be trusted. In key ways we can generally (and *only* generally) trust the stories and events we recall in their broad outline; but the ways in which we interpret them, especially through the doubled dilemma of remembering how we would like things to have been, are part of a highly suspect process. Effectively, we re-write and re-make the past every time we remember it.

Truth goes from bad to worse as soon as we see that the memories that are most meaningful to us are oftentimes the ones we think about the most. We dwell on them and every time we think about a memory, new details are added and others are dropped. It is a given that the more times we tell a story as though it were the truth, the more deeply ingrained our sense of the story's truth becomes. And so it goes. We continue with our versions of remembered truth with unshakeable certitude, even in the face of absolute evidence to the contrary.

Not only do we create false memories by modifying events over time, we can easily assume implanted memories. Numerous scientific experiments have shown that it is much easier than anyone might have previously supposed to implant false memories in a large percentage of the population. Researchers do this in certain ways; law enforcement officers can do it in others. According to Sue Russell, 'Not only can law enforcement unconsciously lead a witness towards identifying a suspect... but they – along with other witnesses or family members – can unconsciously contaminate a witness's memory. What those people say and do can bolster, indeed over inflate, a witness's level of certainty in their identification.' (Russell, 2012a) Misidentification, either through misremembering or by being coerced into a false belief, is far and away the single biggest common denominator in wrongful convictions and a factor in 72 per cent of US cases overturned by DNA. In half of these convictions, eyewitness testimony was not supported by physical evidence or other forms of corroboration.

A recent study conducted by the American Judicature Society found that in police line ups, fillers (people known to be innocent of the crime and placed in the line up to make up the numbers) were picked out 18.1 per cent of the time. (AJS, 2011) Itiel Dror of the University College of London draws on psychological research that shows 'time and time again no correlation between confidence and accuracy' (Doyle, 1998) and still we tend to believe that what people tell us they remember is somehow the truth. Perhaps because to doubt other people's powers of accurate recall is somehow to cast doubt on our own.

Elizabeth Loftus conducted what is now considered a classic experiment in memory research. Her experiment, which became known as 'Lost in the Mall', involved subjects who were given a pamphlet containing three accounts of real childhood events written by family members and a fourth entirely fictitious event of being lost in a shopping mall. Twenty-five per cent of all of the subjects reported remembering the fictitious event, and proceeded to elaborate on it with extensive circumstantial detail. (Loftus, 1993) Subsequent variations of this technique found that an average of 33 per cent of experimental subjects could become easily convinced that they had experienced things in childhood which had never really occurred, and these were often fairly fantastical events that could not realistically have happened at all. In another experiment Loftus led witnesses of a terrorist attack in Russia to recall seeing wounded animals lying nearby. Before the witnesses were debriefed, some had embellished the false memory with numerous details, such as seeing a dismembered cat lying in the dust. Such was the power of imaginary recall that some subjects still claimed to have seen wounded animals even after Loftus had revealed that no such animals had been there. (Loftus & Hoffman, 1989)

It would appear that once we have told a story from our past in a particular way, we do our best to stick to it even in the face of absolute proof that our versions are wrong. This goes beyond the understandable fact that we do not like to admit to being liars or (perhaps worse) easily duped. We convince ourselves of our own truth in direct proportion to the emphasis we place on accuracy in our retellings; and the more people we can get to believe our lies, the more truthful we can believe that we are. In this context, missing-children appeals to the public made by parents who subsequently turn out to be guilty of filicide actually enforce the parents' sense of innocence every time they reinforce that innocence with members of the public.

Many experiments followed those carried out by Loftus, including ones in which 50 per cent of subjects could be convinced that they had survived a vicious animal attack in childhood. One of the more famous examples is the study in which a group of subjects was brought together under the pretext that they would be dealing with fearful experiences. During the course of this particular study, an actor posing as a regular member of the group told a story about being separated from his mother whilst visiting a circus. The actor told the group how he was utterly terrified by a clown he came across. Some months later, the same subjects were invited to a follow up to the study. The subjects were separated and the researcher asked each of them questions about their own memories of frightening experiences. When they are asked whether they had any frightening experiences involving a circus, a high number retold the clown story as though it were their own. Within one year, these subjects had convinced themselves that something that never happened at all had happened to them.

We can discover this easily enough through simple tests. If, for instance, we give people a list of words to memorise that include words like 'toffee', 'candy', 'syrup', 'sugar', 'honey', 'chocolate' and 'ice cream', many people will later quite confidently remember reading the word 'sweet', despite it never having appeared on the list. The same thing happens if we list the words 'dog', 'wild', 'beast', 'bark', 'teeth' and 'savage': we remember reading the word 'bite' because we think it belongs there.

What studies and tests tell us is that, once a false memory has been implanted, the person recalling it will be unaware that it is false: we are unable to differentiate between true memories and false memories. In fact, we trust our memories so emphatically that doubt rarely enters into the equation at all. The more we trust the person implanting the memory, such as is usually the case with a parent, the more likely we are to assume the memory is our own. In describing False Memory Syndrome, Kathleen Flannery suggests that it is 'a condition in which a person's identity and interpersonal relationships are centered on a memory of traumatic experience which is actually false, but in which the person is strongly convinced. When considering FMS, it is best to remember that all individuals are prone to creating false memories.' (Flannery, 2003)

A false memory then is a fabricated and/or distorted recollection of an event that did not actually happen, or which did not happen in the ways that the remembering subject describes. We are living at a time when a television advertisement for a major Australian university (Edith Cowan) carries the tagline 'Where lecturers listen and students come first' and when allegations of abuse from many decades ago are taken at face value. Battered down by this, we have become overly sympathetic to the idea that all words carry equal weight and that the first voice we hear is the voice of truth. When we combine this with our mania for the revelation of victimhood, so that our ordinary lives are seen as extraordinary triumphs over traumatic adversity, it is little wonder that memoirs are as popular amongst us as they are and that the cynicism we carry into every other area of daily life is tempered by our belief that truths are more common than lies.

The neurologist and author Oliver Sacks explores the fallibility of memory in an article in the 2013 issue of the *New York Review of Books*. Citing his own attempts to recall the past to determine the creation of false memories, and discussing the differences between plagiarism, autoplagiarism, and cryptomnesia (when a forgotten memory reappears as an original thought), Sacks sums up: 'There is, it seems, no mechanism in the mind or the brain for ensuring the truth, or at least the veridical character, of our recollections. We have no direct access to historical truth, and what we feel or assert to be true depends as much on our imagination as our senses.' (Sacks, 2013, p.18)

We often think of our own memories as being like video recorders, accurately documenting everything that happens with perfect accuracy and clarity. In reality, and as we have seen, memory is very prone to fallacy. People can feel completely confident that their memory is accurate, but this confidence is no guarantee that a particular memory is correct. Some people, for example, claim that they have memories originating before the age of two, even though science has shown that this is very likely impossible. When a person says that they remember something from before the age of two, this is invariably a reconstructed memory, based on what they have been told by others. Memory does not generally start to form until we learn to speak and there is a strong correlation between the development of memory and the development of speech. The left inferior prefrontal lobe is undeveloped in infants, but is required for any long-term memory. The elaborate encoding required for classifying and remembering events cannot occur in an infant's brain. (French, 2009)

If we cannot always trust the things we think we remember, we cannot imagine anything that we do not first have some knowledge of. Luis Buñuel had it that:

> Our imaginations, and our dreams, are forever invading our memories; and since we are all apt to believe in the reality of our fantasies, we end up transforming our lies into truths. Of course fantasy and reality are equally personal, and equally felt, so their confusion is a matter of only relative importance.
>
> (Buñuel, 1983, p.14)

We need look no further than the former US president Ronald Reagan for proof of this:

> There was a downside to Reagan's emotional intelligence capabilities, as he displayed a certain lack of awareness, if not outright self-deception. At times he seems not to have known the difference between films he had seen or stories he had heard and the actual facts. Reagan once brought tears to the eyes of Yitzhak Shamir, then prime minister of Israel, with a story about his days with the U.S. Signal Corps recording the atrocities of German death camps at the end of World War II. The problem: Reagan spent the entire war in Hollywood recruiting for the army's film units. He had, however, seen footage from the liberated camps and, apparently, convinced himself he'd been there.
>
> (Goleman, 1998, p.83)

Whether Reagan's comments indicated the delusion of FMS or a conscious attempt to delude can never now be known. All that we can say is that fantasy and reality were blurred to the extent that an identity was made subject to a process of fictionalisation. Reagan's assertions and high-profile status were such that the lie could not survive for long without being discovered. For those of us whose assertions are smaller and whose lives are lived beyond the scrutiny of biographers, the truth of any claim is harder to determine. Perhaps we tell the greatest truths about ourselves through the lies we choose to tell? After all, the basic facts of our lives are absolute: all they tell people is where we were born, how old we are, whether we are married or single, employed or unemployed, where we live and what we earn, what car we might drive and how we spend our leisure time. When we lie, we are *choosing* to be seen in particular ways and it is in this yearning to be seen as other than we are that we most emphatically demonstrate *who* we are.

Daniel Schacter has written significant works on memory distortions and in *Searching for Memory* he adds another layer to Reagan's distortions:

> In the 1980 presidential campaign Ronald Reagan repeatedly told a story of a World War II bomber pilot who ordered his crew to bail out after his plane had been seriously damaged by an enemy hit. His young belly gunner was wounded so seriously that he was unable to evacuate the bomber. Reagan could barely hold back his tears as he uttered the pilot's heroic response: "Never mind. We'll ride it down together." The press soon realized that this story was an almost exact duplicate of a scene in the 1944 film *A Wing and a Prayer*. Reagan had apparently retained the facts but forgotten their source.
>
> (Schacter, 1996, p.50)

Montaigne's 'To the Reader' introduces us to a number of key issues, issues for which his subsequent text provides explicit illustration. This occurs because what Montaigne describes is more than (just) an introduction to the idea of the self-reflexivity of his and our time; it also speaks to the ego of those artists who place their signatures not, as is usual in visual art practices, at the bottom right-hand corner of the canvas, at the last point at which a conditioned eye will reach: as the last word. Neither is the author's name on the front cover, title page and spine, eminently visible yet always a part of the frame rather than the work. With Montaigne, the signature, the author's name, is at once enunciator and enunciated and it takes for itself the position of subject proper:

> It is here a book of good faith, reader. It warns you, right from the outset that I here envisaged no end other than a domestic and private one. Here I in no way considered your interests, nor did I look to my own glory. Such a project lies beyond my powers.... I wish to be seen here in all of my simplicity, quite natural and ordinary, without effort

nor artifice: for it is myself that I paint. Insofar here as respect for the public will allow, my flaws will be readily legible here as will my artless shape. For had I found myself amidst those nations that are said yet to live under the gentle freedom of the first laws of nature, I assure you that I would more than gladly have painted myself here in my entirety, and completely naked at that. Thus, dear reader, I am myself the subject of my book.

(Montaigne, 2004)

Montaigne's book of 1580 contained a justification for devoting a book to the 'trivial topic' of himself. Whilst admitting that his topic was relatively unimportant, he argued that this was offset by the fact that he knew his subject so much better than any other author could ever hope to know his. Montaigne's argument was that knowledge of one's self was the most complete and perfect form of understanding. Yet even thinking about the self is not universally regarded as a plausible activity. A blow to self-knowledge came from Richard E. Nisbett and Timothy Wilson who contend that people are not able to know and report on much that happens inside their own minds. People, they argue, may know something of their attitudes and opinions, but they are incapable of knowing how they arrived at them. Furthermore, if they think about their attitudes for any length of time, especially in endeavouring to assess the reasons for them, they are likely to end up in confusion. (Nisbett & Wilson, 1977, p.249)

Working backwards in order to make sense of what we remember falls into Freud's notion of *memoire volontaire*. For Freud, *memoire volontaire* was an act of memory whereas remembrance was about *memoire involontaire*. (Freud, 1963) Whilst memory strives to put the past into some semblance of chronological order, absorbing what is being remembered into a deliberate continuum with the distant past at one end and the present at the other, remembrance destroys the separation of past and present. In other words, at those moments when images from the past are triggered by sensations that are being experienced in the present, remembrance manages to fuse the past *with* the present. Through remembrance, one's past is not made subject to an act of revival so much as one of renewal. As Oscar Wilde informed us, life imitates art to a much greater degree than art imitates life. Artists invent types which are then assimilated into human behavioural patterns. Produced at the close of the nineteenth century, Wilde's epigrammatic style may have lost some of its flavour; yet his comments on the relationship between truth and art are as pertinent now as ever: when

Wilde chastised the artists of his day for presenting for public consumption their 'tedious *document humaines*', he sent a timely warning to all of us who attempt to offer up the barely repackaged self as subject. Within the context of this book and specifically within the context of this chapter, it is no Wildean wordplay to suggest that autoethnography and memoir might be as concerned with the creation of aestheticised lies as with the articulation of truth. What is revealed to the reader is always already mediated and made false by the writer's intentions, judgement and reliance on memories that may not even be real.

The late great performance monologist Spalding Gray's 'I' is clearly his own, just as the actorly Uncle Vanya's 'I' is Chekhov's. The device of 'I' is generally held to be an expression of self, a self that is particular and irreducible, and yet 'I' is available to anyone and everyone. This makes it the least particular of all words. In this way, the self in autoethnography et al. functions as a site wherein the meaning of identity is contested rather than confirmed. Life, like art, is always mediated and the space occupied by the everyday is every bit as much a product of construction as the writing that follows and seeks to record it. According to Kwame Anthony Appiah:

> Every human identity is constructed, historical; every one has its
> share of false presuppositions… invented histories, invented biologies,
> invented cultural affinities come with every identity; each is a kind of
> role that has to be scripted, structured by conventions of narrative to
> which the world never quite conforms.
>
> (Appiah, 1993, p.174)

It is true to say that postmodernism's obsessive drive toward self-reflexivity has resulted in a situation where autobiographical material has become commonplace, where what is on the one hand specific is also representative of a rapidly tiring theme. In contemporary visual art we have seen enlarged endoscopic photographs of Mona Hatoum's internal organs projected onto gallery walls, we have walked around and into Tracey Emin's tent installation, as we have peered at her unmade bed. We have looked at Piero manzoni's canned faeces, *Merda d'artsita, 100% Pure Artist's Shit* in its absolutely literal sense. We have recognised Marc Quinn's heat-reduced heads as well as those that have been deep frozen. We have gazed at Cindy Sherman's relentlessly imaged face, whether in its guise of 1940s film still, pathologist's photograph or Renaissance painting. In performance we have seen Carolee Schneemann's *Interior Scrolls* produced like a conjuror's ace from the artist's vagina; Karen Finlay's down-stage-pointing yam-juiced anus and Annie Sprinkle's *Public*

Cervix Announcement. We have watched Marina Abramovic carve stars into her flesh and scrub clean the bones of dead animals. We have looked up to see Stelarc suspended by hooks through his non-anaesthetised body as he hovers over New York streets. We have seen Orlan subjecting herself (and us) to a series of surgical reconfigurations that place cosmetic plastic surgery as art event, as we have read about Madonna owning a portion of the artist's thigh. To the extent that the self has become the subject, so the subject of self has become an accepted and acceptable theme of contemporary life.

Memory is fallible and deeply subjective. There is no clear mechanism in the mind for ensuring the truth of our recollections. What we feel and say to be true says as much about our imaginations as our senses, and perhaps the stories we tell each other are no further from the false than those memories we keep to ourselves. In the spirit of Joan Didion, many memoirists and autoethnographers would argue that what matters most is emotional truth. The narrative impulse here is not to pursue truth per se, so much as to discover and describe how the events in question felt to them. If this means compromising the reality of what actually happened in order for the writing to speak to its own emotional truth then our concerns with truth slipping away should be tempered with understanding that truth is itself a lie. The concern in creative nonfiction as to whether the writer's obligation is primarily to telling a good story or telling the truth becomes an exercise in chasing one's own tail as soon as we accept that everything we remember and everything we write is at best a partial picture of any event. Every decision is a loss, and as soon as we publish one sentence we lose the possibility of writing another in its place. Ultimately, if what we remember is not a decision we consciously make then what we write is our best attempt to craft something true from something that we only ever really wish it to be. The writing of trauma, however, drifts self-writing away from the relatively harmless toward the potentially problematic.

Memory is itself an error and trusting it completely creates another erroneous act. Memory errors include remembering events that never occurred or remembering them differently from the ways they actually happened. As science has established, there are several different types of memory errors in which people inaccurately recall details of events that did not occur. Obviously, in law the consequences of memory errors can be hugely significant and their implications are severe. In recent years we have witnessed a rise in the phenomenon of adults recovering repressed memories of traumatic events unconsciously retained in the mind; and in the headline-grabbing sense, these often relate to allegations of sexual abuse experienced in the adult rememberer's childhood and only surfacing much later in life.

The recent criminal convictions of generally elderly and wealthy figures from British media and entertainment, namely but not exclusively Stuart Hall, Jimmy Savile, Rolf Harris, Dave Lee Travis and Max Clifford, were widely reported as though they were true long before the cases went to court. The notion of innocence until guilt was proven seemed to dissolve in the public's mind as soon as a plaintiff said 'I remember…', as though allegations based on memories that were repressed for one reason or another are demanding of our sympathy and belief before their truth has been established in court. Innocence until guilt has been proven is a central tenet of our judicial system and yet we are quick to rush to judgement as soon as an accuser's claims appear to be driven by memory. I am not suggesting for one moment that these men were innocent; merely that where criminality is concerned, guilt needs to be established and proven rather than remembered. 'I know, because I was there' is a mantra, not a statement of absolute fact.

Freud described the workings of memory as a series of impressions made on the psychic apparatus. Freud's memory traces differ in the conscious and unconscious realms of the mind whilst remaining in constant contact and communication. Freud made sense of this through his analogy of the mystic writing pad, a slab of wax veiled in a celluloid sheet: impressions become memories precisely because they leave a permanent trace on the underlying wax slab even when they have been removed from the overlaying celluloid. For Freud, the wax slab represents the unconscious that stores every trace made on the mind sheet that directly receives the impressions of everyday life. But, just as traces on the wax slab are only legible in suitable lights, so the imprints on the unconscious only make themselves known in slippages of the tongue, or in speech with an analyst. The problem is that analysis can lead as well as uncover.

Just as there are no records of spiritualism before 1848, when Kate and Margaret Fox began hoaxing in Hydesville, New York, there is no documented writing about repressed memories before the 1800s. The concept of repressed memory originated with Freud in his 1896 essay *On the Etiology of Hysteria*. One of the studies published in his essay involved a young woman referred to as 'Anna O'. Among her many ailments, she suffered from paralysis on the right side of her body. Freud believed that her symptoms were caused by psychological traumas, so that painful memories had separated from her consciousness and brought harm to her body. Freud used hypnosis to treat Anna O and she apparently gained some mobility in her right side. Since this time, repressed memory has remained a heavily debated topic inside of Freud's psychoanalytic philosophy. Our current understanding of the placebo effect in medication forces us to consider the impact a therapist's words can have on a patient's beliefs and it is not currently possible to distinguish a true repressed memory from a false one without corroborating evidence.

Memories *can* be accurate, but they are not *always* accurate. Memories of events are always a mix of factual traces of sensory information overlaid with emotions, mingled with interpretation and filled in with our own conscious and subconscious imaginings. Thus we should always be at least a little sceptical about how valid our memories are as evidence of any factual details. The problem with acknowledging the flawed nature of what we remember is that our memories often work to confirm our sense of bias. Memory bias is the altering influence of present knowledge, beliefs and feelings on memories of previous experiences so that what we remember from the past comes to say more about what we believe, feel and want than about what actually took place. There are at least three types of memory bias. The first, Consistency Bias, occurs when we reconstruct the past to fit the present; the second is Change Bias, which manifests itself in the tendency to exaggerate the difference between what we believe in the present and what we believed in the past; the third, Egocentric Bias, is a derivation of Change Bias inasmuch as it is the tendency to exaggerate the change between the past and the present in order to make ourselves appear somewhat better than we are. It is axiomatic that we are unlikely to recognise these aspects of our own remembering, and less likely still to acknowledge them.

And so bias becomes buried in certitude. And nothing seems more certain than print. Not every sentence we write can end with a question mark in lieu of a full stop but some small acknowledgement that what we know of the past is only ever what we *think* and *wish* would do much to make room for a healthy dose of doubt. We would do well, when we engage in autoethnography or memoir, to question hard the memories we tell ourselves are truths; because memory, assumed without verification to be legitimate, can lay false trails and because the events that for researchers are most worth telling and which carry the most impact for writers to use are the self-same ones that our minds are least likely to acknowledge as inaccurate and laden with bias.

Hard though it is for us to accept, memory does not actually correspond to past events, but to our past experiences; and the act of experiencing rarely corresponds to the reality of the events as they occurred. Because of this we have to acknowledge that our memories are susceptible to distorting effects based on cognitive processes unrelated to the truth of the circumstances in the world as it exists outside of ourselves. Memories are simply imaginative reconstructions of past events and the experience of remembering is determined as much by the remembering subject's expectations regarding what should or could have happened as what actually did. Neither the memoirist nor the autoethnographer provides a record of what took place and when; rather they judge and edit, omit and interpret, reorganise, compose and invent. The idea that there is an essential distinction based on authenticity between works of imagination on the one hand and records of facts and events on the other does not stand up to close examination. All narrative writing is fiction and all (in the non-qualitative sense) is creative. The only genuine distinction that exists is that one form knows (as do its readers) that invention is overt, whilst the other form pretends (as do its readers) that invention is absent. The fact is, these two forms – fact writing and fiction – have their origins in the oral traditions of poetry; and both involve similar processes of mobilising the same faculties of memory and imagination. In this way it can be said that a fiction writer like Shakespeare is the historian of his or her present and the autoethnographer, like Carolyn Ellis, is the novelist of his or her past. Both types of writer invent the truth to suit their needs and each sacrifices documentary detail for narrative expression.

That which we do not willingly sacrifice, we simply lose sight of; and everything we remember exposes the things we forget. The space between the black words and lines is loaded with this white absence. Perhaps the documents we write that are based on memory serve less to conserve what we know as to expel from the archive all of those things we no longer recall. In this sense, we might not write our narratives of truth in order to remember, so much as to deny forever the existence of all of those things we have either forgotten or decided to exclude. If the written text of memoir or autoethnography is a typed out exercise in guesswork, it is also a reinvention of the material we have already forgotten.

Autoethnographers and memoirists draw on personal experiences to inform their writing and the form is defined by researchers including their memories and experiences as data in their work. Regardless of the inclinations of the individual researcher, its embrace is fundamentally postmodern, with ostensibly objective studies of the other morphing into studies of the self's place within certain societies. As researchers we look to relate the intimacies of private life to the sociology of public issues, focusing often on the ephemeral, the hidden and the sub-cultural, and we utilise our own subjectivity in order to bear witness. We do this by observing and reflecting on the experiences of others in ways that fuse our first-person subjective experiences with the third-person worlds we are writing in, offering testimony to, as Andrew Sparkes describes it, 'truth that is generally unrecognised or suppressed'. (Sparkes, 2002, p.221) If this does not lead automatically to the contestation of differing world views, it does reframe and remake events that happen in the world into events that are shaped and skewed by description.

When our studies of other are defined by rather than filtered through our conscious and subconscious sense of self, many issues emerge. We can manage these with all the good will in the world, but disregarding the fact that the things we think we saw and experienced may not quite be so undoes much of this. This does not amount to a throwing of one's hands in the air and a refusal to research and to write. Just as we cannot control what and how we remember, changing what occurred in the act of writing is inevitable. More than this, it is what makes writing work. Autoethnography integrates a personal and cultural lens and its writing (like all writing) is a creative act. Attempts at accuracy and reliability are tempered by the fact that the unreliability of the mind is magnificent, with a seemingly boundless capacity to remember details that did not exist and to fictionalise the things that did. The issue is not that we should not write about what happened because it may not have happened that way and because writing remakes memory; the issue is simply that we would do well to remember that what we remember is not something neutral waiting for a perspective – our perspectives have already determined how we remember.

For Clifford Geertz the function of a researcher's field note is that it inscribes social discourse; that in the act of writing down what he or she sees, the researcher 'turns it from a passing event, which exists only in its own moment of occurrence, into an account, which exists in its inscription and can be consulted'. (Geertz, 1968, p.141) Absolutely so; but because there is always more going on than the researcher can notice, and because we notice the things we are looking for, the act of inscription will create as much as it records. Field notes offer partial, subjective and constructed narratives of events. How could they not? There is no negative issue with partiality; only with partiality and prejudice that does not recognise its own limitations.

The process of taking field notes, Richard Emerson and friends tell us, 'is both intuitive, reflecting the ethnographer's changing sense of what might possibly be made interesting or important to future readers, and empathetic, reflecting the ethnographer's sense of what is interesting or important to the people he is observing'. (Emerson et al., 1995, p.11) Reading my own notes for this book's chapters reveals a top-slicing of ideas that allows me to write what I want in the ways that I want to. Not much neutrality there. Referencing the theorists I draw on and providing an extensive bibliography thus creates accuracy without in any way offering something that is balanced, unbiased and *true*. The knowledge that this book is highly unlikely to be the only book on its subject that its readers will encounter goes some way toward licensing a partiality that is designed to forward a certain view. Writing about a social group when one's writing is the only published work in that field licenses partiality somewhat differently.

Imagination is not possible without memory and the processes of remembering and imagining are not easily distinguished. No bad thing as long as we remain aware of the overlap; and this knowledge puts us in good company. Alexander Graham Bell believed that our most original compositions are composed exclusively of expressions derived from others; and in a pre-Barthes' moment, Mark Twain wrote that 'substantially all ideas are second-hand, consciously and unconsciously drawn from a million outside sources'. (Popova, 2012) As was, I suspect, every line of this chapter that now draws to a close.

Every line of my own, I should stress, rather than every line of Steph Brocken's. In this fourth case study, Brocken cuts to the heart of issues of data collection, through reflecting critically on work with her chosen participant group. Brocken's commitment to developing approaches which aimed at all times for the researcher to hold onto awareness of the effects of her methods on the group she was working with are clear throughout, as is her critique of the idea of the researcher as an *ipso facto* agent of empowerment.

Two Case Studies 'Against Basic Chorus'

Steph Brocken

Based on a Presentation given at 'Drama – The Intercultural Dimension', 16th March 2013, University of Chester

My research focuses on the uses of interdisciplinary and contemporary arts practices in work with children and young people in non-formal education settings and the impact that this can have on young people's social and political development.

I am currently undertaking my second year of study. This year has been primarily focused on the collection of data from my chosen participant group. I elected to use a case-study methodology to collect this data, using the youth theatre (Minerva Youth Theatre) that I run as the research participants. The Minerva Youth Theatre is a group of 16 young people aged between 11 and 18 with varying abilities and experience in the performing arts. I studied them over a period of six months during the creation of a piece of performance that was entitled *Against Basic Chorus*. This was a piece based on the text of *Antigone*, edited, adapted and added to by the young people in line with key themes that they established as part of the process.

The case study is a well-documented method that allows for the collection of in-depth information. 'Case study is the study of the particularity and complexity of a single case, coming to understand its activity within important circumstances'. (Stake, cited by Winston in Ackroyd, 2007, p.41) I decided that this was the method best suited for this study as it allows for the group to be observed in real-life circumstances. This is a pre-existing group of young people that meet regularly once a week during the school term to learn drama skills and work towards plays and performances. The case-study approach allows for their general working process to remain as uninterrupted as possible, enabling me, as the researcher, to gain an accurate perception of the effects of the methods and work that we undertake with them.

Due to the nature of the group as pre-dating the research process and the focus on democracy of process that is integral to the research, I was keen to ensure that the group itself was involved in the research process as much as possible. For me, this goes beyond the notion of simply providing informed consent forms and actually involved, in the first instance, the group choosing their own methods of data collection. This decision was heavily influenced by Kathleen Gallagher's work on co-construction of research methods and her assertion that we should ask our groups what the best way of collecting information from them is.

Gallagher, in her chapter '(Post)Critical Ethnography in Drama Research', talks of Critical Ethnography as being 'openly ideological' and exposing 'the possibilities of human agency'. (Gallagher in Ackroyd, 2007, p.64) I took this as an excellent starting point for establishing the methodologies at work behind this study as we are consciously tying in notions of arts-based learning, albeit in an extra-curricular context, with the social, personal and political awareness and development of the young people involved. Gallagher refers to Quantz's assertion that 'culture should always be understood to refer to both the structured patterns of a group and the meanings members give to those patterns' (Quantz, 1992 cited by Gallagher in Ackroyd, 2007) leading her on to describe how, prior to each observation in the piece of work in question, 'each ethnographer approached a participant and asked her/him the following: How can I best observe you/your work to gain the most insight?' (Gallagher in Ackroyd, 2007, p.70) This idea of asking for the advice of the participant seemed to chime well with the ethos of my research; if we are searching for a democracy in process then we must try to be as democratic as possible in the ways in which we observe and analyse the process.

A further important influence on the notion of co-construction in methodology is the work of Lisa Loutzenheiser. Loutzenheiser's article 'Working Alterity: The Impossibility of Ethical Research with Youth' highlights the use and mis-use of the buzz-term 'giving voice' when working with young people. She asserts that the 'common place usage of terms such as giving voice and empowerment through voice leave in place particular (stereotypical) ideas of young people that perpetuate and exacerbate relations of domination'. (Loutzenheiser, 2007, p.113) This is suggesting that we have a tendency in work with young people to assume that voice is something that can be distributed, in a linear fashion from those with power (us) to those without (the young people); that the young people are somehow incomplete in their ability to articulate experience or opinion. What Loutzenheiser suggests is for research to highlight the pre-existence of the young person's voice without the need for it to be mediated by the researcher. One approach she suggests is the use of Polyvocality, 'upsetting the flow of the academic narrative by interspersing youths' [unedited] text throughout the piece'. (Loutzenheiser, 2007, p.119)

This move towards the precedence of the un-edited voice of the young person dovetails with notions of co-construction, as through asking our participants how they wish to be investigated, we are creating an opening for their voice to be heard in the early stages. Additionally, one of the methods chosen by the young people in my case was video interviewing, allowing me access to the voices of the young people and enabling me in my own work to move towards the polyvocality that Loutzenheiser speaks of.

Details of the workshop that was held can be found below:

> **Games and Warm-up Exercises**: *Round the Circle, Guardian of the Keys, Bomb and Shield, Triangle*

Initial Exercise: Two truths, one lie

Introduce group to purpose of session and refresh the research and its objectives.

Session Introduction: Looking at the media and how we get people to share information with us. In this session you are going to be taking the role of journalists.

The group splits into five groups and each goes to a different corner of the room where there is a recent media story pinned to the wall. Each group will also be given a method through which it is going to collect information about this story. The participants then have 20 minutes to think of how they are going to collect this information whilst staying in role as journalists. The methods are: Focus Group, Unstructured Questionnaire, Solo Structured Interview, Structured Questionnaire, and Solo Unstructured Interview. Each of the methods came with an easy to follow description.

One member (or more) of the group then switches character to become someone involved in the story and the group must try and use its given method on them.

We then shared what we had done and gave feedback on how easy/useful each group thought its method had been.

Observation Exercise: The group then split in two with one half given a task to work on and the other observing. Half of the observer group was instructed to watch and observe generally, the other to look out for particular thing during the group's working process. We then fed back on how this process worked and how successful/useful the group thought it was.

Final Exercise: Sheets were put up around the room with the different choices as to collection methods on them. The group were asked to go around and draw smiley faces next to the ones that they thought were the best and most useful for them. We then discussed the options that they had chosen and made sure that the group were happy with the final outcome.

The results of the workshops were that the group elected to use 'participant observers', two members of the group who would be chosen to 'keep their eyes and ears open' to events and processes in weekly sessions and who, at the end of a two- or three-week cycle, would be interviewed by me. The group was given the choice as to who should devise and conduct the interviews and I was chosen in both cases. At the conclusion of the process, the group also stated that a general semi-structured evaluation questionnaire should be completed.

In her paper with Anne Wessels 'Emergent Pedagogy and Affect in Collaborative Research: A Metho-pedagogical Paradigm', Kathleen Gallagher pinpoints and assesses a concern within drama-based pedagogical research that is extremely relevant to this study. The metho-pedagogical paradigm exists when the lines between the researcher and the facilitator/teacher are blurred; this was extremely relevant in the case of my work as I am at once the researcher and the group's regular director/workshop leader. Gallagher's work highlights the 'alignment of the goals of the research with the goals of the pedagogy'; (Gallagher & Wessels, 2011, p.244) the co-creation between the 'teacher' and 'students' of both the research and the pedagogy; and the involvement of the research team within the process: 'we recorded digital video footage and made fieldnotes but were also fully integrated into every aspect of the pedagogy and class activities as they emerged'. (Gallagher & Wessels, 2011, p.244) In the context of the work that Gallagher describes, there is often a conflict that arises between the 'metho' and the 'pedagogical' in the eyes of both the researcher and the 'student'. Such a conflict may manifest itself, in the context of this project, as a disruption of the focus of the working process – i.e. in myself spending more time on the interviewing/observing elements rather than on teaching/directing the young people; or in the young people beginning to perceive the project as 'boring' if practical elements become secondary.

This was something that I wanted to minimise from the perspective of the young people, but also, if it became an issue for me personally, something I was planning to embrace rather than ignore. As such, the participant interviews that were to take place once every two-to-three weeks were conducted at the start of sessions so as not to isolate either myself or the interviewee from the rest of the group. Additionally, the research itself was rarely referred to during normal practical sessions, only when it was time to choose new participant observers. It was also ensured, as part of weekly planning, that the balance of activity with sessions would always fall in the favour of practical activity rather than long discussions. As such, the group seemed to grow to see the regular interviews as just a natural part of their process, and to see me as very much their director/facilitator and not an outside eye. It was also decided that I would keep a regular journal of the process throughout, ensuring that my observations and experiences were not excluded from the narrative of the project. This serves to underline my involvement within the group and the intrinsic relevance to the project of my own reflections and my own development as a practitioner.

In order to demonstrate some of the emergent themes of this research so far, I will now share two stories from the creative process.

The first features a participant who we will call Participant A (PA). PA was a new member of the group in September. She was outgoing and a little bit boisterous, occasionally disruptive and for a good few weeks seemed unwilling to give 100 per cent to some of the more unusual activities that we do at MYT (Minerva Youth Theatre). She was clearly familiar with drama as an art form and seemed to have quite set ideas as to what she saw 'drama' as, showing enthusiasm when it came to improvisation exercises but also being quite reticent to get up and perform on her own. The reflections in my weekly journal refer to PA's tendency to take a literal approach to any stimuli that I was providing, often leading to group performances involving this member noticeably being less successful than others. It was during weeks 5 and 6 that the problems with PA seemed to really surface in group work and it was evident that her approach was beginning to effectively 'drag down' two of our older and more experienced members. However, after these two weeks there were indications that PA was beginning to show gradual improvement and, by Week 11, it was clear that she had improved in both her performance and interpretation skills and her group work.

The culmination of PA's 'transformation' came in Week 1 of Term 2. That week I had chosen her to take part in the blocking of the first scene of the final piece. This was the first week that we were launching into intensive work with the group and the first experience for the new members of being directed by me. PA was not my first choice to take the role in this scene but the member I had originally wanted was not present that day so I decided to give PA a challenge. She rose to this challenge fully. I feel that the best way of conveying the event is to share the entry that I made in my weekly journal that week.

> As we read through the script and worked through it, I was able to pinpoint
> the elements of it that we needed to highlight for the purposes of our
> interpretation of the piece and the girls seemed to understand well and
> respond to this. It was interesting to observe the effectiveness of the learning
> process that they are going through from their response to direction that is

clearly linked to the themes and ideas that we are exploring. In particular, a section where Ismene speaks about the fact that, as a woman, it is not her place to stand up against authority, I had directed the actor to take on the physicality of a stereotypical woman, upright posture and clasping her hands in front of her. To this, the actor added a marked change in voice, illustrating an awareness of the need for us to highlight this passage as key to one of our themes of feminism and also a sense of freedom in using stark juxtapositions in the performance. She was not worried about it sounding 'odd', simply focussing on making this particular characterisation visible to the audience. This scene was extremely successful and will be very powerful in performance.

This event made me think about the ways in which we can observe and define a learning process. This event also helped to define the different strands of learning that take place during YT sessions, the artistic learning, the thematic learning and the personal learning. This process seems to be an unconscious one, a 'developing familiarity' with the artistic and thematic materials that are presented, facilitated by improvements in the personal sphere. The concept of the four stages of competence, developed by Noel Burch and oft attributed to Abraham Maslow (Chapman, 2007), may be applied here.

The model suggests that we move through four stages when learning something new: unconscious incompetence, conscious incompetence, conscious competence and unconscious competence. It would appear that by this stage PA had reached the unconscious competence stage, reflected in the instinctive responses that she had to both my direction and the text during that rehearsal. However, there would seem to be something else at play here, perhaps more than this approach can tell us. The engagement that PA showed is more in-depth than unconscious competence. The idea of being able to perform a task without thinking both applies and yet fails to apply as the responses are instinctive yet they are at the same time reflective of a deeper thought process at play. Perhaps it is this thought process that is the unconscious competence task.

The second anecdote concerns a participant who we will call PB. PB was also a new member this year but is an older and more experienced young person. PB has always shown a great deal of enthusiasm for all of our activities and always gets stuck in. However, this changed when we held a dance workshop. This workshop was not led by me but by a guest practitioner who was brought in specifically to choreograph a dance opening to the performance. PB initially threw himself into the warm-up activities but when the group was split into smaller groups, he began to show resistance. Their group began literally to follow the stimulus that they were given, that the movement piece was to be based on a fight; and as a result were blocking a far more naturalistic version of a fight scene than we had intended them to do. I went over to the group at this point to try and pull them round to where we needed them to be.

On reflection, it was at this point that I made a big mistake in my use of language by saying to them 'It's a dance, not a fight'. From this point on, PB effectively withdrew from the process, finding it more and more difficult to engage, obstructing his group and not allowing them to explore any further ideas. Initially he asked to be allowed to step out of the process, but this is not something that, as a group, we are keen to allow as we believe that it is important for members to step outside their comfort zones to develop their skills and confidence, so he was encouraged to remain with the group. This process was aided by one of our volunteers who went over to talk to him, trying to encourage him gently to re-engage; but for the remainder of the session he remained fairly detached. Although, when speaking to him at the end of the session, it was clear that he did understand why we had not let him step out, and the importance of trying new things, it was a shocking process to go through with this person who is usually one of the most engaged members of the group.

Although a difficult event to have to deal with, on reflection it did tell me several things about the process that we have been asking our participants to go through. I feel that my own personal use of the word 'dance' in that initial exchange did a lot to exclude PB from the process as the reference to this art form can be off-putting – as with any reference to a specific art form. This highlights a key argument of this study and a way in which we can justify the use of interdisciplinary methods with children and young people: that often terminology serves to exclude young people from engaging with the arts and with whatever themes or ideas one is trying to explore with them. This incident goes to show that even young people who are already engaged in practice in one art form are not immune from this effect of being 'turned off' an activity through it being referred to by its 'official' terminology.

In the work that we do, we are aiming to blur these boundaries to throw out such terminology and encourage our members to become holistic performance makers who are comfortable with stepping outside their comfort zones. However, we must learn from incidents such as this to continue our commitment to refraining from using terminology and also to create a balance between remaining sensitive to our participants' experience and likes and dislikes whilst still pushing them to achieve and stretch themselves.

The key threads that emerged through these two anecdotes – that of defining and characterising the learning process that the young people go through; and the use of art-form terminology – are both areas in which further research will be undertaken in the next stages of the study.

References

Ackroyd, J. (ed.) (2007) *Research Methodologies for Drama Education.* Stoke on Trent and Stirling, USA: Trentham Books Ltd.

Chapman, A. (2007) 'Conscious Competence Learning Model', available from: http://www.businessballs.com/consciouscompetencelearningmodel.htm

Gallagher, K., & A. Wessels (2011) 'Emergent Pedagogy and Affect in Collaborative Research: A Metho-pedagogical Paradigm', *Pedagogy, Culture and Society* 19(2), pp.239–58

Loutzenheiser, L. (2007) 'Working Alterity: The Impossibility of Ethical Research with Youth', *Education Studies* (AESA) 41(2), pp.109–27

The girl I used to be
Has a terrible case of mistaken identity
And yesterday's girl is not what you see
It's a terrible case of mistaken identity

Delta Goodrem

CHAPTER FIVE

Autoethnographic Performance/ Performing Autoethnography

Performativity after Austin; self and solo performance; Lejeune's autobiographical pact and Boal's maieutics; Spalding Gray and fiction as fact; John Leguizamo, Tami Spry and Norman Denzin; feminism and empowerment; postmodern narratology; practice as research; outlaw genres; Jamie Coull's case study

Henri Matisse advised us that whoever wishes to devote a life to painting should begin by cutting out their tongue: warning, if ever we needed it, that doing art and then writing about it are regarded with historical suspicion. If previous chapters had a focus on the fallibility of memory and on the ethics of writing autoethnography, this chapter is on its performance. And at our current point in history this is no simple thing to describe.

As is the case with autoethnography, the term 'performance' remains rigorously unfixed and the idea of performativity even more so. Performativity is regularly traced back to J.L. Austin's references to performative utterance as declarations that, in the moment of being spoken, can cause certain acts to be performed. In the classic and most obvious examples, the words spoken by certain people in certain contexts *make* other people married or under arrest or imprisoned: the words do what they say they will. In this context, saying 'I love you' is not a performative declaration because whilst it may well lead to an outcome, this is not in and of itself prescribed in the words. Saying 'I do' during a wedding service is performative because the words create the deed. A jury declaring a verdict of 'not guilty' in a courtroom is similarly performative in that it frees the defendant both from blame and from consequence. There are remarkably few phrases in the English language that are objectively performative: a police officer saying 'You are under arrest' is perhaps the most obvious example of a phrase performing its own action, i.e. it is a phrase in which the words *are the action*.

Performativity has a wider sense too of describing the daily behaviour of individuals based on habits or social norms. Following Foucault, Judith Butler and Eve Kosofsky Sedgewick have written expertly on the ways in which social norms are strategies of both construction and control, making performativity that which possesses the power to produce the phenomenon that it also regulates and constrains.

These critics are not alone in their exploration of the ways in which gender impacts on the performativity of the narrative act and also on its pragmatic relations. Butler draws on speech-act concepts of performativity in order to reappraise the gendered relation between author, narrator and point of view, arguing for a contextualist narratology that aims to investigate how texts like bodies *perform* sex, gender and sexuality. This approach insists that the performativity of gender in narratives possesses an ideological dimension that cannot be appreciated without attending to the specific social functions in which those narratives take place.

Karen Barad similarly looks to separate performativity from description:

> A *performative* understanding of discursive practices challenges the representationalist belief in the power of words to represent pre-existing things. Performativity, properly construed, is not an invitation to turn everything (including material bodies) into words; on the contrary, performativity is precisely a contestation of the excessive power granted to language to determine what is real. Hence, in ironic contrast to the misconception that would equate performativity with a form of linguistic monism that takes language to be the stuff of reality, performativity is actually a contestation of the unexamined habits of mind that grant language and other forms of representation more power in determining our ontologies than they deserve...
>
> (Barad, 2007, p.133)

In this way, even our seemingly most personal and private acts and desires are seen to be scripted by the hegemony of social convention. In a similar vein, Dwight Conquergood's call for a performative politics that focuses on the culturally lived experiences of the oppressed and the nomadic in situations of upheaval and displacement sees performance as an agency for change and as a process that takes place on the social rather than the theatrical stage.

We can understand performativity then in its Austinesque sense of language doing more than simply stating facts, being also able to function as its own kind of action. Statements such as 'You are under arrest' do not describe a condition so much as make something happen, as with Austin's *performative utterances*; and we can read performativity in its iteration of habitual behaviour. There is, however, another sense of the term. If we look at a map and say, for example, 'this is the route one would take to get from Point A to Point B', the statement can be regarded as performative when it creates the behaviour it describes. The words might not be status changing like those that cause people to be married or put under arrest or found guilty of a crime; but if a path gets worn in the ground between Point A and Point B as a consequence of the words then performative statements do not *reflect* reality, as they do in the case of the declarative statement 'this is a page in a book', but *intervene* in it. Performativity is then an engine for change rather than the record of it and a statement or action becomes performative when its use increases its predictive capabilities.

Performativity and performance are interdisciplinary concepts that have emerged in linguistics and the philosophy of language, in performance, theatre and literary studies, as well as in ethnology, sociology and cultural studies. Although the terms 'performative', 'performance' and 'performativity' are frequently used across a broad range of narratological investigations, and despite the fact that they have received rigorous systematic treatment in this field, to date no authoritative distinctions exist.

In approaching performance as that which hovers between forces of accommodation and resistance, Conquergood denounces continuity, pattern and convention in favour of 'process, change, improvisation and struggle'. (Conquergood, 2013, p.56) In connecting performance with social and cultural life, the politics of identity and everyday behaviour are brought into the light, exposing some of the ways in which categories of race, gender, sexuality and class are determined less by biological imperatives than by social acts of repetition, which are always already innately performative. In an expansion of Austin's term, performativity is thus seen as crucial to disenfranchised communities that function without the privileges afforded to more dominant cultures.

If this goes some way towards connecting performativity with autoethnography, it is matched by autoethnography's urge toward acknowledging the gulf between the researcher and the researched. In theatre, this shift has taken us away from plays about working-class lives, written by predominantly middle-class writers for almost exclusively middle-class audiences in theatres that in every aspect of their being exclude the very subjects they depict. If the reverse of this pornography of class is a tone that is occasionally more patronising than empathic then at least it is a tone of somewhat better intent; and intent does matter, even if it is not always quite *enough*. Concerned as they are with identity construction, conditioning, interaction, the *making real* rather than the *rendering false*, and with *making* rather than *faking*, performance and performativity are at once distinct from dramatisation at the same time as they are inclusive of it. Performance is locating itself increasingly within a sense of interdisciplinarity beyond the arts and into the social sciences; and just as we have given up the security blanket of methodological certainty within research, so have we moved on apace from notions of performance that are limited to learning the lines and avoiding the carefully placed items of on-stage furniture.

Norman Denzin (1997) has argued that there are key requirements that autoethnographic performance should satisfy. For Denzin, autoethnographic performance should unsettle, criticise and challenge taken-for-granted, repressed meanings; invite moral and ethical dialogue at the same time as it reflexively clarifies its own moral positions; engender resistance and offer utopian thoughts about how things can be made different (if not always better); demonstrate kindness; show instead of tell; exhibit interpretive sufficiency and representational adequacy that is authentic; and present political, functional, collective and committed viewpoints. Denzin's views follow Ellis and Bochner's and, along with Tami Spry's various writings, they have become something of a *sine qua non* when it comes to performing autoethnography.

The issue of representational authenticity is no less vexed in autoethnography than in any other form; but for the rest of Denzin's list, wouldn't we say that most good or effective performance attempts this? And if that is the case, then doesn't autoethnographic performance lose precisely the same currency that Denzin et al. are seeking to claim? Showing instead of telling is a given of most performance modes; there would be examples we could find from every period that unsettled, criticised and challenged accepted thought; much theatre strives for social betterment; much is committed; much displays a sense of collective morality and much would see itself as kind. From the Greek theatre of Aeschylus through to the work of our most current post-dramatic moment, performance thrives on the stuff of Denzin's list.

What we find beneath the veneer of Denzin's logic is the essence of most drama that exists beyond the desire only to entertain. If Denzin's criteria provide a list we would do well to follow then every dramatist of weight, along with every poet, novelist and songwriter, is an autoethnographic performer. And if the likes of Dylan and Springsteen, Scott and Coetzee, Kane and Mamet are already doing or have done this work *par excellence* then what might the role of an autoethnographic performance scholar be, other than to make a possibly inferior job of things?

Because Denzin's list is so emphatically *right*, the question is not what autoethnographic performance can *do* (we know well what it can do) so much as what might it do when it is not done particularly well; for this is what happens with deadening regularity when social scientists move into performance with little more than a checklist of dos and don'ts and the urge to lend vocal delivery to the written word. It needs saying that the reverse is also true. Performers are increasingly adopting the techniques of social studies in order to frame their practice in a critical exegesis or otherwise contextualising frame; and just as social scientists do not necessarily make good performers so the creative production of research through performance is often let down by an inability to analyse rather than merely describe.

It would seem an act of common sense to assume that any and all theses by performers (or other creative practitioners) are qualified by dint of their university approval, so that a successful PhD thesis *defines* a work as successful. I am not so sure. For those of us whose research students work in the fields of creative production, the urge to see quality where little of worth actually exists is stronger than we might care to admit. In this sense, creative production as research (which often now means *creative production as thesis*) has assumed an almost religious sanctity so that it is rarely, if ever, challenged from within. On the contrary, its qualities are often exaggerated and its failings reduced. A similar thing happens with autoehnography and memoir: when our academic careers are built on the championing of a certain approach, it is all too easy to adopt a position of entrenchment that sees any criticism as an act of hostility from off-the-pace and old-school colleagues bent on destroying the things that we love. University lecturers thus often defend their own positions through defending the work of their students.

Not all readers will be aware of the ways in which internal and external examiners are determined for PhD theses. It is common practice for supervisors to discuss favoured examiners with their research students, placing potential examiners in order of preference. Under these circumstances the idea of an objective examiner is somewhat questionable. This is not to suggest any academic chicanery, only to say that at many universities the system allows for more manipulation by supervisors and their students than members of the public might think. The aim of supervisors is almost always to see their students pass, not least because promotion is often linked to successful supervisions. At the time of writing, the Australian university at which I have an adjunct role operates a process whereby research points gained in one calendar year allow lecturers to claim against these the following year. In this system, a successful PhD supervision is worth 400 points (the same as for a sole-authored book). An unsuccessful completion, i.e. a student that fails, is worth zero points.

Research points translate into a for-kind cash equivalent, used to fund research trips and such like. Another aspect of successful supervision is that varying levels of appointment (lecturer, senior lecturer, associate professor, reader and professor) carry with them certain expectations, which after time assume the status of demands relating to one's annual research points. Two successful supervisions in any one year would comfortably satisfy the annual expectation of all but those lecturers and professors on research-only contracts. There is a fine line between championing the new and the maintaining of standards, and the line is fine enough for us to dance hither and thither across it in the hope that our chicken-skip steps will not always be seen.

As with research ethics forms, checklists like Denzin's tell us so much, and then they tell us nothing at all. With autobiographical work, performers feel compelled to go public because they believe that their lives matter, that their stories deserve and even need to be told. In both content and form, autobiography is drawn from this moment of realisation, liberation and externalisation. Autoethnography differs in that, whilst it can present an individual performer's perspective, it is one that draws on and connects to a collective understanding. It is a site for recognising communities as well as individuals, for understanding self as something that is innately relational. Autoethnographical research stresses group allegiances, leading to analytical reflections on one's own experiences located within an identified cultural grouping. In the performance terms that apply to this chapter, autoethnography is about work that draws on personal experience and which foregrounds this as a meaning-making endeavour to engage the broader social issues of a given community.

'Truth is what theatre is all about', goes the apocryphal quote, 'and if you can fake that you'll go far.' Wanting to know is always a worthless aim if the aim is not to know the truth. And nowhere is the word 'truth' used with less discretion than in the theatre; so that Brecht is truthful, as are Stanislavski, Shakespeare, Beckett, Grotowski, Kane, Mitchell, Artaud and so on. Actors speak blithely about giving truthful performances whilst directors urge them to find the truth of the moment, the truth of the scene, the truth of the text. In a relativist-obsessed world where the legacy of postmodernism puts truth always in inverted commas, the word is alive, well and unhindered by the punctuation police in countless rehearsal studios as well as in every theatre critic's cut and paste. But what could truth ever be in theatre if it is not the lie well-told? When the mighty David Mamet writes that theatre is the one place in the world (the last place in the world) where we can go to hear the truth, the words seem profound, as well as profoundly true; but really, what life could be worth the living if things were so?

It is worth stressing that we are not talking here about performative events which claim to testify sincerely to certain truths, the type of world that plays host to verbatim theatre; we are considering staged works which explore real experience in order to stress the referential authenticity of the work. Verbatim theatre is itself subject to the playwright's sense of order, edit and tone; and even when the words are hewn directly from everyday *real* life, their utterance in an on-stage world changes everything. What gets changed is not necessarily a reduction: the art might well tell us more, in its concentrated form, than the events ever could. But if this is possible, so too is the reverse. In either case, 'verbatim theatre' remains a more slippery term than most of its followers would wish. In significant part, what gets slipped by us is fiction masquerading as fact, and this is a masquerade we are usually happy to buy into.

In this sense, 'verbatim theatre' is every bit as problematic a term as 'documentary drama' or 'reality television'. We could chase our tails endlessly here, exposing every report as a type of transformation, shifting events to suit the agendas (whether knowing or unknowing) of every reporter; and the extent to which theatre is seen as a potential vehicle for truth or as an innately truthful medium is impossible to measure. For some people, theatre *aficionados* perhaps and a great many of my university theatre colleagues, events are given life in and through performance and the lessons they tell are all the more telling for taking place before our eyes. For others, including another great many of my colleagues, theatrical representation puts an additional barrier between events and understanding.

Richard Norton-Taylor is in the former camp, suggesting that true words 'become stronger still when actors are speaking them on a stage before a live audience'; (Gardner, 2013) so is Robin Soans who believes that 'The normal channels of reportage, wherein we expect some degree of responsibility and truth, are no longer reliable.... Only in the arts is the study of the human condition considered more important than ambition or money, so it is left to artists to ask the relevant questions.' (Hammond & Steward, 2008, p.16) A fine-sounding sentiment, but one that elevates dramatists above journalists for no more reason, perhaps, than that Soans is himself a writer of plays. The expert theatre critic Michael Billington similarly sees verbatim drama 'as a source of uncontaminated information', arguing that British people turn increasingly 'to plays to find out what [is] really going on'. (Billington, 2009) Not good news for Billington's newspaper employer, the *Guardian*. With UK theatre audiences, especially outside London, falling by nearly ten per cent over the last two years, Billington's cultural and knowing elite is massively and increasingly insulated from the rest of the populace.

Writing for London's National Theatre (a knowing contradiction if ever there was one), Robin Belfield does in one page of its 'Discover' pack the same thing as many others, blasting through contradiction as if it were not there. In its section on Verbatim Theatre (the National Theatre is a champion of David Hare and his work in this form), we read 'As the dictionary definition suggests, verbatim theatre uses the exact words from an original source as its playtext.' (Belfield, 2012) A few lines later we read that the aim is 'an authenticity of voice, to represent the experiences, opinions and emotions of those who have been affected', (Ibid.) one in which the writer can exercise a degree of artistic freedom. Not quite the same thing – in fact, not the same thing at all. In a world where we empathise with people who look like they come from somewhere we would call home and where we are drawn endlessly to the pretty, the graceful and the beautifully lit, main-stage theatre deals in too glorious a seduction to pass much muster as fact.

If highlighting the contradictory elements of a national theatre which is reluctant to take its product beyond the M25 that encircles London seems like an unwarranted slur on an institution with fifty years of excellence under its belt, it should be remembered that whilst the National Theatre does at least do some touring (although not much), the English National Opera and the Royal Opera rarely venture out of their London homes. The Royal Ballet does tour, but to America, Australia and Japan rather than to any British cities. Taxpayers across England pay for these London-centric companies without ever having genuine or sustained access to them.

To help us with autoethnographic performance we can look again to Philippe Lejeune who, in his concept of the autobiographical pact, stresses the importance of the author's signature alongside authorial intentions. (Lejeune, 1989) For Lejeune, authors are of fundamental importance in that it is they who create the discursive aspects of an autobiographical pact with the reader. Certainly we need to substitute 'spectator' for 'reader', and 'performer' for 'author', as well as 'autoethnography' for 'autobiography'; but these are simple exchanges and they can be envisaged without damaging the integrity of Lejeune's ideas. One of the immediate consequences of Lejeune's concept is that it demands the participation of at least two parties: the performer/author and the reader/spectator. If this concept implies negotiation, participation and exchange, it also implies a move from autobiography to autoethnography. Highly distinguished performance scholars such as Heddon (2005), Smith and Watson (2001) and Aston and Harris (2006) have so comprehensively theorised self-as-subject presentations that we know well the etymology of autobiography as 'self-life-writing', from 'autos', 'bios' and 'graphe'; we know too that autoethnography differs, and sometimes only slightly, in the switching of 'bios' (life) for 'ethnos', meaning people who share a distinctive cultural identity. It is on this axis of shift that performance is moving away from its recent embrace of catharsis for the artist as an *ipso facto* indicator of worth.

Autoethnographical performance is a form of self-narrative that locates the self within social contexts. In performance no less than in any other field of exploration and expression, effective autoethnography is not simply about the desire to document personal experience so much as the need to deploy one's own uniquely informed yet always partial perspective in order to evoke emotional resonance with the spectator or reader. In this it is both method and text, a form that can be utilised by performers to place the story of their lives within recognition of the social contexts in which they occur, heralding a shift towards art that acts not as an agent of self-awareness or social change so much as a reconsideration of terms such as 'empathy', 'engagement' and 'community'.

Amongst this talk of authenticity and the real re-staged, it is easy to forget that the aim is not to pursue a particularly *genuine* self in a given work of autoethnographical performance. This writer for one (and I suspect like many of us in performance and the wider social sciences) would be painfully unqualified to distinguish the real from the representational other than through the sound-bite knowledge that comes with borrowed terminology and the glib (re) assurance of publication. The intention is to interpret in what ways particular and often localised experiences are represented in the public discourse that is staged performance.

To best describe his legendary theatre practice, Augusto Boal used the term *maieutics*, the process of bringing into consciousness those conceptions that were hitherto latent and unleashed. *Maieutics* is based on Plato's theory of recollection, or *anamnesis*, which holds that knowledge is always awaiting discovery. In this it is an innately pedagogical method based on the idea that truth (that thorny truth) resides in the mind of every human being due to innate reason but that it has to be released by answering intelligently proposed questions or problems. For Boal, empowerment is at the core of the transformative encounter in applied forms of drama and theatre, and the ability to articulate who and what one truly feels and thinks is empowerment in its highest form. The body-in-performance strives for articulation through a type of exhibition even when this is the exhibition of absence. The body strives for difference even when this distinction is made most manifest via a re-framing of the humdrum and the everyday. And this is in part about Boal's view of empowerment.

Jo Bonney has described contemporary culture as the era of the self, a 'product and reflection of a century that has given rise to the hedonism of the twenties, the radical individualism and activism of the sixties and the so-called "me decade" of the eighties.' (Bonney, 2000, p.xiv) For Bonney, 'The nineties finally made room for the previously marginalized, diverse voices of this society, and the solo [performance] form has tracked these developments.' (Ibid.) And solo performance is no small thing. On 31st December 1999, on his forty-ninth birthday, Tehching Hsieh concluded a thirteen-year performance that was never presented to the public. Like his April–April *One Year Performance* of 1980–81, all that the art contained was the body of the artist. Our trust in the artist's integrity is what separates art from artifice: not a suspension of disbelief on our part so much as an act of ongoing belief. And what we believe in is that the work we are seeing (or not seeing) is absolutely not recreational. Performance takes on the significance of religion or politics inasmuch as it is always with us, as work that provides sustenance rather than being something one dips in and out of. In Cocteau's view, shared by Artaud, shared by Grotowski, shared by Beck, art engaged in fully is not so much a pastime as it is a form of priesthood. It becomes logical therefore that life and art, like the self and other, become blurred.

Blurred and also interrogated. If art is part of one's being (of one's self) what is more logical than the self being part of one's art? So Stanislavski makes art his life's work as Artaud makes his life's work art. That is why we tend to give the benefit of the doubt to those radical practitioners and practices that from time to time test both our preconceptions and our patience. We do so because we have faith in their faith and belief in their belief. Because what it is that makes these artists radical is not their demonstration of abilities we can readily applaud so much as their asking of one simple question: What can I do with performance? Simple as the question is, the responses are complex and confusing, cutting as they do to the heart of our contemporary uncertainties regarding the boundary and purpose of this most immediate of all art forms.

The body is ubiquitous (we each have one) and also unique, being the shell of self that we show to the world. Body art tends towards the presentational rather than the representational. In this the performer is likely to function as both story and character – as subject and object. Performers position themselves as objects since they are conscious of the processes in which they are involved. This is a tendency, not a rule. The things that distinguish body art, or live art, or performance art from theatre are tendencies, drifts and perceptions.

Every space is a potential art space, every action a potential event, and this disturbs our conventional understanding of the distinctions between theatre and life, and spectatorship and observation. When on 4th June 2006 an unidentified Ukrainian man climbed into a lion enclosure at a zoo in Kiev shouting 'God will save me', before removing his shoes and subsequently being mauled to death, the people watching this act were what? Spectators? Observers? Witnesses? Who can say with any authority? It is clear that the act of faith (misguided though it plainly was) required an audience of sorts, but what sort of audience? And does being watched (along with the desire to be watched) turn what we do into a performance? Observation generally assumes a calm indifference as opposed to spectatorship's more passionate engagement, but as we shall see these edges blur and fuse like all other elements of performance.

Like it or not and understand it or not, we watch Stelarc's hooked-up body hanging overhead in the same way we watch a jumper on a car-park roof, a high-wire act without a net or a shoeless Christian throwing himself to the lions. We watch with a morbid fascination: part fear, part horror, part hope. In a return to the concerns of this book's opening chapter, our Ukrainian faith-tester brought us no closer to the truth or otherwise of God's existence. In the days immediately following the incident, Christian websites were full of postings citing bible passages such as 'Do not test the Lord your God as you did at Massah', 'Do not put the Lord your God to the test' and 'We should not test the Lord, as some of them did, and were killed by snakes'. Had the lions' mouths stayed closed, like Daniel's beasts in the story from the Hebrew Bible, then surely a great many would have credited that fact as proof of both God's existence and his mercy... a miracle, no less. When he died, those same people saw not of an absence of a higher power so much as confirmation of God's unwillingness to be tested by mortals. In the same week in 2006, fearing the evil portent of 06/06/06, a group of Dutch Evangelists called for a worldwide pray-in against the Devil. When the world spun as normal on 7th June, the group saw this as the proof they had sought. We pay our money, it seems, and we make our choice. But the only truth that emerged in Kiev was that a man made a mistake and then paid for it with his life.

In *Essays on the Blurring of Art and Life*, Allan Kaprow offered a distinction between artlike art and lifelike art. For Kaprow, lifelike art rarely fits within traditional ideas as to what art is: lifelike art can be about moving furniture around a house, dressing or undressing, arranging plants in a garden or merely leaning against a wall. In the 1960s Kaprow wrote 'once the task of the artist was to make good art; now it is to avoid making art of any kind'. (Kaprow, 1993, p.110) In the 1990s he said 'The experimental artist of today is the un-artist'. (Ibid., p.111) For Kaprow, consistently, the point of art is to discover art where nobody knew there was any. This is not dissimilar to Duchamp's statement that art is what happens when an object is taken out of context and given a new thought, and it has echoes in Oliviero Toscani's belief that whilst 'Any idiot can see the beauty in something beautiful... [t]he thing is to see beauty elsewhere. There is beauty everywhere if you are an artist.' (ten Cate, 1996, p.78) Richard Foreman has argued that anything, even a 'jar rolling across the stage', could be afforded the status of theatre. (McDonald, 1993, p.17) Performance is about seeing something differently and this can have as much to do with the spectatorial or autoethnographical gaze as with that which is gazed upon.

The self is suggestive of autobiography, and we can read a relatively simplistic distinction between the actorly concealment of self behind character and the performative revelation of self through the work. As elsewhere, things here are not as simple as they seem. Auto-performance does more than provide actors with the opportunity to make themselves subjects to be seen by spectators; it allows them to see themselves in the process of being seen. Lacan described a state wherein 'the visible me is determined by the look that is outside me'. (Eagleton, 1996, p.133) For Barthes, 'You are the only one who can never see yourself except as an image; you can never see your eyes unless they are dulled by the gaze they rest upon the mirror or the lens'. (Barthes, 1977, p.31) A questioning of self through self's construction: the self as subject does not, we see, amount to the self as given.

Mary Warnock reminds us that the idea of a person is not scientific. Rather it is what she refers to as a 'superficial concept'. 'The word "person" is suggestive of constancy inasmuch as one might assume a binding reference to the past, so that I remain the same *person* I ever was regardless of changes in my situation. One's identity is constructed from labels in ways that one's person is not.' (Warnock, 1987, p.53) For Sartre, self is defined by memory: 'The past is characterized as the past of something or somebody; one *has* a past.' (Sartre, 1990, p.112) In this context, the self's ability to reflect on one's past allows for the possibility of determining what it is that one will become. Conversely, we can say that a postmodern take on the narrative past suggests that it has lost a great deal of its authenticating power. We can probably go so far as to say that the narrative of one's past has inauthenticity as its defining feature. Autoethnographical and autobiographical performances are ultimately authorised fictions, and all that we can know as authentic is the here and now. And no other art form trades on the here and now like performance. The self that was once kept off scene, rendered important only inasmuch as it was possessed of the capacity to dress itself in a costumier's robes in front of paying spectators, has assumed centre stage in all of its small-life mediocrity.

And why should it not? Stage work has moved from Shakespeare's Prince of Denmark to Miller's Willy Loman and on to Butterworth's Silver Johnny, from the machinations and procrastinations of the rich and famous to the day-to-day drudgery of the anonymous and the ordinary; and what could be more vital in its very ordinariness than one's own self? That we continue to be as fascinated as we are with autobiographical performance, to the extent that the form has acquired a position of unprecedented importance over the past thirty years, is because the work relies for its effectiveness upon a unique pact between performers and spectators. Sherrill Grace and Jerry Wasserman cut to the heart of this fascination: 'When we sign on to this pact we expect to be told the truth about someone's life, we believe that the people we encounter are *real*, that they live outside the text and go to the bank and grocery store as we do, and we bring this expectation to autobiography... *despite our realization that we are engaged with art, not life.*' (Grace & Wasserman, 2006, p.13)

As we discussed in Chapter One, the quest for writerly truth is a search without prize, and truth in art has always had a doubled status. On the one hand, we crave the certainty that the signature and the artwork amount to a truth; on the other, we accept that art is (for the most part) no more than a representation of the external truth it depicts. And (for the most part) this seems reasonable enough. Clive Bell insisted that art should have nothing to do with life. His contemporary Edward Bullough wrote in 1912 that 'Explicit references to organic affections, to the material existence of the body, especially to sexual matters, lie normally below the Distance-limit, and can be touched on by Art only with special precautions.' (Tillman & Cahn, 1969, p.403) At these statements, a large part of Euro-American society breathed a sigh of collective relief that all was in order. Everyone, however, did not share Bell and Bullough's views. At the same time as they were making their claims for art's lofty purpose, Marinetti was publishing his 'Manifesto of Futurism', the Dadaists were waiting in the wings and Duchamp was exhibiting his urinal as a readymade. The First World War was about to turn the wrath of machinery on its inventors and art was set to sacrifice its sense of certainty.

Performance, as distinguished loosely from drama, is the domain of the performer who takes no role but her own and is author, subject and director, communicating her own perceptions and ideas through the work. We can say that the performing of oneself is a feature of performance, even something central to it, whereas the submergence of self into character is a defining trait of acting, a phenomenon which Philip Auslander describes as 'The blending of real and fabricated personae and situations that occur when performance personae assume the same functions as *real*.' (Auslander, 1992, p.78) We can also say that, as theatre is the place for the well-told lie, so performance may now be the place for revelations of a new kind of performative truth. What is meant by the term, in this context, is that body art and performance allow for the possibility of performers revealing themselves without the consequences that such revelations would lead to in their daily lives. Performers, no less than the rest of us, can tell secrets to strangers precisely because it does not really matter what those strangers think.

It is in the nature of the work that we, those strangers who watch, are always kept slightly off our guard, always a little uneasy, unsure and undecided. In this sense, being undecided about what to call works of performance emerges as a logical response. Deirdre Heddon advises us that 'Performers have the ability to move in and out of classifications' and that the categorising of genres requires:

> boundaries, and boundaries are constructions which create and depend
> on both the inside and outside to have either. The boundary, though,
> is a point of bleeding, a potential seepage of one into the other.

> Boundaries are neither permanent nor immutable, but are subject to social, historical, political and economic forces.
>
> (Heddon, 2005, p.49)

Marvin Carlson's oft-cited assertion that performance is an essentially contested concept further reinforces the idea that work is no longer easily pinned down into discrete and watertight categories.

The relationship between autobiography, autoethnography and performance is one that is rarely mediated by overt difference. The roles of writer, director and performer may be radically diverse activities but with autobiographical performance they are likely to be adopted by the same person. And there is a clear logic to this. A disempowered subject seeking a platform for her or his voice does not necessarily want that voice diluted by difference: be this through the macro of gender, race, sexuality, nationality or culture or the micro that comes with subtle variations. Far from remaining in the domain of the rich and famous, autobiography has been developed into the chosen form for members of minority and marginalised groups. Furthermore, the deployment of autobiography into performance has often incorporated complex critiques of identity construction.

The here and now suggests solidity, two givens that join at the hip to make performance; but borders are crossed and dismantled in performance as often as they are reinforced and the here-and-nowness of performance can be employed as a means of exploring transience and liminality. The work of a number of performance artists trades on a destabilisation of culturally stereotyped expectations, often by adopting an exaggerated sense of otherness within the work. Accordingly, what we see when we watch work is often no more than our own mirrored expectations and the labels we use to describe it say much about our own spectatorial desires and fears.

Spalding Gray's celebrated monologues such as *Swimming to Cambodia* and *Monster in a Box* traded on the spectatorial and oftentimes critical misnomer that what was being participated in was an intimate and to some eyes *honest* encounter between the watchers and the watched. Gray's carefully crafted texts are a type of heightened, poeticised faux-diary of the writer's own experiences, filtered through his assiduously acted East Coast neurosis. And the work was *acted*, rehearsed, refined and played out (minimally) to maximum effect. Gray's performance writing is at once continuous and fractured, discrete and incremental, revealing the changes in Gray's life at the same time as it takes as its subject the subject of self.

Richard Coe believes that if the writer's self is to be made subject then it needs to be:

> transmuted into something durably significant, it needs to possess a vitality and originality which is very far from common; and it needs further to be spurred on by the imperious urge to impart a message or impart a truth which may not be allowed to vanish, or else by a dose of vanity so strong that never, for one instant, can the author doubt that his own existence, in all its intimate and unmomentous detail, is supremely meaningful to the world at large.

(Coe, 1985, p.26)

The diary or journal provides a means of *creating* a self as well as *expressing* one, of not simply recording an actual daily life so much as offering an alternative to it. Diary-like though it may at first appear, Gray's writing differs inasmuch as diarists tend to write in the moment, without foresight. Gray's texts, whilst often utilising the present tense are written, reflected upon and edited after the event, with the description of events having a more complex relationship with that which might or might not have occurred than Gray's conversational delivery would lead us to assume.

Nothing that is framed by or as performance can ever speak for itself and yet theatre's greatest conjuring trick has been to seduce us away from this fact. Gray's life experiences were the stimulus for his writings but professional performance was the peg on which they hung and his work was always tailored towards this end. Autobiographical performance functions around the 'I' on the page and the 'I' on the stage: one is a paper construct whilst the other is personal, and neither can be true. The forms deny truthful communication precisely because their methods are so innately artificial. We can read this in the light of the distinction Barthes made between the self who writes, the self who was and the self who is: Barthes' challenge to the popular idea of a stable, real and essential self reveals in its place a fabrication, a self that is no more than a fictive truth.

In conversation with Bonnie Marranca, Gray wondered:

> Could I stop acting and what was it I actually did when I acted? Was I, in fact, acting all the time, and was my acting in the theatre the surface showing of that? Was my theatre acting a confession of my constant state of feeling my life as an act? ... Now there was the new space between the timeless poetic me (the me in quotes, the self as poem) and the real-time self in the world (the time-bound, mortal self;

the self as prose). The ongoing 'play' became a play about theatrical transcendence.

(Callens, 2004, p.119)

Gray's musings here are important to our understanding of the role of self and art because, as Gray acknowledged, his work was about the space between a knowingly constructed performance self and a real-time self which, Goffman notwithstanding, is less poetically made.

In fact Goffman was always careful to stress that we put on acts *whether we are aware that we are doing so or not*, and it is this phenomenon of playing roles without being aware of it that distinguishes the self in (performance) quotes from the self or selves of one's daily life. What we saw with Gray's blissfully smart work was the representation of experiences, offered up to us in ways that invited empathy, engagement and *belief* at the same time as we were never quite sure about what the performance persona revealed or obscured. Sherrill Grace and Jerry Wasserman reiterate this when they write of Gray that 'his performance work is created out of what Gray would have the audience see as his everyday life, the quotidian experiences that make up his autobiography.' (Grace and Wasserman, 2006, p.35) In constructing his texts for performance, Gray first relied on recollection, trusting to his memory of events. These memories were spoken onto tape and then, before his words were transcribed Gray would, as he described it, 'listen to a tape of what I said and wonder how I can make it a little more dramatic and funny by juxtaposing a little hyperbole here and play with it a little bit there.' (Ibid.)

Derrida felt that words were to be drawn from the body like blood from a syringe; Harold Pinter said that words are the things we deploy to cover our nakedness. Words and the body: words and the body that bleeds. The body and the self are also centre stage in research. If ethnography amounts to a trying to make sense of cultural groupings, then autoethnography is a trying to make sense of our activity of trying to make sense. It is an innately heuristic and performative activity wherein our learning to learn becomes as important as our understanding of subject. The subject of the research may in fact be the subject of self; or, with more than a(nother) nod to Goffman, the self as subject. In its incorporation of the researcher's own thoughts, feelings and emotions into the study, autoethnography raises questions as to the legitimacy of the self-referential 'I' we use in writing, just as autobiographical performance asks questions of the self-disclosing 'I' we use in the act. The issue of how centrally one chooses to locate one's self in research is misleading: the self that observes is also always looked upon, and not least by the researcher. As a fundamentally relational activity, autoethnography offers nothing if it does not offer writing as a form and process of discovery, as something active rather than passive, as an activity through which we begin learn what it is that we think we might know. And this often results in studies which are written as stories rather than being presented as more clinical, written reports. This is key inasmuch as research stories, like performance, seek almost always to elicit some kind of emotional response in the listener/reader/spectator.

It is key also in that stories are not often seen as the stuff of research papers, and in this sense research and performance can seem to split off into separate worlds. What matters most and most often are the claims made by authors, alongside the place and purpose of publication and one's target audience; and in this regard research papers and performance re-join. Just as one defining feature of an academic paper is its rigorous referencing of other sources and another is the journal, publishing house or conference through which it makes itself known, disseminating its findings to a group of peers, so performance is given a sub-label not least through the seeming pedigree of performer and spectator alongside the particular sanctioning of the work by its venue. Autoethnography then might differ from its more casual cousin autobiography through little more than a shared perception based on features which, whilst subverted, are still recognisably *academic*.

In the same way, performance art is given that label for a variety of reasons, none of which make any *a priori* assumption as to quality. Despite its marginalisation by certain scholars, autoethnography is no more a device for avoiding a rigorous engagement with theory than autobiographical performance is a means of avoiding the difficulties of representation: theory is embedded in ethnography to the same extent that (re)presentation is a given of performance and writing one's self into the work does not mean that all else of value is written out. In prioritising 'I', the work does much to turn everyone involved, presenters, readers and spectators alike, away from 'us' and 'them' into 'we'.

That is a large claim to make and like all claims it looms larger still in print. But we can look to feminism for a type of confirmation. We know that feminism did much to push autobiographical performance into something known, if not quite common, through the stress it places on making particular starting points and experiences a valid and vital part of one's work: and that feminism, through self-evident and embodied connections between the artist and the art, has had a large part to play in the international drift towards autobiographical writing per se. We know, for example, that from the middle of the twentieth-century, feminists abandoned any collective belief in the idea of the genderless mind, recognising instead that imagination is unable to avoid conscious/unconscious impositions of gender. Feminism did much to propel those studies into culture determination which stress the impossibility of separating one's thought processes from the self that has been positioned socially, sexually and historically. Images, readings and representations of women that did not acknowledge the stereotypical assumptions that were implicit in seemingly non-gendered perspectives were exposed through feminism to a new scrutiny: one that would no longer accept the divisive, unequal and oppressive as the objectively arrived at norm. The female experience then began to take on positive affirmations. The Female Aesthetic arose – expressing a unique female consciousness and a feminine tradition in literature – as it celebrated an intuitive female approach in the interpretation of women's texts.

Art, like feminism, has always been about empowerment. Disempowered by the impositions of an adult world, our children play with dolls: items smaller, weaker and more vulnerable than themselves, things that can be manoeuvred and manipulated. And so as adults we opt for art that allows us to speak: to say who we are and to aestheticise and articulate our case to darkened auditoria. The charges of indulgence may pour in but there is nothing more political than this and no form more pertinent than performance.

According to Kristin Langellier (1999), the strength of performance is in its capacity for immediacy and passion, in its evocation of empathy through the performers' and spectators' bodily presence as they share a common space. It is through this sharing that transgression occurs, as personal stories disturb, disrupt and displace both normative narratives and assumptions as to subject. In the same way that visual art is no longer satisfied with the representation of landscapes and still lives, so performance is no longer the prime domain of the well-made play. In its engagement with structurally complex frameworks of representation, recall and relocation, and in its recognition that no all-encompassing notions of identity are able to exist, the peculiar circularity of memory is brought into abrasive contact with the supposed linearity of performance as a time-based durational form. It is this abrasion that results in Carlson's notion of performance as a 'dangerous game' and also as a 'double agent', as a form that is at once private and public, intimate and exposed, complicit and critical. (Carlson, 2004, p.173) These aspects are explored by Jamie Coull in the following section.

Am I Queer (Enough)?

A Discussion of Queerness and its Unstable Definitions

Jamie Coull

Introduction

In an interview with San Francisco based performance artist Monique Jenkinson (aka Fauxnique), I was introduced to the notion of cultural queerness. Monique is married to a cisgendered man, and claims queer as part of her cultural identity. As a heterosexual woman participating in faux queen performance, similar to Monique, I began to ask myself, 'If Monique is queer, am I?' In fact, many women who perform as faux queens are heterosexuals who claim queerness. Yet the category of *queer* is often read as at odds with *heterosexuality*.

In September 2013, I travelled to the USA to compete in San Francisco's Faux Queen Pageant. Prior to my departure I had been grappling with anxiety about whether or not a community of faux queen performers, who identify with many and varied sexual and gender orientations, would accept me into their group as a stranger from Australia who was travelling with her male fiancé. From the first three hours spent in San Francisco, my fears were dissolved and suddenly seemed utterly ridiculous. People were kind and welcoming, and I met with nine faux queens for in-depth interviews who were keen to talk. I spoke at length with each respondent about another concern which was bothering me before I got on the plane: what does queerness mean in San Francisco and is it okay for women with male partners to identify with a sense of queerness? This piece of writing aims to deal with the notion of queerness as it begins to tentatively incorporate opposite-sex-attracted people like me who are involved in queer performance genres.

Eventually, I intend this piece of writing to be the opening of a thesis chapter which negotiates the notion of cultural queerness as an identity category for heterosexual subjects. In the thesis chapter I will begin by contextualising a definition of queerness based on relevant queer theory and attempt to recognise tensions evident between queer theory, feminist theory, and lesbian and gay studies. I will narrow the frame by concentrating on existing conceptualisations of the *heterosexual queer* to understand how other straights might see themselves as queer; functioning as a literature review. Linking a concept of *heteroqueerness* with faux queen performance, I will argue faux queen performance as a conscious expression of queerness and as a queer performative transaction with gay male drag queens. Reading faux queening through this lens, I will make the argument that heterosexual faux queens may claim queer as an identity category, but not, however, without potential consequences and criticism from both LGBT and non-LGBT communities.

The piece I have prepared for this book is a *slice* of my unfinished thesis chapter and not the whole pizza per se. I briefly contextualise how queer is defined in the dominant literature and explore some emerging work which attempts to conceptualise a notion of the queer-heterosexual. My theoretical writing, which here functions as a literature review, is also peppered with verbatim extracts of interview data and at times I shift voice to allow personal experiences and thoughts a space to exist in the discussion. Thank you to Cara Couture, Bea Dazzler, Kentucky Fried Woman, Fauxnique, Frida K Hole, Princess Cream Pie, L Rob Hubby, Vesper Synd and Brandi Amara Skyy whose words are found throughout this work.

Queer Theory and Conceptualisations of *Queer*

Queer theory's ultimate goal is to denaturalise and destabilise sexuality and gender by revealing all identity categories as unstable, non-essential and learned through cultural sedimentation. Predominately, queer theorists work to challenge heteronormativity in all aspects of culture, as well as power relations of hierarchical difference, that is: to destabilise the notion that one difference is more different or more important than another. (Slagle, 2006, pp.313–14) Judith Butler's significant collection of work on the performativity of gender is considered an authoritative theoretical framework through which to destabilise heterosexuality. In her work, she systematically drills down at the apparently *essential* qualities of heteronormative gender and sexuality, revealing them as learned cultural behaviours which consistently work to conceal structural processes at every step. In place of essential gender, Butler argues for an understanding of culturally produced behaviours as gender performativity. That is, all cultural indicators of gender and sexuality are performative: learned scripts which *feel* natural, essential and *real* to an individual's sense of personality and identity, so much so that an assumption of *naturalness* is compelling and often difficult to stray from. (Butler, 1999; Jagger, 2008; Slagle, 2006) Butler's theory of gender performativity has gained many followers, influencing the future directions of queer studies.

Kentucky Fried Woman: When I hear people refer to themselves as queer I feel like it's also kind of placing where they see gender... And I think queers are more likely to get intersectionality and get that we are all composed of really complicated identities based on our race and class and body size and ethnicity and ability level and education, and so I think that in queer spaces I tend to hear lots more conversations that really wrestle with the fact of how complicated all of our identities are.

(K. Smith, personal communication, 8th September 2013)

At the core of queer theory is an understanding that gender and sexuality is performative; they are learned scripts which hide their processes. Importantly, the work of queer theory to debunk stable gender and sexuality categories is indebted to, as Jagose states, 'a specifically lesbian and gay reworking of the post-structuralist figuring of identity as a constellation of multiple and unstable positions'. (Jagose, 1996, p.3)

A definition of queer theory is hard to nail down, and Jagose suggests that it is in fact a category always in process, always in formation. (Jagose, 1996) It is important to acknowledge queer theory's roots in lesbian and gay thought and activism, as well as feminist theory. How we read work as queer or as queering performances and writing is strongly influenced by LGBT and feminist thought. 'Queer' has begun to assert itself as an umbrella term to signify non-heteronormative identity and theoretical frameworks which aim to *queer* literature, art, performance, law, psychology and more. However, LGBT studies and feminism appear to distance themselves from queer theory and the queer umbrella. This distance seems to stem from a concern, or perhaps fear, that the label 'queer' is too far removed from the goals of LGBT activism or feminism and that its umbrella span is too wide, too inclusive.

Princess Cream Pie: I think the word 'queer' encompasses pretty much everyone who is not dead set against the idea.

(Personal communication, 17th September 2013)

Vesper Synd: Queerness means to not want to put yourself into certain boxes of what sexuality is and what gender is.

(Personal communication, 19th September 2013)

Who can stand under the queer umbrella is relatively undefined, unlike LGBT thought where gay, lesbian, bisexual or transgender identity is assumed, or feminism where XX chromosomes are not necessarily a requirement but identification as a feminist is expected. Queer, as a theoretical framework then, is a fluid process, not a solid model with clearly identifiable members. Kirsch explains:

> queer theory was born from the idea that more inclusiveness is better than less. But it holds that the categories presented by gay and lesbian studies are too narrow to encompass the range of behaviour and sexuality that is presented by a wide range of preferences.

(Kirsch, 2006, p.24)

Queer theory aims to make strange all categories and all aspects of culture, rather than normalise what is already assumed *queer*. It therefore must always look ahead to emergent categories, and inwards to itself, challenging normalised categories and revealing their unstable disposition. Roberta Mock notes that in keeping with this goal, queer theory has an inbuilt self-destruct mechanism. (Mock, 2003)ÿÿÿÿÿÿÿF=Zÿÿ Similarly Slagle observes, 'Queer theorists argue that individual identities and differences are constantly being (re)constructed, that identities are not stable, and that identity categories are, therefore, a myth'. (Slagle, 2006, p.325) Further, its primary aim to destabilise and denaturalise means that the use of *queer* as an umbrella term for non-heteronormative lifestyles becomes increasingly broad.

> ***L Ron Hubby:*** *When I think of being culturally queer, I think of anyone being a part of that world in a respectful way.*

(Personal communication, 18th September 2013)

From LGBT activism and feminism's point of view, the concern over queer's wide reaching arms seems, at least in part, to be with regard to this eventual self-destruction, and we must wonder, if everyone and everything becomes queered, what happens to LGBT identity? As Kirsch notes, queer theory's claim to wider inclusivity has also meant that its focus is more narrowly aimed at inquiry of the individual self, given that each individual's experiences are different and potentially non-heteronormative. (Kirsch, 2006). LGBT studies, however, focuses more on the social field of community and political mobilisation.

> **Bea Dazzler:** *The first time I started hearing about it was in San Francisco. For me it was never really used in a derogatory way so for me personally it never really felt like a derogatory thing. It kind of felt like another way to describe the gay, lesbian, transgender, bisexual community.*
>
> (T. Connell, personal communication, 16th September 2013)

As we know, 'queer' has been used as a homophobic slur, and LGBT activists worked to reclaim the word as a term of endearment and political identification. Warner asserts that:

> The preference for 'queer' represents, among other things, an aggressive impulse of generalization; it rejects a minoritizing logic of toleration or simple political interest-representation in favour of a more thorough resistance to regimes of the normal.
>
> (Warner, 1993, p.xxxvi)

Now, it is not unusual to use 'queer' to describe LGBT mobilisations and activities such as 'queer pride parade', 'queer community', 'queer arts festival' or 'queer studies'.

> **Bea Dazzler:** *The first time I really started hearing that word and hearing it being used in context, the context was always really specifically about 'the queer community', people saying that phrase 'the queer community' or 'queer arts' or something like that…*
>
> (T. Connell, personal communication, 16th September 2013)

Personally, I have begun to describe drag and faux queen performance as a 'queer performance genre'. In recent times, *queerness* as an aspect of identity in socially progressive centres such as San Francisco is beginning to represent a kind of cultural orientation with a specifically LGBT focus, rather than a term to indicate LBGT sexuality. The way in which 'queer' is being used more and more, who you sleep with is still considered significant; however, values, lifestyle, relationship status, friends, how you conceptualise gender, your career and political affiliations also become weighty indicators of queerness.

> **Kentucky Fried Woman:** *One thing that I've noticed has happened over the past 10 years is 'queer' has really entered the lexicon; is that it also tends to situate where people are politically.*

(K. Smith, personal communication, 8th September 2013)

To identify as queer under this emergent definition is to find identification with an *emotional* community, a community or culture of queerness, which emerges from and exists within the wider LGBT community.

> Emotional communities whether they be produced by similarities based on sex, gender, race, or class, served as centres of identification, spaces were individuals realize that there are others like themselves and which provide a counter to the alienation caused by rejection and discrimination.

(Kirsch, 2006, p.31)

If the premise of queer theory is to destabilise heterosexuality and the notion of hierarchy, what then is *queerness*? What does it mean to be queer?

> **Fauxnique:** *As a woman who's married to man I don't identify my sexual orientation as queer but I identify my cultural orientation as queer.*

(M. Jenkinson, personal communication, 11th September 2013)

Considering queer thought's emergence from and important links with LGBT thought, it is often assumed that to *be queer* or sense in yourself some sort of *queerness* is to be gay, lesbian, bisexual or transgender. A direct correlation between *queer* and LBGT sexuality/gender identity is often an assumed and sustained position. Speaking with a straight female friend on Skype, I explained about some of the reading I had been doing to prepare for this paper.

> **Jamie:** *So I've been getting ready to write this paper about queerness in San Francisco, because I was talking with this woman and she has a male partner, she's married, but she identifies as queer. I didn't know that straight people could say that, you know, so it's pretty interesting.*

> **My Friend:** *But doesn't 'queer' mean gay?*

Jamie: Well that's what I thought but apparently not always, according to Fauxnique.

My Friend: Oh, so what is queer about her then?

Jamie: Well I guess because she performs as a faux queen, you know she is a female performer who dresses up to look like a man in drag. It's kind of like a cross-dressed gender performance, and lots of her friends are gay and she feels part of the community. So I guess she feels like her lifestyle is queered, like immersed in gay culture, even though she has a husband.

My Friend: Oh right, but I thought 'queer' meant gay? Now I'm confused, like, that is what you grow up hearing from everyone: that 'queer' is another word for gay right? It's hard to change how you understand a word when you've been told it means a certain thing for 28 years.

My friend is not wrong: for many people 'queer' explicitly means gay, or at least LGBT. The notion that 'queer' could apply to straight individuals is, to some LGBT groups and individuals, insulting and disempowering. From this point of view the queer umbrella should **only** extend its shade to those who are LGBT. For some groups and individuals, queer can be inclusive, but not so inclusive that straights are involved. In the context of queer theory, however, *queer* does not mean not-heterosexual, it means not-heteronormative, which is an important point of difference, and a stumbling block for my friend. Queer theory does not alienate people who identify with heterosexuality from *queerness* but it does critique heteronormativity.

Frida K Hole: I think there's something rebellious about being queer because there's this whole idea where you've been kept down, you've been told who you are is bad or you've been closeted and you haven't truly been able to be who you are. And now that you have this freedom, and there's a liberation to it, it's like, 'I'm very much going to be who I am', and so it's very much about claiming who you are.

(L. Tucker, personal communication, 10th September 2013)

It is fair to say that any straight individual could not begin to find identification with *queerness* without first recognising and becoming critical of the overwhelming pressure to be heteronormative and the undeserved privileges awarded to heteronormativity in society and culture.

Conceptualisation of the Heteroqueer

> *All this gender fucking has definitely rubbed off on the heteros, who are ditching the script in favour of writing their own.*

(Taormino, 2003)

In the last decade or so, the notion that an opposite-sex-attracted person might also identify themselves as *queer* has emerged in the cultural and academic spheres. At Beyond Boundaries: An International Conference on Sexuality (University of Amsterdam, 29th July to 1st August 1997), dancer and cultural researcher Clyde Smith gave a presentation titled 'How I became a Queer Heterosexual'. In his paper, he makes reference to an article from 1993 in the *Village Voice* (a free weekly tabloid-format newspaper based in New York) by Anne Powers as the first time he came across the term *Queer Straight*. Smith states:

> Her definition of inclusion in the queer world did not require 'the fundamental acts of intimacy that ground homosexual identity' rather she spoke of 'the projection of a queer attitude [as] enough to claim a place in homosexual culture'.

(Smith, 1997, p.4)

Smith identifies as a queer heterosexual, after long-term involvement with dance institutions and companies where he was often the only straight-identified male. He notes that during his dance career he came to feel part of a 'shifting community of queerness' particularly when based in San Francisco, despite his heterosexuality. Smith explains that his definition of queer heterosexuality (as it was in his 1997 paper) combines Powers' position that queerness is a 'projection of attitude' and Keith Hennessy's definition of queer as:

> an umbrella term which embraces the matrix of sexual preferences, orientations, and habits of the not-exclusively-heterosexual-and-monogamous majority. Queer includes lesbians, gay men, bisexuals, transvestites/transgenders, the radical sex communities, and many other sexually transgressive (underworld) explorers.

(Hennessy, 1992)

In Smith's article, he does not reveal his sexual practices in any more detail than his identification with heterosexuality. In his paper, the juxtaposition of queer and heterosexual is confused by the two definitions he draws on to contextualise his own understanding of this new identity category. Hennessy's definition of queer infers that non-heteronormative sexual practice or gender identity is an important factor of queer identification. The extracts from Powers' article, however, suggest that *attitude and political stance* are indicators of queerness and, as Smith quotes, 'enough to claim a place in homosexual culture'. Further, the title of Smith's presentation infers a queer heterosexual *becoming*, which suggests that queerness amongst straight-identified individuals is a conscious choice.

Although I am on the side of bringing together people of all sexual orientations under a banner of equality and non-prejudicial thinking, I sense that in Hennessy's description of queer there are some assumptions made about the private lives of individuals that he may consider to be heteronormative. Particularly, the inference that all straight people are monogamous by default and that non-monogamy must then come under the banner of queer or sexually radical.

> Does this mean that every straight college student with a fuck buddy or every wife who gives her husband a 'hall pass' at a wedding is fundamentally queer? I noticed a tabloid magazine recently with an image of Khloe Kardashian on the cover. It read something like 'My Open Marriage'. Are Khloe and Lamar queer too?

I perceive an unsure tone in Smith's paper; that he is not certain who fits under the queer banner either, and that he is trying to grasp at the generous definitions of queer posed by some LGBT folk to legitimise a place for himself within this identity category. Smith may feel in himself a sense of queerness, but if anything his paper illustrates how problematic it is to explain and legitimise your sense of queerness, without also being able to say, 'Because I'm gay'.

In 2003, Tristan Taormino published an article in the *Village Voice* titled 'The Queer Heterosexual'. Taormino brings readers attention to the vast changes in identity politics of the LGBT community, particularly since transgender and intersex communities have begun to experience growing understanding and acceptance amongst the wider mainstream population. He insists that LGBT individuals who proudly flaunt their *difference* have encouraged straight-identified people to be more honest about their own sense of queerness, and bring their experiences into the mix. Taormino asks:

> How does one spot a QH? In some cases, it's based on either one or both partners having non-traditional gender expressions… or they actively work against their assigned gender roles. Some queer heterosexuals are strongly aligned with queer community, culture, politics, and activism but happen to love and lust after people of a different gender.
>
> (Taormino, 2003, p.2)

Taormino's brief conceptualisation of queer heterosexuality appears comparable to Anne Power's definition which is drawn upon by Clyde Smith. Again, we come across the notion of attitude rather than sexual desire or sex act as a marker of queerness.

> **Fauxnique**: *It definitely is a part of my identity and maybe queerness too in a 'queer as other', 'queer as alternative', even though the word 'alternative' kind of got co-opted in the '90s as a musical style but this idea of what is 'other' what is 'questioning or rejecting a status quo'.*
>
> (M. Jenkinson, personal communication, 11th September 2013)

Robert Heasley has begun to address the notion of heteroqueerness as it pertains specifically to the male subject. His paper focuses on a typology of men who perform queer masculinities and also identify as straight. Heasley explains how many men perform a queered masculinity and experience ways of being masculine which do not fit within a heteronormative masculinity. (Heasley, 2005) He speaks of his own experiences as a self-identified 'straight-queer' and draws on conversations and narratives provided by students and acquaintances. He argues, convincingly, that 'the queer masculinities of straight men do not have a similar representation [as heteronormative masculinity does], and they lack legitimacy as a form of masculinity'. (Heasley, 2005, p.310) Heasley suggests five categories of queer masculine identity performance amongst straight-identified males: (i) Straight sissy boys, who, 'just cannot "do" straight masculinity. The sissy boy presents to others as queer, though that is not his intention'. (Heasley, 2005, p.315) (ii) Social-justice straight queers who 'take [LGBT centred social-justice] action publically and at the risk of being responded to as if they were gay'. (Heasley, 2005, p.316) (iii) Elective straight queers – 'Males in this category elect to move into queer masculinity as a means of liberating the self from the constrictions of hetero-normative masculinity'. (Heasley, 2005, p.316) (iv) Committed straight queers who 'practice being queer with the intention of benefiting from moving toward queerness as an integral aspect of their sexuality and their masculinity'. (Heasley, 2005, p.317) (v) Males living in the shadow of masculinity who 'are informed about sexuality and masculinity and are likely to understand and support feminism as well as gay rights… [but] unlikely to display nonconforming behaviours or appear in a queer space unless accompanied by a girlfriend or female friend'. (Heasley, 2005, p.317)

> It's easy for me to understand Heasley's anxiety that performing non-heteronormative masculinities can be isolating for men who are straight and do not have a community in which they feel comfortable and accepted. While reading Heasley's paper, I noted some similarities between the behaviours he marks as queered masculinity and the behaviours of my fiancé, as well as other romantic partners of faux queens. In San Francisco I met straight-identified men (boyfriends and husbands of faux queens) who performed similar queer masculinities and were accepted members of the wider queer community. In San Francisco the straight-queers' performance of masculinity was not unusual, but accepted and celebrated.

In a later work, Heasley adds another category to his typology, using David Beckham as an example. Heasley coins the term Stylistic Straight Queers for celebrities who, 'intentionally take on the presentation of self that is traditionally associated with gay male culture'. (Heasley, 2013, p.210) This sort of queered-but-not-queer appearance can be likened to the metrosexual image made popular by early 2000s reality make-over series *Queer Eye for the Straight Guy*. Further, Heasley does not shy away from a discussion of physicality, and marks his own *queerness* by how he physically interacts with male friends through hugging, touching and greeting with a kiss as women and gay men often do. Perhaps not intentionally, Heasley points to a key difference in the heteronormative construction of same-sex friendships amongst straight-identified people. Straight women who snuggle together to watch a film, hug each other deeply, kiss hello and goodbye, share a bed to sleep, or hold hands are not necessarily read as lesbians. They are not seen to be performing femininity in a manner which disrupts heteronormativity. Heasley's discussion of the queer straight suggests, in basic terms, that queerness in heterosexual men is marked by a performance of behaviours which are often considered hetero-feminine and/or gay masculine.

> What about queerness in straight-identified women? Is it the same principle only in reverse? Can straight-identified women only be read as queered

if they present butch aesthetics and behaviours? If queerness in straight women is only marked by performing behaviours which are seen to be heteromasculine then I'm not queer and neither are any of the faux queens I interviewed. However, I'm reminded of the last-place prize handed out at the very first Faux Queen Pageant called The Too Fish Prize. *In the drag world, faux queens who do not perform the aesthetic of a drag queen convincingly are labelled* **too fish**. *A fish is too much like a woman to be a considered a drag queen. In this situation, for cisgendered straight women to be read as queer they must perform a particular gay camp masculinity associated with drag queens; the gay male embodiment of the feminine by the female subject.*

Much of the writing which contextualises a sense of queerness within straight-identified people centres on male sexuality and gay/straight/queer masculinities. Roberta Mock offers an interesting stance on straight women who identify with a sense of camp gay masculinity in their own expression of femininity. Her paper 'explores the efficacy of heterosexual femme performances that attempt to challenge and subvert ideological normatives through their transactions with gay men'. (Mock, 2003, p.21)

> ***Cara Couture:*** *I mean I'm straight, but to be queer, I just feel like for me being queer is accepting all of the gay people around me and gay culture. I guess that is what it would be for me; I fully embrace it… I've always just liked what gay culture provides, the essence of it is more interesting. I can relate to it more. The things that they value compared to straight people, I just like it more.*
>
> (M. Baker, personal communication, 22nd September 2013)

Mock explains that over several years her straight-identified undergraduate female students repeatedly chose to investigate gay masculinity as part of their final-year research projects. She suggests that identification with camp amongst young heterosexual women may be explained as an attempt to position themselves within a format of *femme* behaviour which feels less connected to traditional femininity and the oppression of women.

> I have gradually come to think that the researching of gay male camp is potentially a strategy by which heterosexual young women are not only

reclaiming, but apprenticing, what they consider to be non-oppressive femininity.

(Mock, 2003, p.21)

It is a very interesting analysis of the queered-but-not-queer position of straight women who may feel a sense of queerness in themselves and certainly raises questions about what is queerness per se. For Mock's students, to be queered-but-not-queer seems little to do with sexual desire and more a notion of *attitude*. This attitude may be that of women who are engaged with notions of femininity and feminism and who recognise, to some extent, the role of heteropatriarchal femininity in female gender oppression. A similar argument could be made regarding women in Roller Derby [a female contact sport on roller skates in which players create a costumed persona that incorporates elements of camp and third-wave feminism] and perhaps even some styles of New Burlesque. Importantly, Mock notes that in all of her students' work, a discussion of erotic desire is noticeably absent. Her students do not suggest that they find gay male pornography arousing or that a man in female drag might seem sexually desirable to them. Similar to Smith's conference paper, a discussion of the sexual desires of the writing subject is avoided.

> I wonder why no-one wants to talk about sexual desire? Oh wait, I know why. It's embarrassing and private, and when you admit to something weird you risk raised eyebrows and your socially conservative relatives never talking to you again. Fair enough, that's why I only lasted two meetings at the Rotary Club. But is it really fair enough to ignore your own sexual desire in a discussion of queerness? I feel more and more that it is not fair at all. Why should 'lesbian', 'gay' and 'bisexual' be clear markers of who desires whom, but heteroqueers get to keep their desires private – so much so that nobody knows what a heteroqueer is! When I was talking to Brandi Amara Skyy in an interview recently, we chatted about queerness. I wanted to know her opinion on the heteroqueer, especially as when I have spoken to her before I sensed some discomfort with the notion of straight women performing as faux queens. I do not wish to misrepresent Brandi here, she was very clear in explaining to me that she has no problem with straight faux queens as long as they make the effort to understand the history and culture of drag and enter the performance genre with respect. Nevertheless she did admit to me that accepting straight faux queens has been a 'difficult bridge', and that there is always a tension or duality between wanting to

protect her community, or as she calls it the 'gaybourhood', and promoting inclusiveness within the LGBT world.

It was at this point that I admitted something to her that I had previously kept to myself. I told Brandi my little secret about drag: with some of the drag queens I've seen, I occasionally find them sexually desirable. It's not all drag queens; I usually don't feel that way about the younger queens, especially those who are extremely convincing as a beautiful woman. I tend to like the ones whose physique is stocky; who are over 30 and sometimes you can see hair on their arms and five o'clock shadow creeping through their dense layer of makeup. Their clothes fit awkwardly and attempts to corset their figure have been unsuccessful. Men who drag this way are sometimes referred to as 'butch queens'. I admitted to Brandi that I would really like it if my fiancé dressed in drag, ideally to resemble Tim Curry as Frank 'n' Furter. I'm not sure why I feel this way, nor do I think it is overly important to know. Nonetheless, I told Brandi my secret and she thought it was a bit queer…

I don't believe that it is particularly strange that Mock's *Heteroqueer Ladies* would avoid a conversation about their own erotic desires. There is considerable risk in admitting to something sexual which is non-heteronormative. LGBT individuals have experienced this for a very long time, and the queer- and lesbian-identified women I talk to are very much aware of a real risk of violence and harassment because of their sexual and/or gender identity. An anxiety about the risks of being flagged as *queer* is understandably relevant to young women who sense queerness in themselves. Mock suggests that:

Anxiety appears to be the reflective mirror image of queer. Our anxious selves bite the nails that our queer selves are trying to grow (fashionably manicured with diamanté insets). The fascination that camp holds for my female performance students seems to be an attempt to address a difficult negotiation between cultural 'belonging' and their resistance of gendered expectation, an apolitical embracing of (somebody else's) political positioning.

(Mock, 2003, p.23)

Mock goes on to analyse the work of two performers who she argues engage in a performative transaction with gay men, inasmuch as they perform camp as a critical element of their act. She discusses Bette Midler, who famously apprenticed as a performer in New York's continental bath houses, and Kathy Burke as Linda in *Gimme Gimme Gimme*. She argues that both women intentionally perform as if they were men in drag, and project their sexual desire towards gay masculine men. She marks their *queered* performances as fundamentally different from similar characters such as *Ab Fab*'s Edina and Patsy, in as much as, 'while Edina and Patsy are camp transgressive heterofemme characters who are open to queer readings, they do not embody heteroqueerness'. (Mock, 2003, p.32) Mock illustrates how Midler often suggests in her performances that she is a drag queen; that she was once a man, and underneath her glitter and paint is a gay man with a 'sordid past'.

> Midler thus frames her gendered and eroticized body in a way that
> queers her sexual identity, by citing gay male performance codes rather
> than those usually associated with heterosexual femininity.
>
> (Mock, 2003, p.30)

She goes on to explain the confused sexual desires of *Linda* who is a thirty-something single lusting over gay masculine pop stars, and occasionally projecting her heterosexual fantasies onto her camp gay flat mate.

> All the embodied performative codings I have chosen to reflect upon
> are related in an important sense: they rely on an association with gay
> male cultural products in order to indicate the difference between a
> reification of heteropatriarchal femininity and heterofemme queerness.
>
> (Mock, 2003, p.34)

As I near the end of this contextualisation of the heteroqueer, as it appears in the limited literature which attempts to address it, I find Mock's paper the most relevant in a discussion of faux queens. For a faux queen, the sexed body she plays is deliberately and always flexible, and she intentionally engages in a transaction of gay male performative codes. Some faux queens say they perform as if there were balls under their dress, some say they transform from woman to gay man to drag queen in their dressing process. Others perform in order to cause gender confusion; Brandi has said, 'If someone asks me if I'm a boy or a girl, I've done my job'. (B. Garcia, personal communication, 22nd February 2013)

Even after visiting San Francisco and talking with faux queens about their experiences of queerness, I still feel some discomfort with the insistence on juxtaposing straight with queer or hetero with queer. There is just something which feels tense about the pairing of two words so opposite to each other and so politically loaded. I also still feel uncomfortable with labelling myself *queer* without also putting a marker on my heterosexual identity. It seems unfair for straight-identified people to say 'I'm queer' and send out mixed messages about sexuality and gender identity, which could also be read as disregard for the very real struggles that LGBT individuals face day-to-day. For this reason, I feel the notion of *cultural queerness*, mentioned to me by Fauxnique and L Rob Hubby in their interviews, may quell some of that discomfort. To label oneself as *culturally* queer rather than *sexually* queer acknowledges in some respect that a person can be sexually attracted to the opposite sex but also express an *attitude* of queerness which does not fit with mainstream values, politics and lifestyles in Western society. It also acknowledges that, 'I'm not gay, and I know that I have not and will not face the same struggles as you, but my cultural orientation allies with yours and feels that your struggle is unnecessary and unjust'.

A Brief Conclusion

This piece of writing is intended not as a complete thesis chapter or a journal article, but instead as a *slice* taken from my thesis draft. Not all questions raised are resolved, but instead the writing lets questions emerge to be dealt with in other areas of the thesis document, and in creative work. I aim to complete this chapter by linking a concept of *cultural queerness* with faux queen performance and I will argue faux queen performance as a conscious expression of queerness and as a queer performative transaction with gay male drag queens.

Works Cited and Consulted

Butler, J. (1999) *Gender Trouble*. New York & London: Routledge

Butler, J. (2011) *Bodies that Matter: On the Discursive Limits of 'Sex'*

Heasley, R. (2005) 'Queer Masculinities of Straight Men: A Typology', *Men and Masculinities* 7(310), pp.310–20

Heasley, R. (2013) 'Crossing the Borders of Gendered Sexuality: Queer Masculinities of Straight Men'. In C. Ingraham (ed.), *Thinking Straight: The Power, Promise and Paradox of Heterosexuality*. Hoboken: Taylor and Francis

Hennessy, K. (1992) 'Addressing the Queer Man's Role in the New World Anarchy and the Future of the Men's Movements in the Dis/United States'. San Francisco: Abundant Fuck Publications

Jagger, G. (2008) *Judith Butler: Sexual Politics, Social Change and the Power of the Performative*. London: Routledge

Jagose, A. (1996) *Queer Theory*. Victoria: Melbourne University Press

Kirsch, M. (2006) 'Queer Theory, Late Capitalism and Internalised Homophobia', *Journal of Homosexuality* 52(1–2), pp.19–45

Mock, R. (2003) 'Heteroqueer Ladies: Some Performative Transactions Between Gay Men and Heterosexual Women', *Feminist Review* 75, pp.20–37

Powers, A. (1993 June 29) 'Queer in the Streets, Straight in the Sheets: Notes on Passing', *Village Voice*, pp.24, 30–1

Slagle, R.A. (2006) 'Ferment in LGBT studies and queer theory: Personal ruminations on contested terrain', *Journal of Homosexuality* 52(1/2), pp.309–28

Smith, C. (1997) *How I Became a Queer Heterosexual*. Paper presented at the Beyond Boundaries: An International Conference on Sexuality University of Amsterdam

Taormino, T. (2003) 'The Queer Heterosexual', *Village Voice*

Warner, M. (ed.) (1993) *Fear of a Queer Planet: Queer Politics and Social Theory* (Vol. 6). Minneapolis: University of Minnesota Press

••

Performance, like research, like learning, like life, is a striving to appreciate, create and articulate particular experiences. Truth – or what regularly passes for truth – might well be an aim but it is rarely if ever realised, and validity is ultimately as much a question of context as content. Lived experiences, in their re-telling, become stories of the past and the fact that memory is only ever an act of, and in, the present means that everything becomes sullied by time. We can remember as best we can without ever believing that our memories of events are to be trusted, which is why forms that show doubt and uncertainty are conversely the most honest we can find. There are (if we dare use the term without recourse to inverted commas) realities of the past and realities of the now, but neither one of these travels well.

Despite the deconstructionist ravages of postmodernism, narrative remains the most common way that we disseminate the increasing complexities of life through the expanding fluidity of language. The inclusivity of autoethnography allows for a maximisation of experience, offering multiple and immersive readings from a viewpoint that acknowledges the intrinsically subjective nature of observation, analysis and recall, allowing for the fact that stories are never merely told by the teller. Rather, they are invented and created, fashioned and made, uttered always and often unwittingly in the image of the speaker; and how we are expected to tell our stories has massive import on our ways of telling. The expectations and demands of spectators and readers play a large part in determining the choices we make (or think we make) as tellers. As the once provocative too soon turns into prescription and conventions quickly become conventional, we do well to remember that there are no binaries between the teller and the tale, the performer and the role, the researched and the researcher. There are precious few, either, between the spectator and the spectacle. As spectators we project our own characteristic and character-driven fantasies onto the narratives we watch. These fantasies are more often than not unconscious wishes, which we are unable to bring to easy fruition in our daily lives. In this way, the wishes and desires that we perceive as belonging to on-stage, on-screen and on-page characters are in no small part the result of spectatorial projections.

From this point on, our unconscious desires determine our conceptions, transforming a series of idiosyncratic fantasies into that which we choose to call 'understanding the text'. The phenomenon we refer to as 'scholarly reading' is no different in kind to any other: the scholarly elements, such as they are, stem from the manner of articulation and the ease with which one is able to cross-reference opinions, lending validity and gravitas to the otherwise commonplace. Ethnography is itself a spectatorial act. We watch, we note and we make sense. And like all spectators we have no choice but to alter and construct as we go. Acknowledging one's own subjectivity is not an add-on so much as a stripping away of the subterfuge that comes whenever we seek to present as factual that which is eight parts fantasy fulfilment. Through notions of performative and inscripted space as liminal sites, where the personal is in endless dialogue with the public, autoethnography exists to reacquaint us with that which art always knew and academia too-often forgets. In holding up its mirror, something of the performer's nature is always also captured in the frame. If it is true that we know the artist by the art, it is no less the case that we know the art a little better when we add flesh to the signature at the bottom right of the canvas. Who, after all, would not choose to know the hand that writes and the 'I' that sees?

Where autoethnographical performance demonstrates its innate historical and cultural situatedness through which identity, experience, memory and craft are endlessly negotiated and refashioned, much solo performance work downgrades those same structural inequities which first prompted the actor to articulate the self. These inequities of class, ethnicity, age, appearance, gender, sexuality, finance, education, access and so on are too-often sacrificed to the twin cultures of confession and trauma that are beginning to infuse every aspect of contemporary life. As with the ubiquity of the memoir/momoir, performances dealing with trauma have marked out their territory within the broad realm of victim art through their narration of instances of individual abuse. And there is clearly a legitimate place for work of this kind. Autoethnographical work, however, might be better served by addressing representations of the gendered, classed and raced experience, prompting and engaging ideas of community, individuality and belonging, exploring and exposing the ways in which particular freedoms are granted and/or restricted to particular social groups. It is through the presentation of these experiences of individual social mobility that the ways in which concealed privileges are deployed in order to enable or constrain are exposed to scrutiny, if not quite made ready for change.

A number of performative modes exist with the aim of showing the ways in which identity and self are social constructs and which seek to expose the act of performance as a constructed and value-driven phenomenon. In this way performers are able to critique certain constructs at the same time as they can contextualise them within broader social–political frameworks. Autoethnographical performance is one such mode, one that reveals its material as autobiographical at the same time as it foregrounds the attempt to communicate matters of shared interest to spectators based on societal rather than primarily intellectual or aesthetic concerns.

As we well know, the road to hell is paved with good intentions. And whilst nobody ever sets out to make bad work, other than as a peculiar form of self-knowing critique, our intent is not always matched by creative ability. We set up an instinctive body swerve away from technical accomplishment whenever we focus too strongly on creating frames that justify our practice, rather than letting it stand on its own. We see this in the texts that accompany autoethnographic performance, where the claims for the work begin to stand for the work in itself. And whilst few would seriously diminish the value of contextualising frames, these need ultimately to frame something worth seeing beyond the elegance of their own supporting structures.

Because he has published in the field of autoethnography, because his views are thus in the public domain and because his thesis is excellent work, hari stephen kumar's 2011 MA thesis, *Decolonizing Texts: A Performance Autoethnography* is an appropriate text for this chapter to discuss. This is so not least because the writing talks a very different fight to the one the practice displays. kumar's thesis begins with what is on the face of it a similar series of claims to those made by autoethnographic performers and performative autoethnographers elsewhere. His opening paragraph forms a righteous resistance to the enslavement of ideas and humanity wrought by colonisation and it is worth quoting at some length here. kumar tells us that he writes:

performance autoethnography as a methodological project committed to evoking embodied and lived experience in academic texts, using performance writing to decolonize academic knowledge production. Through a fragmented itinerary across continents and ethnicities, across religions and languages, across academic and vocational careers, I speak from the everyday spaces in between supposedly stable cultural identities involving race, ethnicity, class, gendered norms, to name a few. I write against colonizing practices which police the racist, sexist, and xenophobic cultural politics that produce and validate particular identities. I write from the intersections of my own living experiences within and against those cultural practices, and I bring these intersections with me into the academic spaces where I live and labor, intertwining the personal and the professional. Within the academy, colonizing structures manifest in ways that value disembodied and objectified Western knowledges about people, while excluding certain bodies and lived experiences from research texts.

(kumar, 2011)

All of this is well and good, noble even within a Denzinesque context; but the issue is not whether performance autoethnography *can* form this type of resistance so much as whether it *does*. And, as is often the case with autoethnography where focus is on the methodology, this can often conceal a paucity of research achievement. Indeed one could argue that the focus of achievement is on the ability to strike another autoethnographical notch on the post of research, rather than to add anything significant to our understanding of the subject of the thesis. As long as the subject is the methodology, the approach provides a safety net through which weak research is not easily allowed to fall.

With the *caveat* that kumar's own research is far from weak, on the following page he puts his shoulder to the wheel of his intent, which is namely to 'disrupt acts of academic(s) writing as the textual labor most privileged in the academy. In this thesis I write messy acts of embodied knowledges'. Approximately half of kumar's 150 pages demonstrate rigorously referenced and soundly argued work and the remaining pages are comprised of elegantly constructed performance texts. kumar's thesis does little to disrupt textual labour and, whilst the acts of embodied knowledges he writes are certainly messy, his writing *of them* is extremely neat. In other words, the thesis is neither disruptive nor messy and the structure of the thesis is really quite conventional: events are discussed, analysed and contextualised within historical and current frameworks in ways that coalesce into something that is recognisably a thesis, even if the introduction fails in any significant way to function as the 'stand-alone performance text' that kumar claims. As many have argued (Blau, 1965; Schechner, 1988; Carlson, 2004) and as others, including kumar himself, have shown, the term 'performance text' has no strict definition – no more strict than those of terms like 'art', 'poetry' or 'music', when these operate toward the outer edges of convention. In this sense, describing the introduction to a thesis as performative tells us at once no more than we already know and no more than we have known since Marinetti's Futurist texts. In other words, no more than we have known for a century.

It is worth reiterating here that kumar's thesis is well-written, well-argued and clearly of an extremely high standard. And no critique of the work *as thesis* is intended. What is being critiqued is the sense in which people feel the need to frame what are self-evidently academically acceptable pieces of work as outlaw acts of rebellion (kumar certainly does this and so, elsewhere, have many others, myself included). The battle for methodological flexibility within research has been fought by braver souls in earlier times and there is little need, really, for us to present ourselves as soldiers in a war that has long been won.

As with kumar's work, Barbara Bickel's 2004 thesis for the University of British Columbia, 'From Artist to A/r/tographer: An Autoethnographic Ritual Inquiry into Writing on the Body', begins as an exercise in redundant hyperbole; as with kumar, Bickel's work is well established within the public arena and, as with kumar, it is worth quoting her at some length:

> I have re-appropriated educational language into the language of art.
> I experience performance ritual as pedagogy, recognize art making
> as research and curriculum making, view art as curriculum, and
> work with the body as text.... The question that guides this thesis is:
> What does it mean to me to have an ethical and aesthetic feminist
> art practice? The purpose of this research is to integrate art, text,
> language, and the body. To challenge the dualistic and damaging
> mind–body split that still operates within Western culture, this thesis
> responds to the numerous feminists who call for women to write from
> and with their bodies. Within the third space of ritual, resistances are
> engaged and my body, art and writing are re-forged as interconnected
> language. The question that lies underneath this thesis is: What
> kind of an academic, researcher, pedagogue will I become? Through
> a phenomenological process I embrace anti-pedagogy as an ethically
> resistant stance that teaches between the place of knowing and not
> knowing. Through practicing a psychoanalytic pedagogy within a/r/
> tography, my own internalized dualisms (imperfections) are exposed

and transformed. This thesis engages reflexively on my collaborative aesthetic and ethics and encourages collaboration as an essential feminist educative tool. This a/r/tographic and autoethnographic thesis documents my journey as a spiritual feminist artist, committed to transformative and community-based educational processes, to the expanded identity of an a/r/tographer.

(Bickel, 2005, pp.8–9)

And this is the crux of the matter: with all due respect to Dr Bickel, are many readers likely to care what it means to her to have an ethical and aesthetic art practice? I have certainly never encountered any feminist artists and/or practitioners whose work was *not* concerned with ethics and aesthetics. Come to that, is a reader likely to care what kind of academic, researcher and pedagogue Bickel will become? I suspect the answer is generally going to be no in each case. And why would we? And why should we? How hard might a performer–researcher have to work in order to make a stranger (a disinterested reader) interested in somebody else's 'internalised dualisms' and 'imperfections'? Very hard indeed and too hard for most of us. Once again, the problem is patently not with Bickel's levels of scholarship, nor with the quality of her arguments. The issue is with a self-embrace that might enhance our understanding of the artist and give us an insight into the art but which does little to address any wider issues of knowledge and understanding.

What the work does do is provide a template for subsequent artists to write about their own work in similar ways, so that Artist–Researcher C quotes Autoethnographer B who cites Autoethnographic Performer A. Hard to see a way in which this becomes in any way research that is resistant, unless it is enough to be resistant to members of a different club.

To be regarded as an act of research, a performance must generally meet some form of entry condition, meaning that it will usually be practice conceived and reflected upon in the interests of answering or addressing a clearly defined research question framed on the basis of a sound working knowledge of a particular field, and in the interests of contributing new understandings to it. Not all practice is creative and not all creative practice is research. Pinning the 'research' label to practice does not *ipso facto* make it so. Autoethnography as performance has earned its place at the table of research. It is as valid a framework of application and intent as any other. But this validity does not license the bad, nor does it disguise the shoddy or the cheap. Describing one's work as 'autoethnographic performance' does no more than invite a certain reading; and whilst this invitation is important, once we are into the work it is what we read and what it tells us that matters. The rest is window dressing and it turns autoethnography from a form of research that involves reflexive investigation, and awareness of self in the context of ethnographic field work and presentation, into something as plain, simple and solipsistic as self-ethnography.

To perform autoethnography is to engage in a form of social research that explores the researcher's personal experience and connects the autobiographical story to wider cultural, political and social meanings. In Denzin's view, this results in something that is not so much a method of gathering information as 'a vehicle for producing performance texts and performance ethnographies about self and society' in which 'text and audience come together and inform one another'. This leads to an innately relational situation where research methods in the social sciences do not simply describe the world as it is, but also enact it. The results are performative inasmuch as they have effects, make differences and enact realities: in essence, we can say that they can help to bring into being what they also discover. Kip Jones goes so far as to write that 'to the extent social science conceals its performativity from itself it is pretending to innocence that it cannot have'. (Jones, 2007)

If Jones's text displays the type of self-aggrandisement that has become common amongst autoethnographers – for example, when he writes that 'These qualitative investigators [such as Jones himself] are courageously developing arts-based research methods and dissemination techniques in order to both investigate deeper and reach wider audiences' – it also, and quite rightly, identifies performance as that which has become a 'catchphrase for the work of qualitative researchers no longer satisfied with typical PowerPoint conference presentations or journal restrictions'. (Ibid.) His comments on the ways in which new forms of dissemination can do justice to narrative interview material are astute and well made. Well-made arguments aside, Jones's paper hinges on the reframing of an after-dinner story he has told countless times as a newly located piece of performance autoethnography. In many ways, we have become used to this in performance academia, where back catalogues of occasionally ordinary practice are rehashed, heated up and served as examples of practice-led research, as though the application of the term alone was enough to make it so.

Jones refers to a story, told from his perspective, of being a gay man in a straight New York nightclub in 1965. Because the story is being morphed from a funny tale into something that alludes to performance autoethnography, Jones describes it as a celebration of 'being an outsider, seeing oneself from outside of the "norm", and the interior conflicts of "coming out" within a continuum as a (gay) male in a straight world.' (Ibid.) Jones notes that his narrative observations are set within a flux period of great social change, one in which sexuality could be viewed within 'the wider culture's need to set up a sexual binary and force sexual "choice" decision-making for the benefit of the majority culture'. (Ibid.) Furthermore, Jones points out that the piece does not unpack or analyse these phenomena, but rather is descriptive, a reflective interpretation of the confusion and self-doubt that such rites of passage typically present for gay and lesbian youths. Moreover, the presentation itself engages its audience in its own introspection and interpretation in a creative way. As autoethnography, it documents minor transient personal moments of everyday life: something transitory, lasting a day. Through the device of the fleeting moment, the story interrogates the certainties and uncertainties of the norms of modernity and sexuality. Such, at least, is Jones's belief. Readers can make their own minds up as to whether his work achieves this by locating the text for themselves.

It is clear that that the bulk of published autoethnography is concerned not just with the outsider status of Jones's narrative, nor even the desire to be seen as outside, but also with fatality, disease, cruelty and/or health problems – and this latter to such an extent that titles like Sophie Tamas's 'Writing and Righting Trauma: Troubling the Autoethnographic Voice' (2009) are ubiquitous. Fixated as it often is with the death of someone loved, physical disability, mental illness and/or drug dependency, violent sexual abuse and the general field of traumatic memories, this creates a kind of victim art that is difficult to criticise without appearing to attack the experience of the writer. Quite simply, the text is so drenched in tears that what it is saying becomes obscured by the seeming need to speak. The series of Left Coast Press books *Writing Lives: Ethnographic Narratives* epitomises this with titles such as *The Remains of Spousal Abuse*; whilst Tami Spry cites autoethnography as a form and process that allowed her to make 'critical, political, and personal sense of [her] experiences with sexual assault, grief, mental illness, and White privilege'. (Spry, 2001, p.711) Reasonably enough, Patricia Clough has had enough of this, going so far as to suggest that autoethnographers making work about the experiences of 'drug abuse, sexual abuse, child abuse, rape, incest, anorexia, chronic illness and death' are making autoethnography 'symptomatic of the trauma culture that has been outrageously presented in television talk shows'. (Clough, 2000) If it is possible to be critical of trauma art without appearing dismissive of the trauma itself, then the time to make oneself heard may well be now; for there is only so much woe-is-me tragedy that autoethnography can support before it mutates into the trivia of daytime television soap – with the only difference being that soap operas tend to be better performed.

Michael Hemmingson addresses this smartly in his 2008 article 'Make Them Giggle: Auto/Ethnography as Stand Up Comedy – A Response to Denzin's Call to Performance'. Here Hemmingson sends out his own call for the employment of stand-up comedy methods when performing autoethnographic texts. Arguing that autoethnography is often therapeutic in intent and that the best medicine is laughter, Hemmingson suggests that many comedians are 'already engaging in auto/ethnography, they simply do not know it or give it that label'. (Hemmingson, 2008, p.4) Perhaps the best performance autoethnography exists somewhere between Kip Jones's reframed after-dinner story of New York nightclubs, replete with the customary endnotes that mark the work as knowingly 'academic' even as its teller works against this, and a commitment to performance in which authenticity exists in the skilful telling of the tale, ethical concerns are determined by a home-town audience rather than a university panel, and spectators are offered more than the opportunity to witness a public act of self-healing.

Where a self-defined autoethnographer like Jones might appear to be stretching an elastic band to the moon, recycling a much-told story into something that can be submitted as an act of creative scholarship, works of certain others can stand as examples of emphatically effective practice. Hemmingson refers to the classic examples set by Lenny Bruce, Richard Pryor and, to a somewhat lesser extent, Freddie Prince Jr., each of whom used background stories of abuse, poverty and racism in ways that deconstructed what is uncomfortable and ugly and looked to make members of an audience, in a very Brechtian way, think about the subject at the same time as they were laughing at the comic's delivery. By exploring past pains, Hemmingson reminds us, these practitioners were operating in an autoethnographic mode that made their comedy therapeutic and healing at the same time as it was critically successful and effective. Indeed, Hemmingson reminds us that many comedians are already engaging in autoethnographic performance without knowing that they are, and without giving their work that label. If Whoopie Goldberg, Eric Bogosian and Spalding Gray provide the missing link between the comic raconteur and the performance artist who moves into the mainstream, the well-known film actor John Leguizamo is someone whose live work takes him back from Hollywood to his roots and his audience in New York City.

As the site in which the represented other of character is made manifest through the viscerally authentic performer, live work has always shown a tension between self and the shadows it throws; and no form is at the same time as shadowy and substantial as autoethnography. As with written autoethnography, the search for the defining features of autoethnographical performance has become something of a sub-industry in itself, to the extent that the struggle to equate facts, subjectivity, honesty and artifice folds in on itself like a Möbius Strip.

The emphasis at this point in the chapter is on representing aspects of a person's life through autoethnography in ways that speak to wider communities, and that do so whilst acknowledging performance in its fullest sense: not as a means through which one can escape from the realities of life through sentimentalised entertainment, but as a method through which we are encouraged to contemplate life imaginatively, deeply and with increased shifts in understanding. These shifts occur as soon as we acknowledge understanding as a 'series of perspective shifts' rather than as a 'once-and-for-all act'. At its best, we witness this with autoethnographers – or autoperformers, to borrow Michael Kirby's term – those practitioners whose work conforms to post-structuralist ideals by presenting material that acknowledges and investigates the relationships between subjective perspectives and the social–historical manifestations of construction.

The most important questions within autoethnographic performance are not about how accurately a specific work reflects the look of life, or how heavily the blood flows from a performer's self-lacerations, nor even how zeitgeist-connecting we find the *mise en scène*. What matters is how much the work allows, supports and encourages spectators to understand and grapple with the meanings of life as we/they live it. The challenge is to create from autoethnography a new ethically informed practice: one that approaches self as a social subject rather than self as self-justification. What matters most in autoethnographical performance is not necessarily a work's record of an authentic historical past (assumedly the lived experience of the author–performer) so much as the ways in which it functions as a form that is fundamental to the construction of modern life. The approach to performance adopted by John Leguizamo in his December 2003 Broadway Theatre performance of *Sexaholix… A Love Story* illustrates this.

Sexaholix is at once an example of autobiographical catharsis, through its reconstructing and revisiting of a life history, at the same time as it is an autoethnographical study of representation, translation and authorial agency. Where autobiography looks to tell the unique life experiences of an individual 'I', the same 'I' becomes plural through autoethnography. It does so inasmuch as the performance is made to stand for a community of people who share a common identity and representative experiences. Works like these are the 'outlaw genres' identified by Caren Kaplan, (1992) performances which compose strategically staged events for those artists who position themselves or who are themselves positioned beyond the parameters of normative theatrical empowerment. The term implies a shifting of the autobiography-by-rote of elitist postmodern performance towards a complex body of exchange between spectacle and spectator that explores issues of identity, self-representation and self-recognition. That this approach demands a different understanding of fitness for purpose is axiomatic.

Fundamental to our reading of Leguizamo's work as autoethnographical (despite his own occasional claims against such loaded terms) is our knowledge that social roles and their attendant values are communicated and absorbed through a chain of symbolic actions that are central to that which might elsewhere be usefully termed 'the body politic' and which, for the purposes of this chapter, we can describe as 'the body social'. This is not intended to mark some crude distinction between society and politics so much as it is a way of noting the performing autoethnographical body as the locus where cultural groups are able to share in, preserve and perpetuate their values. When Leguizamo describes his childhood experiences of the 'Fresh Air Fund', an organisation 'that takes poor underprivileged inner-city kids and sends them to a rich white family in the country for two weeks', his Broadway audience is split between those who laugh at the delivery of the line and those who laugh differently at what the line delivers, seeing their own experiences played back to them. (Leguizamo, 2008, p.93) Alan Read points to certain types of performance that take as their material 'the neglected and the undocumented' and this is what *Sexaholix* provides. (Read, 1993, p.2)

Perhaps the desire to make autoethnographic performance denies its own intent. Perhaps what it is that makes Leguizamo's work so effective is precisely its lack of academic pretention. An audience paying top dollar is unlikely to be satisfied with work that is earnest and noble and badly performed. Perhaps Bob Dylan and Bruce Springsteen are the autoethnographers that they are *because* they would never claim to be. They are first and foremost skilled storytellers and the fact that the stories they tell matter as much as they do has more to do with their skill and their craft than with their astute social concerns. When Brecht told us that a good idea, badly presented, dies a long time he could have been sounding a warning about autoethnographic performance that is glorious in intent and tragic in delivery.

Leguizamo's performative rhetoric is open to spectators rather than being closed off or solipsistic. Through work that is endlessly contingent, flexible and rooted in a play of communicative forms, the one thing we are not witnessing here is a prioritising of the idea of catharsis for, by and in honour of the artist. On the contrary, we experience, according to Mary Brewer, the type of performance through which we witness 'one of the cultural frameworks within which the spectator may recognise his/her location and level of complicity in... social conventions'. (Brewer, 2005, p.xiii) The postmodern rejection of the idea that assertions about the natural or social world can be objectively (and hence transculturally) true or false falls into disrepute when one considers Bertrand Russell's claim that the 'concept of "truth" as something dependent upon facts largely outside human control has been one of the ways in which philosophy hitherto has inculcated the necessary element of humility. When this check upon pride is removed, a further step is taken on the road towards a certain kind of madness'. (Russell, 1991, p.652)

Whilst an autoethnographical performance writer like Leguizamo might have an initial intent to explore aspects of self, this is also about the need for a place to share that voice. In the context of performance, creating text as a form of self-knowledge is always more than writing the individual self: it is about voicing that which power has silenced. In working the material of a life through autoethnographical forms, the individual's story is made to connect with those of others. The writer/performer is possessed of an individual voice, but this is made to connect to a collective experience and a collective voice, and it is at this point that a sense of community can be born through autoethnography. Shifting our focus from performative self-orientation as intrinsically private activity for public spaces, we are able to view autoethnography in the context of reigniting common values: of tapping into the values of communities through sharing stories that matter to more than just the storyteller and that speak from the body of individualistic recall to the body of collective experience.

Tami Spry is correct in her belief that good autoethnographic performance 'is not simply a confessional tale of self-renewal [but] a provocative weave of story and theory'. (Spry, 2001) The issue is what, precisely, each manifestation of autoethnographic research strives to provoke, because provocation without an end game amounts to nothing much at all. It is not enough for us to hide behind arguments that the work makes us think, or that the work allows us to better understand ourselves. Like Spry, Bochner is correct in his argument that no paradigm exists to determine valid and significant knowledge but even now, when research has been partly stripped of its old-school sense of purpose, the word still demands a certain intent to do more than fill in gaps in our knowledge: the gaps themselves need to be worth filling in the first place. If public consequence is linked to social commitment then autoethnographic performance needs to demonstrate its own commitment to society, and this involves more than playing to a society of scholars and like-minded sycophants.

Ultimately, autoethnographical performance is as much about a socio-philosophical ideal as a direct echo of experience. We know, after all, that it is not necessary to have the exact same experience as someone in order to connect with their stories, just as we know that empathy is possible through both similarity and difference. What matters most is that performance based on reconstructions of lived experience is harnessed to transformational identity politics in ways that pursue connections with spectators, rather than performers regarding us as being fortunate simply to witness their work.

Richard Courtney suggests that 'The kind of feeling carried by dramatic acts is usually beyond the reach of language.' (Courtney, 1964) Autoethnography is often about staging the ordinary and this comprises a challenge to the Barthesian ideal of the spectator or reader as someone who is 'without history, biography, psychology; he is simply that *someone* who holds together in a single field all the traces by which the written field is constituted.' (Ibid.) With autoethnography, the spectator's history, biography and psychology are central to the constitution of the work and central to its completion. In a Derridean sense, we can argue that it is the readers and spectators who literally *make sense* of the work they encounter, rather than that sense being placed there by the writer. Without some sense of being *simpatico* to the work, viewers and spectators can only function like non-believers at a religious service, observing what takes place before them without the sense of engagement that the work will generally require.

If successful theatre stills external conflict through some notion of cathartic release then perhaps the job of research is likewise to still conflict, to settle an issue, if only temporarily; and if not this, then to agitate debate, to stir the waters of public concern. All of which is to say that autoethnography needs to matter to the people it plays to as much as to the researcher who plays. We can indulge ourselves as far as our writing and performing goes without falling into the abyss of self-indulgence and the very best autoethnographic performance shows us how this can be achieved, even if not it does not quite give evidence of what it is that can be achieved by and through it. The opposite is also worth considering because, when our work neither settles nor stirs, it is healthy to step back and take some stock of what it is that we are actually trying to do and what it is that our work is hoping to achieve.

As we saw in Chapter One, Charles Marowitz likens writing about theatre to masturbation, an act that serves no fertile end (he said it, of course, in a book). Maybe he is right, at least inasmuch as creative practice, when *driven* by the need for research outcomes (which, let us not forget, are outcomes that appear in certain privileged sites and venues), denies the very thing it purports to seek. When we search for research outcomes, we can lose sight of the principles of research in false pursuit of the prize of promotion. It is a trap that both I and many of my colleagues (more than would care to admit it) do not so much fall into as seek out and throw ourselves upon with abandon.

This book is being published at a time when ideas of practice-led, practice-based and artistic research are at once both fiercely fought over and ubiquitous. At worst, this ubiquity has threatened to turn the search for appropriate and effective theatre research methodologies into a type of fashion statement, so that daring to engage in research in ways that do not amount to a practice-led methodology is both a glaring cultural faux pas and an ignominious form of career suicide.

It should be stressed that I am in no way *against* performance-led research: just the opposite in fact. My concern is not with performance as a means of knowing so much as with the ways in which knowing has been ambushed by performance. It is possible to be supportive of creative research at the same time as we are aware of the ideas of superiority that are wrapped up in the language we use and in the ways we describe ourselves. We read regularly now of 'live research', with all of its attendant view of the flipside as somehow inert, out of date, dead, even; of practice-led research and its researchers as being brave, innovative trail-blazers, engaged in precarious activities. These are the terms that we commonly use. We need to be careful that we do not use descriptions like these as terms that provide their own misleading guarantee.

The question with research is who gains from our work and how is its value defined? If our critical analyses are not published, they remain insignificant; if our practice is insignificant then it remains critically invisible and self-serving. What remains is confirmation bias linked to the lure of practice. Descartes' *'Je pense donc je suis'* says one thing; 'I practice therefore I am a practitioner' says something else – and something, I fear, rather less. (Germay & Poirrier, 2013)

Writing and live performance are in many ways as opposed as any two forms of expression could ever be. We write words in the moment for other people to read in other countries and contexts and times, knowing that the paragraphs and line breaks we suggest will be disrupted by the rhythms that different readers bring. We make performance in the moment, knowing that we are seeking to control time and experience for other people. When we want darkness, the lights go out; when we want collective surprise, we manufacture it; and everybody hears the lines we speak at the exact time we choose. Spectators are free to leave but we have more control over them than we can ever exert over readers. Creative practice forms its own articulation and practitioners tend to do their best speaking in and through their work For this reason, making performance as part of an autoethnographical submission requires something of a split personality.

Universities will generally ask that the written or critical part of a practice-led PhD will form part of a thesis, accompanying the creative or literary work or series of works. This critically written element will not generally exceed 40,000 words excluding appendices, tables and illustrative matter, on the assumption that a PhD will be regarded as equivalent to 80,000 words. The exegesis, then, is defined in most universities (and for the moment at least) as something amounting to not more than half of a traditional thesis.

A common approach in contemporary Australian universities to understanding the nature and shape of the exegesis defines it as a discussion of the context for the creative work. In this format, the student submits a written document that rehearses the historical, social and/or disciplinary context(s) within which the student developed the creative or production component of her or his thesis. Examples of this model in university documents provided by Alan Mann and Julie Fletcher are illuminating:

> At one university the creative or production-based thesis is described as an *amalgam* of studio-based research and the theorising of that research and the exegesis as a written document that presents relevant contemporary critical debates and practices which inform and position the studio work; at another, the thesis is comprised of an exhibition and a research paper [that] *supports and complements* the exhibition; and – a last example – still another university indicates that the written thesis accompanying the exhibition will be *on art theory, history or practice.*
>
> (Mann & Fletcher, 2000)

The exegesis is conceived as an explication of or comment on the creative production, and in this sense researchers absolutely need to be able to analyse their processes and to be as innately critical of their own approaches as they are aware of the critical contexts in which their own work is placed. This demands rather more than self-justification (although that is a part of it). It requires the ability to locate one's work within a thorough academic and aesthetic context, and it demands the type of self-analysis that autoethnography elsewhere champions. As in any other discipline, the thesis presents the results of an independently undertaken research project. In the case of autoethnographical performance, the result of the research is the submission and/or presentation of a work of creative practice. The exegesis exists to articulate the research framework. This framework will not necessarily be evident to viewers/spectators; indeed, performance makers will often seek to load ambiguity into their work rather than make their meanings overt. The exegesis functions then as a way of making hidden meanings overt and of exposing exactly what qualifies the work as *research*.

Viewed in this way, the imperative to write about one's work is neither reductive nor onerous; rather it is an opportunity to chronicle the processes of performance in ways that disambiguate method and meaning. It is our opportunity to guide the reader/viewer/examiner toward our own interpretation of what makes the work tick at the same time as honouring other perspectives.

Writing about Rose English's *The Double Wedding*, Geraldine Harris explains that 'the theoretical terrain in which this piece appears to be placed, in and of itself, suggests that in the final analysis this is a show which cannot be interpreted, only described.' (Harris, 1999, p.23) This is a negation of the fact that all description is interpretative. What it is that Harris chooses to describe is the result of an interpretative act, not vice versa. To suggest otherwise is to argue for a type of factual reporting that we know is impossible and ultimately undesirable. What makes Harris's reading of English interesting is the perspective she brings. If we accept that any reading of any culturally manufactured product, of any art, is an act of interpretation, then we are also recognising that the meaning of the work is interpreted and that all meaning is interpretative and personal. Every performative act can be consumed in multiple ways and the ways in which performance is interpreted are subject to innumerable variations of perspective. Meaning can no longer be discussed without referring to the questions of *who* reads the work, and *where*, *when* and *how* they do so. The circle is thus interactive and anticipatory in nature, with the spectator approaching the performance with the inevitability of projecting certain meanings onto and into it.

The codes on which performances are built are complex and, semiotics notwithstanding, the ways in which these codes are deciphered are never absolute. Italian art critics coined the term *inesspressionismo* to describe art which aspires to a state in which it means whatever the viewer chooses it to mean. For those of us who regard the Derridean idea that things may not mean what their creator intended as an eminently acceptable philosophical position, *inesspressionismo* or inexpressionism can still seem like a leap into an excess of liberality. In reality, inexpressionism differs little from the negotiated readings inherent in all forms of communication, with the perceiver incorporating intended and accidental responses to any given subject. As indeterminate works, performances cannot but leave spaces that the spectator will fill, and fix in, in the process of spectating.

Inexpressionism fails as a philosophical as well as a critical phenomenon because of the impossibility of creating an entirely open text: indications always exist, whether they are recognised as such or not. Meanings are suggested by the rigidity or otherwise of the codes in operation and these codes will, for the most part, be manipulated by the artist, by the creator of the work. An exegesis allows us to be honest and open about the ways we seek to manipulate and shape the spectators' response.

It is a characteristic of language that webs of meaning are generated and that any and all texts are necessarily self-contradictory. Performances are no different. They are, in Wittgenstein's terms, language games, (Lechte, 1994, p.247) works which, in seeking to utilise the language of performance, are handicapped 'because the attempt to do so itself constitutes a [further] language game.' (Ibid.) This contradiction is a part of making performance. The printed word has a permanence (and a status) that is usually denied to the ephemerality of performance. However, the existence of live performance in the *now* imbues it with a different relationship to truth. The work seen may be illusory, but the *seeing of it*, in this space and at this time, is rarely if ever in doubt. Readers of words written are not usually witnesses to the process of writing. Words, no matter how truthfully they may read, are constructed in the elsewhere whereas performances, no matter how other they may seem, are constructed in the here and now. Where performance charts a wrestling with the contradictions between truth and lies, these contradictions can be usefully explored in an exegesis, and its power and purpose should not be underestimated.

As with performance, so it is with documentation. The words you are reading, flat on the page or screen, strive to evoke ideas about performance at the same time as they are antithetical to much that is performative. In discussing performance-in-denial-of-closure, I seek now to close this book with an emphasis that hopes, against itself perhaps, that some of my thoughts are also yours: that the reader is able to trust both the teller and the tale.

As ever, of course, readers will think what they will.

Contributors

Dr Rebekka Kill is Head of School at the Leeds School of Art, Architecture and Design at Leeds Beckett University. Her research interests include disciplinary constructions of academic identity, practice-based research, festival performance and social media.

Dr Kill is a practising visual and performance artist, a social-media enthusiast and also works as a nightclub DJ. Her DJ gigs have included an underwater disco and a performance work where she played seven-inch records in alphabetical order for 24 hours without stopping. Rebekka's TED-style performance 'Facebook is like Disco and Twitter is like Punk' (2012–14) has had worldwide interest online and can be viewed on her blog http://djtheduchess.wordpress.com.

Niz Jabour has a unique position as a poet, theatre worker and investigator, stemming from his upbringing in Iraq, his training in the arts and his subsequent lengthy and involved experiences in exile, where he worked with local and exiled multi-ethnic communities in Australia, Iran and Pakistan.

Jabour was a child at the coming to power of the Ba'ath regime and a university student at the inception of Saddam Hussein's leadership. As an Iraqi artist, he studied theatre and directing for many years, only to see any possibilities for a future disappear as he lived through the sacking of libraries and the destruction of books. Jabour seeks to retrieve the buried experiences of Iraqi artists through engaging performers in a process of collaborative and exploratory theatre-building and shared dialogue.

Kate Rice is an award-winning Australian playwright. She trained as a professional actor at Victorian College of the Arts and then studied playwriting at NIDA (National Institute of Dramatic Art). Rice has been commissioned by Curtin University, Deckchair Theatre Company, Agelink Theatre Company, Black Swan Theatre Company, Barking Gecko Theatre Company, Darwin Theatre Company, Darwin High School and Corrugated Iron Youth Arts.

She has also written for children's television and several short films. Kate is currently researching a practice-led PhD through Curtin University on the ethics of creating theatre based on real stories.

Steph Brocken is currently in her third year of studying for a part-time PhD at the University of Chester. Her work looks at the ways in which influences from contemporary performance can help to encourage social, personal and political development in young people participating in youth theatre.

Brocken combines her research with professional practice as a drama facilitator, project manager and businesswoman, having run her own arts organisation, Minerva Arts, since 2009. She has studied at the University of Chester since 2006, undertaking both BA and MA studies in the English Department where, in 2009, she won the Valedictory Prize for Academic Achievement. Her research interests lie in the interaction between the arts and citizenship education, the role of self-employment and entrepreneurialism in young artists and the performance of magic in the nineteenth century.

Jamie Coull is a PhD candidate in the School of Media, Culture & Creative Arts at Curtin University in Perth, Western Australia. Her research interests include identity formation in performances of desire and fantasy, imaginative persona play in adulthood, emergent concepts of queerness, and how notions of private, public and the act of performance might be challenged in the age of online media and Web 2.0.

Coull's current research project towards her PhD is an autoethnography which critically explores these notions with reference to her personal interest in Faux Queen Drag.

Research Proposal Guidelines

How you write a research proposal for your research degree will be determined by a number of factors, not least the area of study and your previous experience of it. Writing a research proposal is one of the first tasks to be undertaken by all research programme students at university. The final word count for a PhD thesis is generally 80,000 to 100,000 words.

It is important to note that the comments that make up this appendix comprise an approximate guide and not a rule for research proposal writing. The notes focus on particular research traditions and will not necessarily address the requirements of other research centres or approaches. For practice-led and/or creative production theses, researchers are recommended to read appropriate literature in the field, examples of which are given at the end of this appendix. Whether you are studying for a PhD (Doctor of Philosophy), DCA (Doctor of Creative Arts) or MPhil (Master of Philosophy), a research proposal will allow you to focus your work and find a suitable supervisor. A proposal is therefore an important starting point for your research journey and not just a hoop to be jumped through.

Your writing of a research proposal will be dependent upon a number of factors. Before you commence, it is important that these factors are explored and identified, if possible with your potential research supervisor. The option discussed in this guide on writing a research proposal is to approach it as a mini project, meaning that your research proposal writing project has its time deadlines, quality benchmarks and associated costs. The information in this example draws on developing a PhD study research proposal that would be used for submission in most universities.

Dependent on your experience of the subject area, the average time allocated to writing a proposal could be anything from a couple of days (for someone who has just finished their master's degree and plans to develop their dissertation into a PhD) to many weeks (perhaps where you have found a new area of interest and want to take your career in this direction). For example, if you have recently graduated with a master's degree in an area in which you would like to develop your work further, the PhD research proposal could be the natural progression of your dissertation; in this case, you could start with the conclusions chapter where you reflect on your findings and identify new areas of study. Alternatively, you might have developed a new concept and would like to test it further in different settings. What is important is that you set yourself realistic expectations and also a target that beckons: that is to say, a target that is achievable *through the research* rather than in advance of it.

It is always advisable to see your research proposal writing as a first step to advancing your future career and not simply as writing a research proposal for its own sake. There are a number of reasons for this, not least the financial necessity to fund your work and the potential use of your findings for wider purposes in the future. Also, unless your work is unique, the contribution to knowledge (which is a basic requirement of a PhD) would be difficult to achieve. Although there are exceptions to this, and there are some researchers who simply take their degree to gain a research qualification, it is important that you are interested in the research area yourself and are not considering it simply because of your potential supervisor or a journal paper that mentioned that a specific area is important. What is of utmost importance is that the problem you set yourself (most PhD work will address a problem) is capable of being satisfactorily researched. For example, is there enough extant research for you to build your work on? Do you possess the requisite skills, or are you likely to develop these in time? Will you have adequate access to the research material? What will your research add to existing research in the field?

A research proposal is not something that should be submitted without a longer-term perspective and there are a number of issues that have to be considered before you submit your research proposal draft.

Given the chance, prospective students should initiate the process by briefing the Head of Research in the relevant University School on possible topics and gaining the director's reactions. The Head of Research (or equivalent) is the first recourse for the prospective PhD student and s/he will generally guide the overall thesis process. The next step is to write a draft of the proposal and submit it to the director in both hard copy and electronic form.

There is often no minimum or maximum word count for the proposal, but typically it is 15 to 20 pages. It should include a cover page with the title and the student's name, information that identifies it as a proposal for the given area.

It should go without saying that the submission of a poorly prepared draft can delay the thesis process considerably.

The purpose of the proposal is to make clear the student's thinking about the research on a topic that s/he intends to pursue. It should be unambiguous about how the dissertation will be an original contribution to conceptualisation and to the field's corpus of knowledge overall. It should focus on how the student will use original (e.g. survey data, ethnographic studies, observations) or primary (e.g. government documents, historical records, philosophical texts) source material to approach the topic. The proposal is not written in cement. Assuming it is approved by the School's research committee and a supervisor or supervisory team is allocated, the prospective student can make modest adjustments during the research phase. However, any major deviations from the proposal would normally need to be approved by the committee. The proposal should identify the prospective theoretical and methodological boundaries of the dissertation. What material and time restrictions would prevent the student from doing more than s/he intends to do?

The proposal should contain in outline form a timeline of anticipated steps in the dissertation process, from beginning to end. It should also contain a description of sites where the student anticipates gathering her/his material. Examples of sites are archives containing special documentary information, places where a survey is to be conducted, and specific contexts in which empirical observations are to be made. If the dissertation is to rely mainly on archival material, the proposal should identify the archives that are to be researched. If the dissertation is to rely on ethnographic or survey methods, the proposal should describe the research population and the locale(s) in which the research is to take place.

The proposal should usually be organised in sections rather than chapters and, if appropriate, subsections, with appropriate headings and subheadings. The first section should be an introduction that clearly defines or identifies the general topic, issue or area of concern, and thereby establishes a well-reasoned context for reviewing the relevant literature. It should explain the topic's scope and why the student has chosen the topic. Finally, it should lay out the organisational pattern of the proposal overall.

The second section is often the theoretical framework. This should describe relevant trends in published research on the topic along with any gaps in scholarship and conflicts in theory, methodology or conclusions.

The third section might consist of a thesis or a set of hypotheses, propositions or questions that the student intends to pursue. It should draw directly upon the previous two sections, so that the basis for addressing the thesis, hypotheses, propositions or questions is clear.

The fourth section is likely to focus on a procedure of the methods to be used to address the proposed thesis, hypotheses, propositions or questions. If the thesis proposes to test hypotheses, this section should describe the methods to be used for that purpose. If the thesis proposes to address a set of propositions or questions, it should describe the analytical procedure to be used. A thesis may rely on mixed methods, including both quantitative and qualitative approaches. If human subjects are involved, the student should outline in this section how s/he intends to satisfy ethics requirements.

The fifth section should describe the limitations of the proposed thesis. That is, what are the theoretical and methodological boundaries? What material and time restrictions would prevent the student from doing more than s/he intends to do?

The sixth section should be a tentative timeline for the thesis in outline form. It should show the overall anticipated beginning and ending dates as well as the beginning and ending dates for each phase of the thesis the student intends to complete.

The seventh section should describe the proposed research sites. For example, if the thesis is to rely mainly on archival material, the proposal should identify the archives that are to be researched. If the thesis is to rely on ethnographic, autoethnographic or survey methods, the proposal should describe the research population and the places in which the research is to be undertaken.

The final section should include a bibliography. When primary sources are to be used extensively, the bibliography should clearly differentiate the primary from the secondary sources that the student intends to examine.

Proposing a PhD project that utilises an autoethnographic approach is considerably less problematic now than it used to be. Most arts, humanities, and health and social sciences divisions will include members of staff who are supportive of autoethnography and who will generally embrace writing that is personal and experimental. Key to autoethnographic research is that it is always much more than a diary of experience.

Creative Production and Practice-led Research

The following books address practice-led research and are useful starting points for higher-degree-by-research proposals. An increasing number of articles are also available, and university websites offer their own reading lists and requirements.

Barrett, E., & B. Bolt (2010) *Practice as Research: Approaches to Creative Arts Enquiry*, London: I.B. Tauris & Co Ltd.

Freeman, J. (2010) *Blood, Sweat & Theory: Research through Practice in Performance*, Faringdon: Libri

Kershaw, B., & H. Nicholson (2010) *Research Methods in Theatre and Performance (Research Methods for the Arts and Humanities)*, Edinburgh: Edinburgh University Press

Nelson, R. (2009) *The Jealousy of Ideas: Research Methods in the Creative Arts*, Ellikon: Fitzroy

Nelson, R. (2013) *Practice as Research in the Arts: Principles, Protocols, Pedagogies, Resistances*, Hampshire: Palgrave Macmillan

Sample Ethical Clearance Form

Date:
Name of applicant:
Research project title:

Complete this form if you are a member of staff or a postgraduate research student who plans to undertake a research project which requires ethics approval via the University Ethics Review Procedure.

Or

Complete this form if you plan to submit a generic research ethics application (i.e. an application that will cover several sufficiently similar research projects).

PLEASE NOTE THAT YOUR SCHOOL, SUBJECT AREA OR DEPARTMENT MAY USE A VARIATION OF THIS FORM: PLEASE CHECK WITH THE ETHICS ADMINISTRATOR IN YOUR DEPARTMENT

This form should be accompanied, where appropriate, by all Information Sheets, Written Scripts and/or Covering Letters which you propose to use to inform the prospective participants about the proposed research, and/or by a Consent Form where you need to use one.

Once you have completed this research ethics application form in full, and other documents where appropriate, check that your name, the title of your research project and the date are contained in the footer of each page and email it to the Ethics Administrator of your academic department. Please note that the original signed and dated version of Part B of the application form should also be provided to the Ethics Administrator in hard copy.

I confirm that I have read the current version of the University's Ethics Policy Governing Research Involving Human Participants, Personal Data and Human Tissue, as shown on the University's research ethics website.

1. **Title of research project:**

2. **Contact person** (normally the Principal Investigator, in the case of staff-led research projects, or the student in the case of supervised postgraduate research projects):
   Title:
   Post:
   Email:
   Name:
   Department:
   Telephone:

3. **Is this a postgraduate researcher project? If yes, please provide the Supervisor's contact details:**
   Title:
   Post:
   Email:
   Name:
   Department:
   Telephone:

4. **Other key investigators/co-applicants** (within or outside University) where applicable – please list all (add more if necessary):
   Title:
   Post:
   Email:
   Name:
   Department:
   Telephone:

5. **Proposed Project Duration:**
   Start date:
   End date:

6. **Does your research involve:**
   - vulnerable adults or those with mental incapacity or mental illness?
   - prisoners or others in custodial care (e.g. young offenders)?
   - children or young people aged under 18 years of age?
   - using samples of human biological material collected before for another purpose?
   - taking new samples of human biological material (e.g. blood, tissue)?
   - testing a medicinal product?
   - taking new samples of human biological material (e.g. blood, tissue)?
   - additional radiation above that required for clinical care?
   - investigating a medical device?
   - social care research?

It is recommended that you familiarise yourself with the University's Ethics Policy Governing Research Involving Human Participants, Personal Data and Human Tissue before completing the following questions. Please note that if you provide sufficient information about the research (what you intend to do, how it will be carried out and how you intend to minimise any risks) this will help the ethics reviewers to make an informed judgement quickly without having to ask for further details.

7. **Briefly summarise:**

The project's aims and objectives:

(This should be in language comprehensible to a lay person i.e. somebody from beyond your research area and subject.)

The project's methodology:

(This should be in language comprehensible to a lay person.)

8. What is the potential for physical and/or psychological harm/distress to participants?

9. Does your research raise any issues of personal safety for you or other researchers involved in the project?

(Especially if taking place outside working hours or off University premises)

If yes, explain how these issues will be managed.

10. How will the potential participants in the project be:
    Identified?
    Approached?
    Recruited?

11. Will informed consent be obtained from the participants?

If informed consent or consent is NOT to be obtained, please explain why.

12. This question is only applicable if you are planning to obtain informed consent:

How do you plan to obtain informed consent? (i.e. explain your proposed process):

Remember to attach your consent form and information sheet (where appropriate).

13. What measures will be put in place to ensure confidentiality of personal data, where appropriate?

14. Will financial and/or in-kind payments (other than reasonable expenses and compensation for time) be offered to participants?

(Indicate how much and on what basis this has been decided.)

15. Will the research involve the production of recorded media such as audio and/or video recordings?

16. This question is only applicable if you are planning to produce recorded media:

How will you ensure that there is a clear agreement with participants as to how these recorded media may be stored, used and (if appropriate) destroyed?

Title of Research Project (including any subtitle):

I confirm my responsibility to deliver the research project in accordance with the University's policies and procedures and, where externally funded, with the terms and conditions of the research funder.

In signing this research ethics application form, I am also confirming that:

The form is accurate to the best of my knowledge and belief.

The project will abide by the University's Ethics Policy.

There is no potential material interest that may, or may appear to, impair the independence and objectivity of researchers conducting this project.

Subject to the research being approved, I undertake to adhere to the project protocol without deviation, unless formally agreed after resubmission of all forms, and to comply with any conditions set out in the letter from the University ethics reviewers notifying me of this.

I undertake to inform the ethics reviewers of significant changes to the protocol, by contacting my academic department's Ethics Administrator in the first instance.

I am aware of my responsibility to be up to date and comply with the requirements of the law and relevant guidelines relating to security and confidentiality of personal data, including the need to register when necessary with the appropriate Data Protection Officer.

I understand that the project, including research records and data, may be subject to inspection for audit purposes, if required in future.

I understand that personal data about me as a researcher in this form will be held by those involved in the ethics review procedure (e.g. the Ethics Administrator and/or ethics reviewers) and that this will be managed according to Data Protection Act principles.

If this is an application for a generic project, all the individual projects that fit under the generic project are compatible with this application.

I understand that this project cannot be submitted for ethics approval in more than one department, and that if I wish to appeal against the decision made, this must be done through the original department.

Name of the Principal Investigator (or the name of the Supervisor if this is a postgraduate research project):

Signature of Principal Investigator (or the Supervisor):

Date:

Bibliography

Ackroyd, J. (ed.) (2007) *Research Methodologies for Drama Education*, Stoke on Trent and Stirling, USA: Trentham Books Ltd

Adkins, B. (2009) 'PhD Pedagogy and the Changing Knowledge Landscapes of Universities', *Higher Education Research and Development* 28(2), 165–77

Agar, M. (1996) *The Professional Stranger: An Informal Introduction to Ethnography*, Academic Press

Alexander, B.K., C. Moreira & h. kumar (2012) 'Resisting (Resistance) Stories of Father: An Intertwined Triple Autoethnography', *Qualitative Inquiry* 9(3), 369–73

Allen, C. (1997) 'Spies Like Us: When Sociologists Deceive Their Subjects', *Lingua Franca*, November 1977, available from: http://linguafranca.mirror.theinfo.org/9711/9711.allen.html

American Judicature Society (2011) *Eyewitness Identification Reform*, available from: https://www.ajs.org/judicature-journal/editorial/eyewitness-identification-reform/

Anderson, L. (2006) 'Analytic Autoethnography', *Journal of Contemporary Ethnography*, 35(4), August 2006, pp.373–95

Appiah, K.A. (1993) *In My Father's House: Africa in the Philosophy of Culture*, New York: Oxford University Press

Aston, E., & G. Harris (eds) (2006) *Feminist Futures? Theatre, Theory, Performance*, Palgrave Macmillan

Auslander, P. (1992) *Presence and Resistance: Postmodernism and Cultural Politics in Contemporary American Performance*, Ann Arbor: University of Michigan Press

Austin, J.L. (1962) *How to Do Things with Words*, Oxford: Clarendon Press

____ (1970) 'Performative Utterances', *Philosophical Papers*, London: Oxford University Press

Australia Council (2013) *New Work: Eligibility and Selection*, available from: http://www.australiacouncil.gov.au/grants/2013/theatre-new-work [accessed 8 August 2013]

Bakhtin, M. (1986) 'Response to a Question from the *Novy Mir* Editorial Staff' in C. Emerson and M. Holquist (eds), *Speech Genres and Other Late Essays*, trans. V.W. McGee, Austin, TX: University of Texas Press, pp.1–7

Banes, S. (2001) *Subversive Expectations: Performance Art and Paratheater in New York 1976–85*, Ann Arbor, MI: University of Michigan Press

Barad, K. (2007) *Meeting the Universe Halfway: Quantum Physics and the Entanglement of Matter and Meaning*, Durham, NC: Duke University Press

Barnett, R. (2009) 'Knowing and Becoming in the Higher Education Curriculum', *Studies in Higher Education* 34(4), pp.429–40

Barthes, R. (1977) "The Grain of the Voice', *Image, Music, Text*, trans. S. Heath, New York: Hill and Wang, pp.179–89

———— (1986) *The Rustle of Language*, London: Blackwell

———— (1989) *The Reality Effect: The Rustle of Language*, New York: Hill & Wang

Barton, B. (2006) *Stripped: Inside the Lives of Exotic Dancers*, New York: New York University Press

———— (2011) 'My Auto/Ethnographic Dilemma: Who Owns the Story?' *Qualitative Sociology* 34(3), pp.431–45

Bass, E., & L. Davis (2002) *The Courage to Heal: A Guide for Women and Men Survivors of Child Sexual Abuse*, London: Vermilion Books

BBC News (2000) *Lockerbie Trial Hears Diary Evidence*, available from: http://news.bbc.co.uk/2/hi/957306.stm

Behar, R. (1996) *The Vulnerable Observer: Anthropology that Breaks your Heart*, Boston, MA: Beacon

Behar, R., & L.M. Suárez (2008) *Anthologies: The Portable Island: Cubans at Home in the World*, New York: Palgrave

Belfield, R. (2012) *The Power of Yes*, The National Theatre Discover Pack, London: National Theatre

Bell, D. (2008) 'Is there a doctor in the house? A riposte to Victor Burgin on practice-based arts and audiovisual research', *Journal of Media Practice*, http://search.ebscohost.com/login.aspx?direct=true&db=ufh&AN=34909837&loginpage=Login.asp&site=ehost-live&scope=site

Bellah, R.N., R. Madsen, W.M. Sullivan, A. Swindler & S.M. Tipton (1985) *Habits of the Heart: Individualism and Commitment in American Life*, Berkeley, CA: University of California Press

Bennett, S. (2004) *Susan Bennett's Workshop Autoethnography: Writing about the Self Analytically*, available from: http://www.humboldt.edu/~cpf/autoethnography.html

Bickel, B. (2005) 'From Artist to A/r/tographer: An Autoethnographic Ritual Inquiry into Writing on the Body', *Journal of Curriculum and Pedagogy* 2(2), pp.8–17

Bierman, J. (1979) 'Three Places in Rhode Island', *Drama Review* 23, pp.14–30

Billington, M. (2009) *Review of the Decade*, available from: http://www.theguardian.com/world/2009/dec/08/review-of-the-decade-theatre

Blackmore, J. (2009) 'Academic Pedagogies, Quality Logics and Performative Universities: Evaluating Teaching and What Students Want', *Studies in Higher Education* 34(8), pp.857–72

Blair, J. (2004) *Burning Down My Masters' House: My Life at the New York Times*, New York: New Millennium Press

Blau, H. (1965) *The Impossible Theater: A Manifesto*, New York: Macmillan

Blumer, H. (1969) *Symbolic Interactionism: Perspective and Method*, Englewood Cliffs, NJ: Prentice-Hall

Bochner, A.P. (2000) 'Criteria Against Ourselves', *Scholar Commons*, Florida: University of South Florida, available from: http://scholarcommons.usf.edu/cgi/ viewcontent.cgiarticle=1011&context=spe_facpub

Bolt, B. (2012) 'Back and beyond the sublime: Catastrophe in contemporary art', in: *CREATEC Symposium 2012 – Catastrophe and Creativity*. Perth, Western Australia

Bonney, J. (2000) *Extreme Exposures: An Anthology of Solo Performance Texts from the Twentieth Century*, New York: Theatre Communications Group

Boud, D., & A. Lee (2005) 'Peer Learning as Pedagogic Discourse for Research Education', *Studies in Higher Education* 30(5), pp.501–16

Bourriaud, N. (2002) *Relational Aesthetics*, Dijon, France: Les Presses du Reel

Bowman, R.L. (1998) 'Performing Social Rubbish: Humbug and Romance in the American Marketplace' in D. Pollock (ed.), *Exceptional Spaces: Essays in Performance and History*, Chapel Hill, NC: University of North Carolina Press, pp.121–41

Brewer, M. (2005) *Staging Whiteness*, Middletown, CT: Wesleyan

Bruner, J. (2004) *Making Stories: Law, Literature, Life*, Cambridge, MA: Harvard

Buñuel, L. (1976) in D.G. Zinder, *An Approach to a Surrealist Aesthetic of Theatre*, Michigan: UMI Research

_____ (1983) *My Last Sigh*, New York: Alfred A. Knopf

Burgin, V. (1986) *The End of Art Theory: Criticism and Postmodernity*, London: Macmillan

Butler, J. (1993) *Bodies that Matter: On the Discursive Limits of Sex*, London & New York: Routledge

_____ (1997) *Excitable Speech: A Politics of the Performative*, New York: Routledge

_____ (1999) *Gender Trouble: Feminism and the Subversion of Identity*, NewYork: Routledge

_____ (2004) 'Changing the Subject' in S. Salih & J. Butler (eds), *The Judith Butler Reader*, pp.325–56, Malden, MA: Blackwell

Callens, J. (ed.) (2004) *The Wooster Group and its Traditions*, Brussels: Peter Lang, pp.118–19

Carlson, M. (2004) *Performance: A Critical Introduction*, 2nd edn, New York: Routledge

Carr, C. (1993) *On Edge Performance at the End of the Twentieth Century*, Hanover: University Press of New England

Cary, L.J. (1999) 'Unexpected Stories: Life History and the Limits of Representation', *Qualitative Inquiry* 5(3), pp.411–27

Casey, K. (1995) 'The New Narrative Research in Education', *Review of Research in Education*, Vol. 21, AERA

Castro, J. (2008) *On Memoir and Money*, available from: http://joycastro. com/2008/07/on-memoir-and-money.html

Ceglowski, D. (2002) 'Research as Relationship' in N.K. Denzin & Y.S. Lincoln (eds), *The Qualitative Inquiry Reader*, Sage: Thousand Oaks, CA, pp.5–24

Chang, H. (2008) *Autoethnography as Method*, Walnut Creek, CA: Left Coast Press

Chaplin, S. (1900) 'Stained Glass Political Platform', *Century Magazine*, available from: http://www.weaselwords.com.au/

Chapman, A. (2007) 'Conscious Competence Learning Model', available from: http://www.businessballs.com/consciouscompetencelearningmodel.htm

Chatham-Carpenter, A. (2010) 'Do Thyself No Harm: Protecting Ourselves as Autoethnographers', *Journal of Research Practice* 6(1)

Chenhall, R., K. Senior & S. Belton (2011) 'Negotiating Human Research Ethics: Case Notes from Anthropologists in the Field', *Anthropology Today* 27(5), pp.13–17

Chomsky, N. (1993) *Year 501: The Conquest Continues*, Boston, MA: South End Press

Clandinin, D.J., & F.M. Connelly (1990) 'Stories of Experience and Narrative Inquiry', *Educational Researcher* 19(5), pp.2–14

_____ (2000) *Narrative Inquiry: Experience and Story in Qualitative Research*, San Francisco, CA: Jossey-Bass

Clark, R., & R. Ivanič (1997) *The Politics of Writing*, London & New York: Routledge

Clifford, J. (1986a) 'Introduction: Partial Truths' in J. Clifford & G.E. Marcus (eds), *Writing Culture: The Poetics and Politics of Ethnography*, Berkeley, CA: University of California Press, pp.1–26

_____ (1986b) 'On Ethnographic Allegory' in J. Clifford & G.E. Marcus (eds), *Writing Culture: The Poetics and Politics of Ethnography*, Berkeley, CA: University of California Press, pp.98–121

Clough, P. (2000) 'Comments on Setting Criteria for Experimental Writing', *Qualitative Inquiry* 6(2), pp.278–91, available from: http://qix.sagepub.com/content/6/2/278

Coe, R. (1985) *When the Grass was Taller: Autobiography and the Experience of Childhood*, London: Yale University Press

Coetzee, J.M. (1993) 'Confessions and Double Thoughts: Tolstoy, Rousseau, Dostoevsky', *Doubling the Point*, Cambridge, MA: Harvard University Press

Coffey, A. (1999) *The Ethnographic Self*, London: Sage

Conquergood, D. (2013) *Cultural Struggles: Performance, Ethnography, Praxis*, E.P. Johnson (ed.), University of Michigan Press

Corrigan, M., & P. Chapman (2008) 'Trust in Teachers: A Motivating element to learning', *Radical Pedagogy* 9(2), Spring 2008

Courtney, R. (1964) *Drama for Youth*, London: Sir Isaac Pitman & Sons

Crapanzano, V. (1986) 'Hermes' Dilemma: The Masking of Subversion in Ethnographic Description' in J. Clifford & G.E. Marcus (eds), *Writing Culture: The Poetics and Politics of Ethnography*, Berkeley, CA: University of California Press, pp.51–76

curezone.com (2012) 'I Suspect I was sexually abused, but have no specific memory, but all the Symptoms', *Educating Instead of Medicating*, available from: http://curezone.com/forums/am.asp?i=1120706

Curzon-Hobson, A. (2002) 'A Pedagogy of Trust in Higher Learning', *Teaching in Higher Education* 7(3), pp.265–76

Dandby, S., & A. Lee (2012) 'Researching Doctoral Pedagogy Close Up: Design and Action in Two Doctoral Programs', *Australian Universities' Review* 54(1), pp.19–28

Davies, B., & S. Gannon (2006) *Doing Collective Biography*, Berkshire: Open University/McGraw-Hill

de Botton, A. (2002) *The Art of Travel*, London: Hamish Hamilton, p.15

Delamont, S. (2007) 'Arguments against Auto-Ethnography', Paper presented at the British Educational Research Association Annual Conference, Institute of Education, University of London, 5–8 September 2007, available from: http://www.leeds.ac.uk/educol/documents/168227.htm

DeLeon, A.P. (2010) 'How Do I Begin to Tell a Story that Has Not Been Told? Anarchism, Autoethnography, and the Middle Ground', *Equity & Excellence in Education* 43(4), pp.398–413

Deleuze, G., and F. Guattari (1987) *A Thousand Plateaus: Capitalism and Schizophrenia*, Minneapolis, MN: University of Minnesota Press

Denzin, N.K. (1989) *Interpretive Biography*, Newbury Park, CA: Sage

_____ (1997) *Interpretative Ethnography*, Newbury Park, CA: Sage

_____ (1999) *Cultural Studies: A Research Annual*, Volume 4, Bingley: Emerald Group Publishing

_____ (2001) 'The Reflexive Interview and a Performative Social Science', *Qualitative Research* 1(1), pp.23–46

_____ (2002) *Symbolic Interactionism and Cultural Studies*, Oxford: Blackwell

_____ (2003a) 'The Call to Performance', *Symbolic Interaction* 26(1), pp.187–207

_____ (2003b) 'Performing [Auto] Ethnography Politically', *Review of Education, Pedagogy, and Cultural Studies* 25, pp.257–78, available from: http://www.kakali.org/memphiswebsite/kakaliorg1/8562/PerformanceEthnography/Denzin.%20Performing.pdf

_____ (2005) *Performance Ethnography: Critical Pedagogy and the Politics of Culture*, Thousand Oaks, CA: Sage

Denzin, N.K., & Y.S. Lincoln (2005) *The Sage Handbook of Qualitative Research*, Thousand Oaks, CA: Sage

Denzin, N. (2006) 'Analytic Autoethnography, or Déjà Vu all Over Again', *Journal of Contemporary Ethnography* 35(4), August 2006, pp.419–28

Derrida, J. (1978) *Writing and Differènce*, trans. Alan Bass, Chicago, IL: University of Chicago Press

Dick, B. (2012) '*What is Action Research?*' *Action Research and Action Learning for Community and Organisational Change*. Available from: http://www.aral.com.au/

Domínguez, D. (2007) *An Autoethnographic Approach to Fieldwork at the Centre for Qualitative Research*, Bournemouth University, Summer 2006, available from: http://www.bournemouth.ac.uk/ihcs/rescqrddr.html

Douglas, K. (2001) '"Blurbing" Autobiographical: Authorship and Autobiography', *Biography* 24(4), pp.806–26

Doyle, J.M. (1998) 'No Confidence: A Step Toward Accuracy in Eyewitness Trials', *Champion*

Eagleton, T. (1996) *Literary Theory: An Introduction*, Minneapolis, MN: University of Minnesota Press

Eakin, P.J. (1998) 'Relational Selves, Relational Lives: The Story of the Story' in G.T. Couser and J. Fichtelberg (eds), *True Relations: Essays on Autobiography and the Postmodern*, Connecticut: Greenwood Press

_____ (1999) *Making Selves: How Our Lives Become Stories*, Ithaca, NY: Cornell University Press

_____ (2004) 'What Are We Reading When We Read Autobiography?' *Narrative* 12(2), pp.121–32

Earl, R. (2013) 'Why I Want my Diaries Burned', *Guardian*, 16 September 2013, available from: http://www.theguardian.com/books/shortcuts/2013/sep/16

Eco, U. (1994) *Six Walks in the Fictional Woods*, Cambridge, MA: Harvard University Press

Edwards, R. (2006) 'A Sticky Business? Exploring the "and" in Teaching and Learning', *Discourse Studies in the Cultural Politics of Education* 27(1), pp.121–33

Eisner, E. (1991/1998) *The Enlightened Eye: Qualitative Inquiry and the Enhancement of Educational Practice*, New Jersey: Prentice Hall

Eliot, T.S. (1932) *Selected Essays, 1917–1932*, New York: Faber & Faber

Ellingson, L., & C. Ellis (2008) 'Autoethnography as Constructionist Project' in J.A. Holstein & J.F. Gubrium (eds), *Handbook of Constructionist Research*, pp.445–66, New York: Guilford Press

Ellis, C. (1993) '"There are Survivors": Telling a Story of Sudden Death', *Sociological Quarterly* 34, pp.711–30

_____ (1995) *Final Negotiations*, Philadelphia: Temple University Press

_____ (1996) 'Maternal Connections' in C. Ellis & A.P. Bochner (eds), *Composing Ethnography: Alternative Forms of Qualitative Writing*, Newbury Park, CA: Sage

_____ (2000) 'Creating Criteria: An Ethnographic Short Story', *Qualitative Inquiry* 6(2), pp.273–7

_____ (2004) *The Ethnographic I: A Methodological Novel About Autoethnography*, New York: Altamira Press

Ellis, C., T. Adams & A.P. Bochner (2010) 'Autoethnography: An Overview', *Qualitative Social Research* 12(1), Art. 10, available from: http://nbn-resolving.de/urn:nbn:de:0114-fqs1101108

Ellis, C., & A.P. Bochner (2000) 'Autoethnography, Personal Narrative, Reflexivity: Researcher as subject' in N.K. Denzin & Y.S. Lincoln (eds), *The Handbook of Qualitative Research*, second edition, pp.733–68, Newbury Park, CA: Sage

Emerson, R.M., R.I. Fretz & L.S. Shaw (1995) *Writing Ethnographic Fieldnotes*, Chicago: University of Chicago Press

Fabio (2007) *The Day Alvin Gouldner Punched a Guy*, available from: http://orgtheory.wordpress.com/2007/09/24/the-day-alvin-gouldner-punched-a-guy/

Fine, G.A. (1993) 'Ten Lies of Ethnography', *Journal of Contemporary Ethnography* 22(3), pp.267–94

Finley, S. (2005) 'Arts Based Inquiry: Performing Revolutionary Pedagogy' in N.K. Denzin & Y.S. Lincoln (eds), *The Sage Handbook of Qualitative Research*, third edition, Thousand Oaks, CA: Sage

Flannery, K. (2003) *False Memory Syndrome and The Brain*, available from: http://serendip.brynmawr.edu/bb/neuro/neuro03/web2/kflannery.html

Fleming, P. (2005) *The Ethics of Tragedy: Plot Victims are People Too!*, available from: http://www.writing-world.com/fiction/ethics.shtml

Flynn, E. (1961) *My Wicked, Wicked Ways*, New York: Dell Publishing

Foucault, M. (1978) *The History of Sexuality: Volume I*, trans. Robert Hurley, New York: Vintage

_____ (1980) *Power/Knowledge: Selected Interviews and Other Writings 1972–1977*, London: Harvester

_____ (1982) 'The Subject of Power' in H.L. Dreyfus & P. Rabinow (eds), *Michel Foucault: Beyond Structuralism and Hermeneutics*, pp.208–28, Chicago, IL: University of Chicago Press

_____ (1991) 'Questions of Method' in G. Burchell, C. Gordon & P. Miller (eds), *The Foucault Effect: Studies in Governmentality*, Chicago, IL: Chicago University Press

_____ (2000) *Power*, New York: New Press

Finley, S. (2005) 'Arts-based inquiry: Performing revolutionary pedagogy', in N.K. Denzin & Y.S. Lincoln (eds), *The Sage Handbook of Qualitative Inquiry*, third edition, Thousand Oaks, CA: Sage

Fox, R. (2013) *The Perils, Politics, and Economics of Publishing Autoethnography*, available from: http://raganfox.wordpress.com/2013/04/28/the-perils-politics-and-economics-of-publishing-autoethnography/

François, P., T. Syrjämaa & H. Terho (2008) *Power and Culture: New Perspectives on Spatiality in European History*, Pisa: PLUS-Pisa University Press

Freeman, J. (2007) 'Making the Obscene Seen: Performance, Research and the Autoethnographical Drift', *Journal of Dramatic Theory & Criticism*, Spring 2007, pp.5–14

_____ (2010) *Blood, Sweat & Theory: Research Through Practice in Performance*, Faringdon: Libri

French, C. (2009) *Families are Still Living the Nightmare of False Memories of Sexual Abuse*, available from: http://www.guardian.co.uk/science/2009/apr/07/sexual-abuse-false-memory-syndrome

Freud, S. (1963) *General Psychological Theory*, New York: Scribener

_____ (1985) *Art and Literature*, London: Penguin Books

_____ (1995) *Moses and Monotheism*, New York: Vintage

Fusco, C. (1995) *English is Broken Here: Notes on Cultural Fusion in the Americas*, New York: The New Press

_____ (1999) *Corpus Delecti: Performance Art of the Americas*, London and New York: Routledge

_____ (2001) *The Bodies That Were Not Ours: And Other Writings*, London and New York: Routledge

Gallagher, K., & A. Wessels (2011) 'Emergent Pedagogy and Affect in Collaborative Research: A Metho-pedagogical Paradigm', *Pedagogy, Culture and Society* 19(2), pp.239–58

Geertz, C. (1968) 'Thinking as a Moral Act: Ethical Dimensions of Anthropological Fieldwork in the New States', *Antioch Review* 28, pp.131–68

Genslinger, N. (2011) 'A Moment of Silence, Please, For the Lost Art of Shutting up', *New York Times Sunday Book Review*, 28 January 2011

Gentile, J.S. (1989) *Cast of One: One-Person Shows form the Chautauqua Platform to the Broadway Stage*, Chicago, IL: University of Illinois Press

_____ (2003) 'A *TPQ* Interview: Tim Miller on Autobiographical Storytelling', *Text and Performance Quarterly* 23, pp.271–87

Germay, R., & P. Poirrier (2013) *Le Théâtre Universitaire: Pratiques et Expériences*, Éditions Universitaires de Dijon

Gilmore, L. (2001) *The Limits of Autobiography: Trauma and Testimony*, New York: Cornell University Press

Gingrich-Philbrook, C. (1997) 'Autobiographical Performance Scripts: Refreshment', *Text and Performance Quarterly* 17, pp.352–60

_____ (1998) 'Autobiographical Performance and Carnivorous Knowledge: Rae C. Wright's *Animal Instincts*', *Text and Performance Quarterly* 18, pp.63–79

Gladwell, M. (2002) *The Tipping Point: How Little Things Can Make a Big Difference*, New York: Back Bay Books

_____ (2008) *Outliers: The Story of Success*, London: Penguin Books

Goffman, E. (1959) *The Presentation of Self in Everyday Life*, Garden City, NY: Doubleday

_____ (1963) Behaviour in Public Places, New York: Free Press

Goldberg, R. (1988) *Performance Art from Futurism to the Present*, New York: Thames and Hudson

Goldner, V. (2006) *Girl's Diary Evidence in Sex Case*, available from: http://www. rickross.com/reference/kenja/kenja17.html

Goleman, D. (1998) *Working with Emotional Intelligence*, London: Bloomsbury

Gómez-Peña, G. (1994) *Warrior for Gringostroika*, Saint Paul, MN: Graywolf Press

_____ (2000) *Dangerous Border Crossers: The Artist Talks Back*, London and New York: Routledge

_____ (2004) 'In Defence of Performance Art' in A. Heathfield (ed.), *Live: Art and Performance*, London: Tate Publishing

_____ (2005) *Ethno-Techno: Writings on Performance, Activism and Pedagogy*, London and New York: Routledge

Goode, E. (2010) *Deviant Behaviour*, Upper Saddle River, NJ: Pearson Education

Gornick, V. (2001) *The Situation and the Story: The Art of Personal Narrative*, New York: Farrar, Straus and Giroux

Grace, S., & J. Wasserman (2006) *Theatre and Autobiography*, Vancouver: Talon Books

Grand, S. (2003) *Creation: Life and How to Make It*, Cambridge, MA: Harvard University Press

Gray, R.E. (2003) 'Performing on and Off Stage: The Place(s) of Performance in Arts-Based Approaches to Qualitative Inquiry', *Qualitative Inquiry* 9(2), pp.254–67

Grimes, D.M. (2010) 'O.J. Simpson and the Evolution of Domestic Violence Cases', available from: http://www.grimesandwarwick.com/DV_cases

Grosz, E. (2005) 'Bergson, Deleuze and Becoming', *Parallax* 11(2), pp.4–13

Gruske, K. (2011) *What is the Importance of a Daily Journal in Family Law Cases?* available from: http://wiki.answers.com/Q/ WhatistheimportanceofadailyjournalinFamilyLawcases

Guba, E.G. (1967) *Proposal for the development and testing of new theories and methods of evaluation in field contexts*. Submitted to the U.S. Commissioner of Education for support through the Bureau of Research. (Bloomington, Indiana University and the National Institute for the Study of Educational Change)

Gubrium, J. (1988) *Analyzing Field Reality*, Newbury Park, CA: Sage

Haggis, T. (2009) 'What Have we Been Thinking of? A Critical Overview of 40 Years of Student Learning Research in Higher Education', *Studies in Higher Education* 34(4), pp.377–90

Hall, S. (2010) *Ethnographers' Interviewing Techniques*, available from: *http://www.ehow. com/way_5632833_ethnographers-interviewing-techniques.html*

Halliday, M.A.K. (2003) 'On Language in Relation to the Evolution of Human Consciousness' in J. Webster (ed.), *On Language and Linguistics*, Vol. 3, pp.390–433, London and New York: Continuum

Halliday, M.A.K., & J. Webster (eds) (2009) *Continuum Companion to Systemic Functional Linguistics*, New York and London: Continuum

Hammond, W., & D. Steward (2008) *Verbatim Verbatim: Techniques in Contemporary Documentary Theatre*, London: Oberon

Harris, G. (1999) *Staging Femininities*, Manchester: Manchester University Press

Hayano, D.M. (1979) 'Auto-Ethnography: Paradigms, Problems and Prospects', *Human Organization* 38(1), pp.99–104

He, M.-F. (2000) *A River Forever Flowing: Cross-Cultural Lives and Identities in the Multicultural Landscape*, Charlotte: Information Age Publishing

Heasley, R. (2005) 'Queer Masculinities of Straight Men: A Typology', *Men and Masculinities* 7(310), pp.310–20

Heasley, R. (2013) 'Crossing the Borders of Gendered Sexuality: Queer Masculinities of Straight Men', in C. Ingraham (ed.), *Thinking Straight: The Power, Promise and Paradox of Heterosexuality*, Hoboken, NJ: Taylor and Francis

Heddon, D. (2005) *Devising Performance: A Critical History*, London: Palgrave

Hedgecoe, A. (2008) 'Research Ethics Review and the Sociological Research Relationship', *Sociology* 42(5), pp.873–86

Heider, K (1975) *Ethnographic Film*, Austin, TX: University of Texas Press

Hemingway, E. (1987) *The Complete Short Stories*, New York: Simon & Schuster

Hemmingson, M. (1997) *Driving Somewhere: A Play in Three Acts*, San Francisco, CA: Ventana Productions

_____ (2008) 'Make Them Giggle: Auto/Ethnography as Stand Up Comedy – A Response to Denzin's Call to Performance', *Creative Approaches to Research* 1(2), pp.9–22

Hennessy, K. (1992) 'Addressing the Queer Man's Role in the New World Anarchy and the Future of the Men's Movements in the Dis/United States', San Francisco: Abundant Fuck Publications

Hill, D.T. (2007) 'Ethics and Institutions in Biographical Writing on Indonesian Subjects', *Life Writing* 4(2), pp.215–29

Hofling, C.K. (1966) 'An Experimental Study of Nurse–Physician Relationships', *Journal of Nervous and Mental Disease* 141, pp.171–80

Holbrook, A., & S. Johnston (eds) (1999) 'Supervision of Postgraduate Research in Education', *AARE*, Vol. 5, Melbourne: Victoria Press

Holman Jones, S. (2005) 'Autoethnography: Making the personal political' in N.K. Denzin & Y.S. Lincoln (eds), *The Sage Handbook of Qualitative Research*, third edition, pp.763–92, Thousand Oaks, CA: Sage

Humphreys, M. (2005) 'Getting Personal: Reflexivity and Autoethnographic Vignettes', *Qualitative Inquiry* 11(6), pp.840–60

Humphreys, M., A.D. Brown & M.J. Hatch. (2003) 'Is Ethnography Jazz?' *Organization* 10(1), pp.5–31

Hylton, H. (2007) 'Oprah vs James Frey: The Sequel', *Time Entertainment*, available from: *http://content.time.com/time/arts/article/0,8599,1648140,00.html?cnn=yes*

Hymes, D. (1974) *Foundations in Sociolinguistics: An Ethnographic Approach*, Philadelphia, PA: University of Pennsylvania Press

Jagger, G. (2008) *Judith Butler: Sexual Politics, Social Change and the Power of the Performative*. London: Routledge

Jagose, A. (1996) *Queer Theory*, Victoria: Melbourne University Press

James, W. (1948) *Sameness in the Self as Known*, New York: World Press

Janke, T. (1996) 'Protecting Australian Indigenous Arts and Cultural Expression: A Matter of Legislative Reform or Cultural Policy?' *Culture & Policy* 7(3)

Jones, K. (2006) 'A Biographic Researcher in Pursuit of an Aesthetic: The Use of Arts-based (Re)Presentations in "Performative" Dissemination of Life Stories', *Qualitative Sociology Review*, April, available from: http://www.qualitativesociologyreview.org/ENG/index_eng.php

____ (2007) 'How Did I Get to Princess Margaret? (And How Did I Get Her to the World Wide Web?)' *Forum: Qualitative Social Research* 3, available from: http://www.qualitativeresearch.net/index.php/fqs/article/view/281/618

Junger, S. (2007) *The Perfect Storm: A True Story of Men Against the Sea*, New York: Harper Perrenial

Kaplan, C. (1992) 'Resisting Autobiography: Out-Law Genres and Transnational Feminist Subjects' in S. Smith and J. Watson (eds), *De/Colonizing the Subject: The Politics of Gender in Women's Autobiography*, Minneapolis, MN: University of Minnesota Press

Kaprow, A. (1993) *Essays on the Blurring of Art and Life*, Berkeley, CA: University of California Press

Karuth, N. (2011) '*Evolution of the exegesis: the radical trajectory of the creative writing doctorate in Australia*', *TEXT* 15(1), April 2011, available from: http://www.textjournal.com

Keneally, T. (2003) *The Borrowers*, available from: http://www.theage.com.au

Kimmel, A.J. (2007) *Ethical Issues in Behavioral Research: Basic and Applied Perspectives*, Hoboken: John Wiley & Sons

Kirby, M. (1969) *The Art of Time: Essays on the Avant-Garde*, New York: E.P. Dutton

Kirsch, M. (2006) 'Queer Theory, Late Capitalism and Internalised Homophobia', *Journal of Homosexuality* 52(1–2), pp.19–45

Klein, T.W. (2012) 'The Assumption: A Lie That Tells the Truth' in *America: The National Catholic Review*, available from: http://americamagazine.org/node/128643

Krauth, N. (2011) 'Evolution of the Exegesis: the Radical Trajectory of the Creative Writing Doctorate in Australia', Text 15(1), April 2011, available from: http://www. textjournal.com.au

kumar, h.s. (2011) Decolonising Texts: A Performance Autoethnography, Amherst, MA: University of Massachusetts, available from: http://scholarworks.umass.edu/ theses/692/

Langellier, K.M. (1999) 'Personal Narrative, Performance, Performativity: Two or Three Things I Know For Sure', Text and Performance Quarterly 19, pp.125–44

Langlois, A.J. (2011) 'Political Research and Human Research Ethics Committees', Australian Journal of Political Science 46(1)

Law, J., & J. Urry (2004) 'Enacting the Social', Economy and Society 33(3), pp.390–410

Layton, J. (dir.) (1982) Richard Pryor Live on Sunset Strip, Los Angeles, CA: Columbia Pictures

Lea, M., & B. Street (1998) 'Student Writing in Higher Education: An Academic Literacies Approach', Studies in Higher Education 23(2), pp.157–71

Lechte, J. (1994) Fifty Key Contemporary Thinkers, London: Routledge

Leguizamo, J. (2007) Pimps, Hos, Playa Hatas, and All the Rest of My Hollywood Friends: My Life, New York: Harper

_____ (2008) The Works of John Leguizamo: Freak, Spic-o-Rama, Mambo Mouth, and Sexaholix, New York: Harper

Lejeune, P. (1989) 'The Autobiographical Pact' in Eakin, P. (ed.), On Autobiography, Minneapolis, MN: University of Minnesota Press

Leslie, I. (2012) Born Liars: Why We Can't Live Without Deceit, London: Quercus

Levi, P. (1987) If This is a Man, London: Abacus

_____ (1997) Conversations with Primo Levi and the Voice of Memory: Interviews, 1961–1987, New York: Polity Press

Lillis, T., & M. Scott (2007) 'Defining Academic Literacies Research: Issues of Epistemology, Ideology and Strategy', Journal of Applied Linguistics 4(1), pp.5–32

Lincoln, Y.S. (2002) 'Emerging Criteria for Quality' in N.K. Denzin & Y.S. Lincoln (eds), The Qualitative Inquiry Reader, Thousand Oaks, CA: Sage, pp.5–24

Locke, J., & P.E. Sigmund (2005) The Selected Political Writings of John Locke, New York: W.W. Norton & Company, Norton Critical Editions

Lodge, D. (1990) After Bakhtin: Essays on Fiction and Criticism, London: Routledge

Loftus, E. (1993) 'The Reality of Repressed Memories', American Psychologist 48, May, pp.518–37

Loftus, E.F., & H.G. Hoffman (1989) 'Misinformation and Memory: The Creation of Memory', Journal of Experimental Psychology: General 118, pp.100–4

Lopate, P. (ed.) (1994) The Art of the Personal Essay, New York: Anchor

Loutzenheiser, L. (2007) 'Working Alterity: The Impossibility of Ethical Research with Youth', Education Studies (AESA) 41(2), pp.109–27

Luke, A. (2003) 'After the Marketplace: Evidence, Social Science and Educational Research', *Australian Educational Researcher* 30(2), pp.87–107

Madison, D.S. (1999) 'Performing Theory/Embodied Writing', *Text and Performance Quarterly* 19, pp.107–24

Mann, A., & J. Fletcher (2004) 'Illuminating the Exegesis: A Discussion of the Exegesis Component of the Creative Thesis in Australian Research Higher Degrees', Griffith University, *TEXT*, Special Issue No. 3

Maréchal, G. (2010) 'Autoethnography' in A.J. Mills, G. Durepos & E. Wiebe (eds), *Encyclopedia of Case Study Research*, Vol. 2, pp.43–5, Thousand Oaks, CA: Sage Publications

Marginson, S. (2007) *Global Setting, National Policy and Higher Education in 2007*, Melbourne: University of Melbourne, Web of Science

Marowitz, C. (1991) *Recycling Shakespeare*, London: Applause Theatre Book Publishers

Martin, J. (1990) *Voice in Modern Theatre*, London and New York: Routledge

Martin, J.R. (1993) 'Life as a Noun: Arresting the Universe in Science and Humanities' in M.A.K. Halliday & J.R. Martin (eds), *Writing Science: Literacy and Discursive Power*, pp.221–67, London: Falmer Press

McCasland, G. (2012) *Daily Journals: A Key to Success*, available from: http://www.squidoo.com/DailyJournalsKeyToSuccess

McClatchky, J.D. (1990) *The Vintage Book of Contemporary American Poetry*, New York: Vintage

McCullough, C. (1998) *Theatre Praxis: Teaching Drama through Practice*, London & New York: Routledge

McDonald, E. (1993) *Theatre at the Margins*, Ann Arbor, MI: University of Michigan Press

McEvoy, W. (2003) 'Finding the Balance: Writing and Performing Ethics in Theatre du Soleils' *Le Dernier Caravanséril'*, *New Theatre Quarterly* 22, pp.211–26

McTaggart, R. (1991) 'Principles of Participatory Action Research', *Adult Education Quarterly* 41(3), pp.168–87

McQuire, A. (2012) *No longer flora and fauna: NSW government commits to heritage legislation*, available from: http://tracker.org.au/2012/11/no-longer-flora-and-fauna-nsw-govt-commits-to-heritage-legislation/

McWilliam, E., D. Sanderson, T. Evans, A. Lawson & P.G. Taylor (2006) 'The Risky Business of Doctoral Management', *Asia Pacific Journal of Education* 26(2), pp.209–21

Medford, K. (2006) 'Caught With a Fake ID', *Qualitative Inquiry* 12(5), pp.853–64

Meyers, J., & M. Simms (eds) (1989) *The Longman Dictionary of Poetic Terms*, New York: Longman

Miller, C. (2012) *Pages in Your Diary: Supreme Court of West Virginia Badly Errs in Deeming Diary Entries Admissible Despite Rape Shield Rule*, available from: http://

www.feministlawprofessors.com/2012/12/pages-diary-supreme-court-west-virginia-badly-errs-deeming-diary-entries-admissible-despite-rape-shield-rule/

Minh-ha, T.T. (1989) *Woman Native Other: Writing Postcoloniality and Feminism*, Bloomington, IN: Indiana University Press

Mock, R. (2003) 'Heteroqueer Ladies: Some Performative Transactions Between Gay Men and Heterosexual Women', *Feminist Review* 75, pp.20–37

Montaigne, M. (2004) *The Essays*, trans. C. Cotton, available from: http://oregonstate. edu/instruct/phl302/texts/montaigne/montaigne-essays—4.html ('The Era of Great Voyages', ed. B. Uzgalis)

Moriarty, B., et al. (2008) 'Freire and dialogical pedagogy: a means for interrogating opportunities and challenges in Australian postgraduate supervision', *International Journal of Lifelong Education* 27(4), pp.431–42

Morrison, B. (2007) *And When Did You Last See Your Father?* London: Granta Books

Morson, G.S. (1994) *Narrative and Freedom: The Shadows of Time*, New Haven, CT: Yale University Press

Morson, G., & C. Emerson (1990) *Mikhail Bakhtin: Creation of a Prosaics*, Stanford, CA: Stanford University Press

Mortimer, J. (1971) *A Voyage Round My Father*, London: Penguin Classics

Muncey, T. (2005) 'Doing Autoethnography', *International Journal of Qualitative Methods*, available from: http://ejournals.library.ualberta.ca/index.php/IJQM/article/view/4454

Nash, R.J., D.L. Bradley & A.W. Chickering (2008) *How to Talk About Hot Topics on Campus*, Jossey-Bass

National Health and Medical Research Council, A.R.C., Australian Vice-Chancellors' Committee (2007) *National Statement on Ethical Conduct in Human Research*, Australian Government: Canberra

Nelson, R. (2009) *The Jealousy of Ideas: Research Methods in the Creative Arts*, Ellikon: Fitzroy

Nisbett, R., & T.D. Wilson (1977) 'Telling More Than We Can Know: Verbal Reports on Mental Processes', *Psychological Review* 84, pp.231–59

Norton-Taylor, R. (2011) 'Verbatim Theatre lets the Truth Speak for Itself', *Guardian*, 30 May 2011

Oliver, K. (2001) *Witnessing: Beyond Recognition*, Minneapolis, MN: University of Minnesota Press

Osgood, C. (2005) *The Osgood File*, CBS 9 March 2004, LexisNexis Academic, Louisiana State University, Louisiana Online University Information System, 16 February 2005, available from: http://80-web.lexis-nexis.com

Owens, A. (2007) 'The Magic Bullet: Metaphors for Thinking through Applied Drama Practice', Keynote Address, *Drama Education 16th World Congress*, IATA, Scheinling Castle, Austria

Park-Fuller, L. (1995) 'Narration and Narratization of a Cancer Story: Composing and Performing *A Clean Breast of It*', *Text and Performance Quarterly* 15, pp.60–7

_____ (2000) 'Performing Absence: The Staged Personal Narrative as Testimony', *Text and Performance Quarterly* 20, pp.20–42

Pearson, M. (2010) *Site-specific Performance*, Basingstoke: Palgrave MacMillan

Pedersen, H., & B. Woorunmurra (2000) *Jandamarra and the Bunuba Resistance*, Broome: Magabala Books Aboriginal Corporation

Penner, J. (2005) 'Stage Death: Remembering a Painful Evening with Spalding Gray', *Houston Press*, LexisNexis Academic, Louisiana State University, Louisiana Online University Information System, 16 February 2005, available from: http://80-web.lexis-nexis.com

Pennycook, A. (2007) 'The Rotation Gets Thick. The Restraints get Thin: Creativity, Recontextualisation and Difference', *Applied Linguistics* 28(4), pp.579–96

Peretz, E. (2008) 'James Frey's "Morning After"', *Vanity Fair*, available from: http://www.vanityfair.com/culture/features/2008/06/frey200806

Peters, J.D. (1999) *Speaking into the Air: A History of the Idea of Communication*, Chicago, IL: University of Chicago Press

Phelan, P. (1988) 'Spalding Gray's Swimming to Cambodia; The Article!' *Critical Texts* 5, pp.27–30

_____ (1993) *Unmarked: The Politics of Performance*, London: Routledge

Phillips, T. (1985) *The Heart of a Humument*, Cologne: Hansjorg Mayer

Pineau, E.L. (1992) 'A Mirror of Her Own: Anais Nin's Autobiographical Performances', *Text and Performance Quarterly* 12, pp.97–112

Plummer, K. (2001) 'The Call of Life Stories in Ethnographic Research' in P. Atkinson, A. Coffey, S. Delamont, J. Lofland & L. Lofland (eds), *The Handbook of Ethnography*, London: Sage

Pollock, D. (1998) 'Introduction: Making History Go' in D. Pollock (ed.), *Exceptional Spaces: Essays in Performance and History*, Chapel Hill, NC: University of North Carolina Press, pp.1–45

Popova, M. (2012) *Mark Twain on Plagiarism and Originality*, available from: http://www.brainpickings.org/index.php/2012/05/10/mark-twain-helen-keller-plagiarism-originality/

Powers, A. (1993 June 29) 'Queer in the Streets, Straight in the Sheets: Notes on Passing', *Village Voice*, pp.24, 30–1

Poynton, C. (2000) 'Linguistics and Discourse Analysis' in A. Lee & C. Poynton (eds), *Culture and Text*, pp.19–39, St Leonards: Allen and Unwin

Pratt, M.L. (1986) 'Fieldwork in Common Places' in J. Clifford and G.E. Marcus (eds), *Writing Culture: The Poetics and Politics of Ethnography*, Berkeley, CA: University of California Press, pp.27–50

Prince, R. (2010) 'Janet Cooke's Hoax Still Resonates After 30 Years', *The Root*, available from: http://www.theroot.com/blogs/pulitzer-prize/janet-cookes-hoax-still-resonates-after-30-years

Read, A. (1993) *Theatre and Everyday Life*, London and New York: Routledge

Reed-Danahay, D. (1997) *Auto/ethnography: Rewriting the Self and the Social*, Oxford: Berg

_____ (2007) 'Autobiography, Intimacy and Ethnography' in P. Atkinson et al. (eds), *Handbook of Ethnography*, London: Sage

Rhodes, H. (1956) *Alphonse Bertillon: Father of Scientific Detection*, New York: Abelard-Schuman

Richards, A. (1995) 'Performance as Research/Research by Means of Performance', a discussion paper Presented to the Australasian Drama Studies Association Annual Conference, Armidale NSW, available from: http://www.adsa.edu.au/research/performance-as-research/performance-as-research

Richardson, L. (1994) 'Nine Poems', *Journal of Contemporary Ethnography* 23(1), pp.9–19

_____ (2000) 'Poetics, Dramatics, and Transgressive Validity', *Sociological Quarterly* 35, pp.695–710

Rose, J. (1986) *Sexuality in the Field of Vision*, London: Verso

Ruddick, L. (1990) *Reading Gertrude Stein: Body, Text, Gnosis*, Cornell University Press

Russell, B. (1921) *The Analysis of Mind*, London: George Allen & Unwin

_____ (1991) *History of Western Philosophy*, London and New York: Routledge

Russell, S. (2012a) 'Litigating Lineups: Why the American Justice System Is Keeping a Close Eye on Witness Identification', *Pacific Standard*, available from: http://www.psmag.com/legal-affairs/litigating-lineups-47504/

_____ (2012b) *Why Police Lineups Can't be Trusted*, available from: http://www.salon.com/2012/09/29/why_criminal_lineups_cant_be_trusted/

Sacks, O. (2013) 'Speak, Memory', *New York Review of Books*, 21 February 2013

Said, E.W. (1978) *Orientalism*, New York: Vintage Books

Saldana, J. (ed.) (2005) *Ethnodrama: An Anthology of Reality Theatre*, Lanham, MD: AltaMira

_____ (2011) *Ethnotheatre: Research from Page to Stage (Qualitative Inquiry & Social Justice)*, Los Angeles: Left Coast Press

Salih, S. (2002) *Judith Butler*, London: Routledge

_____ (2002a) Gen'Ferment in LGBT Students and Queer Theory: Personal Rumination on Contested Terrain' in K.E. Lovaas, J.P. Elia & G.A. Yep (eds), *LGBT Studies and Queer Theory: New Conflicts, Collaborations and Contested Terrain*, Binghamton, NY: Harrington Park Press

Sartre, J.P. (1990) *Being and Nothingness*, London: Routledge

Sayre, H.M. (1989) *The Object of Performance: The American Avant-Garde Since 1970*, Chicago, IL: University of Chicago Press

Schacter, D. (1996) *Searching for Memory: The Brain, the Mind and the Past*, New York: Basic Books

Schechner, R. (1986) *Between Theatre and Anthropology*, Philadelphia, PN: University of Pennsylvania Press

_____ (1988) *Performance Theory*, London and New York: Routledge

_____ (2002) 'My Art in Life: Interviewing Spalding Gray', *Drama Review* 46(4), pp.161–76

Schieffelin, E.L. (1998) 'Problematizing Performance' in F. Hughes-Freeland (ed.), *Ritual, Performance, Media*, New York: Routledge, pp.194–205

Scholten, K.G. (2007) *When Art and Celebrity Collide: Telling the Dixie Chicks to 'Shut up and Sing'*, Berlin: VDM Verlag Dr. Mueller e.K.

Schön, D.A. (1984) *The Reflective Practitioner: How Professionals Think in Action*, New York: Basic Books

Seale, C. (1999) *The Quality of Qualitative Research* London, Sage

Sedgewick, E.K. (2003) *Touching Feeling: Affect, Pedagogy, Performativity*, Durham, NC: Duke University Press

Sellers, H. (2010) *Creative Writing Now*, available from: http://www.creative-writing-now.com/memoir-writing-interview.html

Shoemaker, S. (1963) *Self-knowledge and Self-identity*, Ithaca, NY: Cornell University Press

Shreeve, A. (2009) '"I'd rather be seen as a practitioner, come in to teach my subject": Identity Work in Part-Time Art and Design Tutors', *JADE* 28(2), pp.151–9, London: Blackwell

Slagle, R.A. (2006) 'Ferment in LGBT studies and queer theory: Personal ruminations on contested terrain', *Journal of Homosexuality* 52(1/2), pp.309–28

Slater, L. (2000) *Lying*, New York: Penguin Books

Smith, C. (1997) *How I Became a Queer Heterosexual*, paper presented at Beyond Boundaries: An International Conference on Sexuality, University of Amsterdam

Smith, S., & J. Watson (2001) *Reading Autobiography: A Guide for Interpreting Life Narratives*, Minneapolis, MN: University of Minnesota Press

Sobol, J. (1999) *The Storytellers's Journey: An American Revival*, Chicago, IL: University of Illinois Press

Sokal, A. (2008) *Beyond the Hoax: Science, Philosophy and Culture*, Oxford: Oxford University Press

Sotorin, P. (2010) 'Autoethnographic Mother-Writing: Advocating Radical Specificity', *Journal of Research Practice* 6(1), Article M9

Sparkes, A. (2002) *Telling Tales in Sport and Physical Activity: A Qualitative Journey*, London: Human Kinetics

_____ (2007) 'Embodiment, Academics, and the Audit Culture: A Story Seeking Consideration', *Qualitative Research* 7(4), pp.521–50

Sparrow, J.L., & D.M. Wegner (2011) *Google Effects on Memory: Cognitive Consequences of Having Information at Our Fingertips*, available from: http://www.sciencemag.org/content/333/6043/776

Spradley, J. (1979) *The Ethnographic Interview*, Belmont, CA: Wadsworth Publishing Co. Inc.

Spry, T. (1997) 'Skins: A Daughter's (Re)construction of Cancer: A Performative Autobiography', *Text and Performance Quarterly* 17, pp.361–5

_____ (2001) 'Performing Autoethnography: An Embodied Methodological Praxis', *Qualitative Inquiry* 7(6), pp.706–73

Starfield, S., & L. Ravelli (2006) 'Self and Structure in New Humanities Research Theses', *Journal of English for Academic Purposes* 5, pp.222–43

Stein, G. (1995) *The Making of Americans*, Normal, IL: Dalkey Archive Press

Strine, M.S., B. Whitaker Long & M.F. Hopkins (1990) 'Research in Interpretation and Performance Studies: Trends Issues, Priorities' in G.M. Philips and J.T. Wood (eds), *Speech Communication: Essays to Commemorate the 75th Anniversary of the Speech Communication Association*, Carbondale, IL: Southern Illinois UP, pp.181–204

Sword, H. (2012) *Stylish Academic Writing*, Cambridge, MA: Harvard University Press

Taft-Kaufman, J. (2000) 'Critical Claims, Critical Functions: Autoethnography and Postscholarship', *American Communication Journal* 4(1), Fall 2000, available from: http://ac-journal.org/journal/vol4/iss1/special/taft.htm

Tamas, S. (2009) 'Writing and Righting Trauma: Troubling the Autoethnographic Voice', *Forum: Qualitative Social Research* 10(1), available from: http://nbn-resolving.de/urn:nbn:de:0114-fqs0901220

Taormino, T. (2003) 'The Queer Heterosexual', *Village Voice*

ten Cate, R. (1996) *Man Looking for Words*, Amsterdam: Theater Instituut Nederland

Threadgold, T. (2003) 'Cultural Studies, Critical Theory and Critical Discourse Analysis: Histories, Remembering and Futures', *Linguistic Online* 14(2), pp.5–37

Tierney, G. (1998) 'Constructing Knowledge: Educational Research in Gay and Lesbian Studies' in W. Pinar, *Queer Theory in Education*, New Jersey: Lawrence Erlbaum Associates

Tierney, G., & Y. Lincoln (1997) *Representation and the Text: Re-framing the Narrative Voice*, New York: State University of New York Press

Tillman, F., & S. Cahn (1969) *Philosophy of Art and Aesthetics from Plato to Wittgenstein*, New York: Harpers & Row

Tolich, M. (2010) 'A Critique of Current Practice: Ten Foundational Guidelines for Autoethnographers', *Qualitative Health Research*, London: Sage, available from: http://qhr.sagepub.com/content/early/2010/07/19/1049732310376076

Torres, P.M. (1994) 'Interested in Writing about Indigenous Australians?' *Australian Author* 26(3)

Twain, M. (1880) *On the Decay of the Art of Lying*, available from: http://www.online-literature.com.o.henry/1320/D

Tzara, T. (1920) Feeble Love & Bitter Love, II, in Tzara, T. (1981) *Seven Dada Manifestos and Lampisteries*, London: Calder Publications

Van Den Hoonaard, W.C. (2006) 'New Angles and Tangles in the Ethics Review of Research', *Journal of Academic Ethics* 4, pp.261–74

Vatican (2011) 'Truth, Proclamation and Authenticity of Life in the Digital Age', *Message of His Holiness Pope Benedict XV for the 45th World Communications Day*, Rome: Libreria Editrice Vaticana, available from: http://www.vatican.va/holy_father_benedict_xvi/messages/communications/documents/hf_ben-xvi_mes_20110124_45th-world-communications-day_en.htm

Warner, M. (ed.) (1993) *Fear of a Queer Planet: Queer Politics and Social Theory*, Volume 6, Minneapolis, MN: University of Minnesota Press

Warnock, M. (1987) *Memory*, London: Faber & Faber

Westbrook, D.A. (2008) *Navigators of the Contemporary: Why Ethnography Matters*, Chicago, IL: University of Chicago Press

White, N. (2012) *Trust Me, I'm an Artist*, available from: http://www.artscienceethics.com/

Whitehead, T.L. (2005) 'Basic Classical Ethnographic Research Methods', *Cultural Ecology of Health and Change*, available from: http://www.scribd.com/doc/152274890/Ethnography

Wilde, O. (1995) *The Decay of Lying*, London: Penguin Books

Windschuttle, K. (2010) *Holes in the Rabbit-Proof Fence: The 10 big fictions of Rabbit-Proof Fence*, available from: http://www.quadrant.org.au/blogs/history-wars/2010/05/holes-in-the-rabbit-proof-fence

Winlow, S.H. & Steve Hall (2012) 'What is an "Ethics Committee"? Academic Governance in an Epoch of Belief and Incredulity', *British Journal of Criminology* 52(2), pp.400–16

Wood, M. (2003) 'On Edward Said', *London Review of Books*, October, p.3

Zinsser, W. (2001) *On Writing Well: The Classic Guide to Writing Nonfiction*, London: HarperCollins

Index